Simple & Classic

Simple & Classic

123 step-by-step recipes   Jane Hornby

What to Cook and How to Cook It

When people meet a real live cookery writer, there are a few questions that come up again and again. After food photography trade secrets, and whether anyone is ever brave enough to cook me dinner, usually the next question is "What's your signature dish?" That's a hard one. Like many things in life, it depends: on the season; the time I have; who I'm cooking for; and, even my current flavor or equipment crush. But, if making an intense tangle of Spicy Shrimp (Prawn), Fennel, and Chile Linguini (see page 186) on a summer's evening is a good enough answer, then take it. Or maybe it's the Vanilla Celebration Cake (see page 482) I make time and again for weddings and big parties. My signature dish would, most probably, be something simple and classic—and I suspect it's the same for most of us.

And so *Simple and Classic* has come about. This book is a collection of tried and tested recipes created from my Phaidon cookbooks over the last 10 years, carefully chosen to help you become a better cook.

Step by step and easy to follow, the recipes are ideal for food lovers with some practical skills, but who need a little hand-holding here and there. Or beginners, of course.

I often turn to the original books myself when I need a reminder of technique, for example, the perfect hollandaise (see page 20) and also for exact baking instructions and a recipe I know I can rely on. I've added in amendments and new hints and tips noted down over the years.

There's nothing more fulfilling than turning out a delicious meal or gorgeous cake. But I won't assume you have endless ingredients, pans, cooking space, and expensive equipment and gadgets to achieve it. A good pantry, smart shopping, and a few pieces of equipment are enough.

The recipes are designed to make the most of your time in the kitchen, with chopping instructions in the recipe instead of in the ingredients list. This saves you time in preparing the ingredients to start with, when there is time that can be filled later. There are plenty of make-ahead tips, too, to be helpful as possible. As I draft this introduction in various windows of time, often while my toddler catches 40 winks, I can't help but reflect that this is all the more relevant to me these days.

So, what about the food? We've chosen a list that reflects both classic cooking and newer flavors; a book to take you through family meals to drinks with friends, to holiday baking with the children and more. But the first hurdle, of course, is often not *how*, but *what* to cook. The recipes are arranged around meal type rather than ingredient to make the decision easier. A clear photo of the ingredients also helps to jog the memory about the ingredients hiding in the refrigerator and freezer, or pantry. It is also a perfect prompt to help avoid food waste, too.

I hope this book will open up new ways to think about eating; replacing a weekend roast with all the trimmings for a simple Roast Chicken with Tarragon Sauce (see page 204), for instance, will gain you time and a new method to employ next time.

Making a menu? I've included a list of menu ideas to get you started on page 506, matching recipes that sit together really well, if not exclusively.

Step-by-step recipes have really come back into favor, I'm glad to say, and are no longer just for beginners. Think about how many food blogs and vlogs there are online, with step shots and walk-throughs. It's about that visual cue, a definite in the fluid world of the recipe, where things can fluctuate depending on ingredient, the kitchen, and even the mood of the cook. The words and photos together replace the guesswork of cooking with a solid reference point.

Food is always moving, with trends changing, one ingredient in focus, easier, faster, better (sometimes). But at its heart, good homecooking is about feeding people well, with recipes that earn their place in the kitchen. And time and again the food is classic, simple, and based on good ingredients, treated well.

I hope you look to this book often, both for inspiration and to resolve any number of cooking dilemmas. It's a new reference for your kitchen—and mine, too.

Oh, and in case you were wondering, we did eat all of the food in these photos. And if I'm cooked for, I'm always grateful, even if it's just a bowl of soup. That Chicken Noodle Soup on page 80 might be nice…

–Jane Hornby

How to Make the Recipes Work for You

Read the recipe from start to finish before you begin cooking. It is particularly important for baking and desserts.

Unless you're a confident cook, don't change the ingredients in a recipe. You can always make it again once you're familiar with it. If you do make swaps, use like for like; white sugar for brown, for instance, not honey or sweetener (in baking). For more on ingredients, see pages 11–13.

Weigh and measure carefully. American cup measures are followed by European metric grams. Having worked in both cups and grams, I would still say that using a scale and cooking in grams is best, with less room for mistakes. Whichever method you prefer, stick to one method within a recipe. Australian readers should note that your tablespoons are 20 ml (4 teaspoons) as opposed to 15 ml (3 teaspoons) in the USA and UK, so please use 3 teaspoons in place of 1 tablespoon where needed. There is more information on measuring for baking below. I urge you to read this before you measure any flour, in particular, because the method you use to fill your cup will drastically alter how much it holds.

Take note of the instructions alongside each ingredient. Softened butter should be soft, almost like mayonnaise from a jar. Meat should be allowed to come up to room temperature for a while or your cooking times won't match mine. Eggs should usually be at room temperature before baking.

Where possible, I've tried to reduce the amount of fine chopping and replace it with slicing instead.

The prep time for each recipe is the time it will take you to collect the ingredients and equipment, and any preliminary cooking, such as browning meat. The cooking time is the final time in the oven or pan. Set a timer, it will be your friend.

Get to know your oven. Always preheat it, and keep the door closed as you cook (although some broilers [grills] need to have the door open, so check the instructions if you're not sure). Avoid the urge to peek in every few minutes, because it will just slow the cooking down (and possibly deflate a cake). An oven thermometer is helpful if you're not sure it's calibrated correctly. For more information see pages 9–10.

Try to get cakes into the oven as soon as you can after the batter has been mixed (not to panic, but just don't go and make a phone call). This prevents large bubbles or a flat cake and heartache.

Weighing and measuring (especially for baking)

If you read only one thing before you get started with recipes from this book, make it this. It's so important to measure accurately, especially in baking.

In the USA, most ingredients are measured by volume in cups. Cups are less accurate than measuring the weight on a scale and need careful attention to get the best results.

One standard American measuring cup will hold 240 ml, or 8 fl oz, or 16 tablespoons. Buy a good quality set of sturdy metal cups and measuring spoons from a reputable cookware shop. Make sure you fill the cup to the top and level it off. Use the right cup for each measurement, instead of, for example, measuring ½ cup in a 1-cup measure by eye.

For liquids, use a liquid measuring cup with a pouring lip and markings on the side. It's best to use a 1-cup liquid measuring cup for small liquid measures, because the markings will be more accurate than those on a large cup, and check the ingredient against the markings at eye level.

To measure fine, dry ingredients, such as flour and confectioners' sugar, use the fluff-spoon-sweep method for my recipes, because this is how I measured when I developed the recipes:

- Start by aerating it by fluffing and swirling it in the package or box with a spoon or fork.
- Hold the cup over the package or a bowl to catch any excess.
- Gently spoon heaping spoonfuls into the cup measure.
- Keep going until the flour or sugar is mounded in the cup, and is at least as high as the edge of the cup all the way around.
- Take a straight-edged blunt knife and lightly sweep away the excess.
- Don't pack or press the flour, or scoop it with the cup straight from the bag, because this compacts it into the cup and your baked item could end up with too much flour in it.

For measuring small amounts, such as 1 tablespoon, just scoop from the bag with the measuring spoon, then level off.

To measure regular granulated or superfine (caster) sugars, spoon into the cup and level the top. They do not need the fluff-spoon-sweep method.

Dark and light brown sugars are measured packed. Spoon the sugar into the cup and press down with the back of the spoon to level the top of the cup. To measure butter in the USA, use the markings on the side of the stick wrapper to cut off the appropriate amount of tablespoons. One stick is 8 tablespoons or 112 g. Don't try and press it into a spoon measure.

For eggs, unless otherwise stated, the recipes call for US large eggs (UK medium-size), which weigh about 2¾ oz (60 g) in their shells, and yield 2 oz (50 g) when cracked, or 3 tablespoons (45 ml) once beaten.

If you don't have the right egg size at hand, allow 3 tablespoons (or 50 g) beaten egg for every egg used.

For thick or sticky liquids, such as molasses, I find it helpful to first very lightly oil the measuring spoon or cup and the spoon I'm using for scooping from the jar. This helps them flow out of the measuring cup or spoon and you get the right quantity in your recipe.

All other dry ingredients have been spooned into the cups, not packed down, then leveled off.

Kitchen Equipment
A little knowledge about your oven and some well-chosen pieces of kitchenware will serve you well.

Ovens
If you're new to cooking, please familiarize yourself with your oven first. The temperatures in this book are for conventional ovens. Conventional ovens are hotter at the top and/or bottom, closer to the heating elements. It's best to bake cakes and cook large roasts (joints) in the middle of the oven. For food you want to crisp up a little, use the top third of the oven.

Convection and fan-assisted ovens
Convection ovens have an element at the back of the oven and a fan that blows the heat into and around the oven. Fan-assisted ovens have a fan that moves the air around the oven, but the heat comes from the elements

at the bottom and/or top. Both ovens cook more quickly than conventional, and if you have a convection or fan oven, you will need to cook at 25°F (20°C) lower than the conventional temperatures given in this book. But, check your oven booklet, because some ovens do the adjustment for you. They tend to need less time to preheat.

Gas ovens
These have roughly three areas of heat, coolest at the bottom, hottest at the top. Cook anything that needs to be browned in the top third, use the middle for baking and roasting, and reserve the bottom third for gentle cooking.

Mixers, blenders & processors
I use a small set of handheld electric mixers for many tasks. They are more affordable than a stand mixer, and take up less space. If you have a stand mixer, you can use it instead for beating, whipping, and kneading. I can live without a stand mixer, but I use my food processor a lot. It chops quickly and makes good pastry because the blade works the dough together fast and helps to reduce the amount of liquid you'll need to add (both good things for short, delicious pastry). It is ideal for prep work, such as chopping onions, celery, and carrots together for a sauce, or rubbing in butter and chopping nuts. A handheld immersion (stick) blender is as good as a freestanding or blender attachment for general cooking, and it also saves on space. Use to puree, either in the tall pitcher (jug) it will have come with, or in a deep pan—being careful with hot liquids, of course. Some have a mini chopper attachment which can be really useful.

Cutting (chopping) boards
I use one for raw food and one for cooked food and food that is to be eaten raw, such as salads. Plastic boards are hard-wearing and easier to clean, whereas wooden boards are more pleasing to chop on, but more costly and harder to keep in good condition.

Knives
A chef's knife of about 8 inches (20 cm) is ideal for the average hand, but go bigger if you are bigger. It is best to buy from a cookshop—try a few in hand as your choice of knife should be based on personal preference. Add to that, a small knife, a serrated knife, a bread knife, and a spatula (palette knife) and you're ready to chop, shred, slice, or spread anything.

Bowls
Large, medium, and small are all useful, and if they stack, that's better. Pyrex are good because they can withstand heat and their depth means fewer splashes.

Measuring cups, spoons, and pitchers
Metal or plastic cups and spoons are fine. Look for a set of cups with 1 cup (240 ml), ½ cup (120 ml), ⅓ cup (80 ml) and ¼ cup (60 ml). I always take mine off the ring to avoid washing up the whole set when I've used only one.

One each of small, medium, and large liquid measuring cups will be useful if you plan to cook a lot. Glass is best so you can clearly see the level.

Scales
If you want to buy kitchen scales, go for a digital set that measures in increments of at least 5 g, that can be easily wiped clean and that has a "tare" or zero function so you can weigh one ingredient on top of another. You can measure liquids as well as dry goods on your scale, because 1 ml of water, juice or milk weighs 1 g. I like to weigh thick liquids, too, because it can be hard to get an accurate measurement in a cup or pitcher (jug).

Pans & dishes

All pan sizes are specified in my recipes. Personally, I like to use sturdy stainless steel saucepans with a copper layer inside the base, and anodized nonstick skillets or frying pans, all with handles that are ovenproof. Roasting pans should be sturdy so that they don't warp. A couple of large ceramic dishes (about 11 x 8 inches/28 x 20 cm) are useful, too. Make sure you line baking pans carefully using nonstick baking parchment paper, the kind with silicon coating (not wax/greaseproof). Reuseable mats are also a good investment if you like to bake a lot.

Ingredients & Shopping

Don't worry, I don't assume you'll be at the farmers' market every day. These recipes can be created entirely from the supermarket and by visiting a farmers' market or local specialty store, butcher, and deli whenever or if you can. Shop smart for your pantry and staples, then spend whatever you can afford on meat, eggs, and dairy produce—you'll notice the difference.

Meat

Your butcher will prepare meat if you ask. If you need to, take a shot of the recipe you're cooking from and show them. Choose where you buy your meat wisely, from a traceable source and animals that have been well cared for. Buying as good as you can for your budget is the aim, and free-range and organic, the ideal. Beef should be well-marbled with fat and with a natural (not bright red) color, and ideally well hung for flavor. All meat and poultry should have no discoloration or sliminess, and definitely no bad smell. Be especially careful with poultry. Storage: Keep in at the bottom of the refrigerator on a tray for up to 3 days, so that no drips can reach other food below. Defrost frozen meat overnight in the refrigerator in the same way.

Fish

It can be really hard to know what's sustainable and what isn't as the fish-to-eat lists change so regularly. Choose fish labeled as sustainably caught, and be prepared to try something new. Whole fish should be bright eyed and firm, with red gills and no fishy smell. Fillets are harder to gauge for freshness, but look for flashing bright scales and firm flesh. Dismiss anything that looks mushy or dull. Frozen fish can often be fresher than unfrozen and a good choice if you are shopping ahead of time. Storage: Buy fish and seafood from the fish dealer on the day you need it, or follow use by dates on prepacked fish. Defrost as for meat.

Eggs

Again I'd advocate organic or cage-free. Look for the longest sell by dates on the carton because these will be the most fresh on the shelf. Storage: Keep chilled, away from strong-smelling foods.

Fruit and vegetables

Wash before use. Go for what's in season because it will always taste best. Choose fruit that feels heavy for its size. The odd blemish is normal, but leave anything with squashy patches or bruising. Leafy vegetables should be lively, not wilting. Leave skins on for best flavor or peel carefully, because much of the flavor and nutrients lie just beneath the skin. Storage: In a cool, dark place or the refrigerator, the exception being those that need to ripen, plus bananas, which will go black if they get cold. Take tomatoes, avocados, and any fruit from the refrigerator at least an hour before eating because the cold will otherwise dull their flavor and texture. Citrus are easier to squeeze from room temperature; choose unwaxed if you are to use the zest, wash well in warm soapy water before zesting.

Dairy produce
Generally milk, yogurt, soft cheese, and cream will keep for about a week. If you eat cheese uncooked, it's more flavorful, and will have the correct texture, if served at room temperature. Unless stated, milk is whole, and yogurt and cheese in these recipes are whole (full fat)—mainly because they are more predictable for cooking and taste better. Heavy (double) cream can be swapped for whipping cream or regular (full fat) crème fraiche in some instances. Don't boil light (single or reduced-fat) cream or sour cream, because they will split.

The Pantry
Arm yourself with a basic store.

Oils and butter
Keep olive oil (or vegetable oil) for general cooking, and use extra virgin olive (or cold-pressed canola/rapeseed oil) for finishing and dressings. Sunflower oil and vegetable oil are good for frying, because they will not burn at high temperatures. Unsalted butter is the best for baking and buttery sauces, because you are able to determine the level of salt in your recipe.

Cans, jars, and tubes
I often use canned tomatoes and tomato puree (passata), plus tomato paste (puree) is one of my all time essentials. Canned beans (pulses) such as chickpeas, cannellini, and black beans, can be interchanged easily. Roasted peppers, prepared artichokes, olives, and other antipasti vegetables come in handy, too. My favorite olives for cooking are the small, dried Provencal type, which are pitted (stoned) for convenience. Once opened, keep jars in the refrigerator and make sure that the top layer is covered with liquid to keep air out. Coconut milk is a good standby for curries and pomegranate molasses for finishing Middle-Eastern style recipes.

Pasta, noodles, rice, and cornmeal
All of these will last almost indefinitely. Most pasta shapes can be substituted for another, so I tend to store one long shape and one short shape. If you enjoy Asian-style food, then pick up a package of rice noodles and also egg noodles. I like using couscous (often whole wheat/wholemeal) for its almost instant-ness, plus quinoa and spelt, as sustaining whole grains for salads and pilafs. When making risottos, try to use carnaroli rice. Cornmeal (polenta) should be the quick-cooking variety.

Flour
Try to use good-quality flour, because this is the foundation of most of your baking. I've mainly used all-purpose (plain) flour and added my own leavening (raising) agents (baking powder or bicarbonate of soda or both), however a few recipes use self-rising (self-raising) flour. If you can't find it, then mix every 1 cup (125 g) all-purpose flour with 1½ teaspoons baking powder. It's best to make a full cup, sift them together well, then measure what you need, instead of trying to guess proportions for the quantity of flour the recipe includes. You can keep the leftover flour for another time. If you do have USA self-rising flour, note that it contains ¼ teaspoon salt per cup, and you will not to need to add the salt that is listed in the recipe.

Spices and spice pastes
Dried chili flakes, ground or whole cumin seeds, coriander, turmeric, chili powder, paprika (both smoked and ordinary), cinnamon, nutmeg, and ginger are all regulars here. Try to buy spices in small quantities, because they lose their potency after a couple of months, and store them in a cool, dark place. Curry pastes are invaluable for the time-pressed cook. Try to pick authentic imported brands for the best flavor. Whole vanilla beans (pods) are

ideal when you want to see flecks of vanilla as well as taste their superior flavor, but they are expensive. You can use vanilla paste or extract instead.

Dried herbs
When fresh herbs aren't available, use 1 teaspoon dried herbs to every small bunch of fresh where they can reasonably be substituted, such as in long, slow cooking. Dried rosemary instead of fresh is fine in a marinade (go easy, it's strong), but dried parsley isn't right in a couscous salad.

Dried fruit, nuts & seeds
Look for plump dried fruit. Good-quality golden raisins (sultanas) tend to have fewer crunchy stems (stalks). Nuts, especially ground nuts, can turn rancid within months, so don't stock up.

Mustards
Whole-grain mustard and Dijon are the commonly used mustards in cooking, because they have a gentle, rounded flavor. English mustard is more fiery.

Garlic
Choose garlic with tight, papery, and unblemished skin. I always choose bulbs with larger cloves.

Anchovies & capers
I prefer anchovies in oil and small capers in brine, because they don't need to be rinsed before use.

Flavored oils
Sesame oil adds a rich nuttiness to Asian and other dishes, and walnut oil gives bitter-sweet flavor to salad dressings. Flavored oils need to be kept in a cool place away from direct light.

Salt & pepper
I use flaky sea salt (coarse kosher salt is fine) and crush it between my fingers. I freshly grind black peppercorns to get the maximum flavor and aroma.

Vinegars
Choose a bottle of good-quality white or red wine vinegar—it will last for months and give your salad dressings and sauces perfect piquancy. I've used apple cider vinegar and rice wine vinegar in some recipes when looking for sweeter flavor—but if you can't find or afford them, white wine vinegar and a pinch of sugar will do fine. Balsamic is sweeter, normally a little thicker, and good for dressing as well as cooking.

Broth (Stock)
The better the broth (stock), the better the dish. Good-quality store-bought liquid broth (or, better still, homemade) is the best option for meat gravies, because it will contain some of the natural gelatine from the bones used to make it. If you buy organic meat, choose organic broth, too. However, broth made by dissolving a cube or bouillon powder in hot water is fine to add to most everyday recipes, as are concentrated liquid broths.

Alcohol
A bottle of white wine or dry sherry is useful. Don't buy anything too expensive for cooking, but don't add any rough old wine or liquor (spirit) either; your food deserves better.

Sauces
Worcester sauce, soy sauce, Tabasco, and ketchup are all useful to have on hand, as are harissa or chili paste. Thai fish sauce is essential for a Thai flavor.

Chocolate
Chocolate with 70% cocoa solids has an intense cocoa hit and works well for desserts and more decadent baked items. Usually, I like to bake with chocolate that has 60% cocoa solids, because it has a deep chocolate flavor but is easy to work with. It can be harder to find, so I use half 50% and half 70% to hit the right percentage.

Breakfast & Brunch

Cinnamon Rolls

Preparation time: 35 minutes,
plus 1½ hours for rising
Cooking time: 20 minutes
Makes 12

Here's something really worth getting out of bed for. As with most dough-based recipes, these sticky rolls take a little while to put together, but this recipe cuts out any lengthy kneading. The rolls are best eaten warm, so if you want to make them the night before, follow the getting ahead note on page 18.

4 cups (500 g) all-purpose (plain) flour, plus extra for shaping the dough

1 tsp salt

¼ cup (50 g) superfine (caster) sugar

2 tsps (7 g) instant dry (fast-action) yeast

1¼ sticks (150 g) soft unsalted butter, plus extra for the pan

1 cup (240 ml) milk, plus 2 tbsp for the icing

2 large (UK medium) eggs

vegetable oil, for greasing

½ cup packed (100 g) light brown sugar

1 tsp ground cinnamon

½ cup (85 g) golden raisins (sultanas), raisins, or a mixture of both

½ cup (50 g) pecan nuts

1¼ cups (150 g) confectioners' (icing) sugar

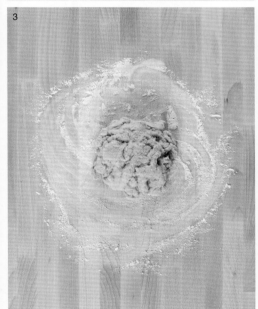

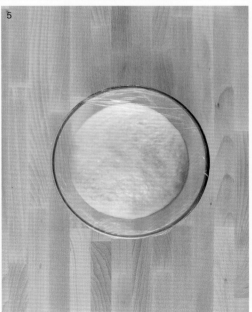

1

Put the flour, salt, superfine (caster) sugar, and yeast into a large bowl. Melt 3½ tablespoons (50 g) of the butter in a small saucepan then add 1 cup (240 ml) milk. When the milk is warm, take from the heat and beat in the eggs using a fork.

2

Quickly mix the wet ingredients into the dry ones until you have a rough, sticky dough. Cover with plastic wrap (clingfilm), then set it aside for 10 minutes.

3

Sprinkle a little of the flour over the work surface, then scrape the dough out of the bowl.

4

Dust the top of the dough with a little flour. With dry, floured hands, knead the dough into a smoother, springy ball. This should take 3 minutes or so.

HOW TO KNEAD
Hold the left edge of the dough down with one hand, then grab the farthest edge with the other and push it away from you. Fold the dough back on top of itself, press it down, give the dough a quarter turn, then repeat. After a few turns, the dough will be smooth and elastic. Use more flour if the dough sticks.

5

Rub a little oil around the inside of a large bowl, then put in the dough. Lightly oil a sheet of plastic wrap and cover the bowl. Put the bowl in a warm (not hot) place. After 1 hour, the dough will have doubled in size.

6

Flour the work surface and your hands, then turn the dough out. Press the dough into a rectangle of about 16 × 12 inches (40 × 30 cm).

7

For the filling, spread the remaining soft butter over the dough, then sprinkle with the light brown sugar, cinnamon, and golden raisins (sultanas) or raisins. Chop the pecans and sprinkle over.

8

Take hold of one of the long sides, then roll the dough around the filling, as though you're rolling up a carpet.

9

Using a sharp knife dipped in a little flour, cut off the very ends of the roll and discard them, then cut the rest of the roll into 12 equal slices.

10

Use a little butter to grease the inside of a baking or roasting pan measuring around 9 × 13 inches (23 × 33 cm). Put the rolls into the pan, cut sides up, spaced apart.

11

Rub a little vegetable oil over a sheet of plastic wrap, then loosely drape it over the rolls. Leave them in a warm place for 30 minutes, or until the dough looks puffy and the rolls have grown together. Preheat the oven to 350°F/180°C/Gas Mark 4.

12

Bake the rolls for 20 minutes, until risen and golden. Cool in the pan for 15 minutes, then turn out and put them onto a cooling rack. Sift the confectioners' (icing) sugar into a bowl, then mix with 2 tablespoons milk to make a smooth, runny icing. Spoon it over the rolls while they're still warm.

GETTING AHEAD

Make the dough the day before, then put the rolls into the refrigerator at the end of step 10. They will rise, but at a slower rate.

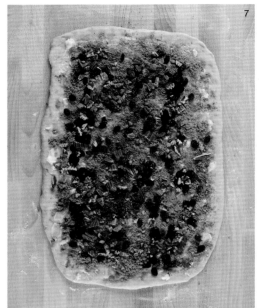

Eggs Benedict

Preparation time: 15 minutes
Cooking time: 15 minutes
Serves 2

Start the weekend in style with this
classic brunch dish. Hollandaise
has a reputation for being difficult,
but follow this method and you'll
have a rich, smooth sauce without
any stress. Choose the freshest eggs
possible—look for the carton with
the longest use-by date. The fresher
the egg, the more the white and yolk
will cling together as it poaches.

---

7 tablespoons (100 g) unsalted
    butter, plus extra for spreading
6 large (UK medium) eggs
½ tsp plus 1 tbsp white wine vinegar
½ lemon
1 tsp salt
1 pinch cayenne pepper, plus
    extra to serve
2 English muffins
2 slices cooked ham
salt and pepper

1
Melt the butter in a small saucepan, then keep it warm over the lowest heat the stove can manage. In the meantime, boil a medium saucepan filled halfway with water.

2
Separate 2 of the eggs, putting the yolks into a medium heatproof mixing bowl. When the pan of water is simmering, sit the bowl on top of the pan, ensuring the bottom of the bowl does not touch the water. Add ½ teaspoon vinegar to the yolks.

3
Using an electric mixer, or a whisk, whisk the yolks for about 3 minutes, or until they have thickened and have turned pale in color. Make sure that the water below is simmering, not boiling.

4
Keep whisking, then pour in the warm butter in about 6 batches, whisking well after each addition until creamy. Remove the pan from the heat when all the butter has been added and the sauce is silky, thickened, and spoonable. If the sauce splits and turns runny, don't worry: Scrape it into a cold bowl and whisk in a spoon of cold water until it comes back together. Failing that, try whisking the split mixture into another egg yolk in a clean bowl.

5
Squeeze the lemon, then stir 1 teaspoon of the juice into the sauce with the cayenne pepper. Season with a little salt and more lemon, if you like. The sauce should have a good balance of richness and tanginess. If it seems too thick, add 2 teaspoons hot water. Cover the surface of the sauce with plastic wrap to prevent a skin from forming on the top. It will stay warm over the pan while you poach the eggs.

6

To poach the eggs, half-fill a saucepan with hot water. Bring to a boil, add 1 teaspoon salt and 1 tablespoon vinegar, then turn the heat down to a very gentle simmer, with a bubble rising to the surface every now and then. Crack 1 egg into a cup. Fill a bowl with cold water and set to one side for later. Using a slotted spoon, stir the water in the pan into a whirlpool.

7

Gently slide the egg from the cup into the middle of the swirling water. Don't worry if it looks messy to begin with—it will become a neater, rounder shape as it spins and cooks.

8

Keep the water at a gentle simmer for 3 minutes, until the white is set and the yolk is still soft. Don't disturb the egg as it cooks. Now use the slotted spoon to carefully lift the egg from the pan and into the bowl of cold water. Poach the remaining eggs and set them aside in the water as each one is cooked.

9

Slice the muffins in two, then toast them and spread with butter. Fold half a piece of ham onto each piece of muffin. Return the eggs to the hot water to reheat briefly, then lift them out one by one with the slotted spoon. Hold a paper towel under the spoon for a few seconds to absorb any drips of water (these could make the muffins soggy). Ease the egg on top of the ham, then repeat with the rest of the eggs.

10

Spoon over plenty of the hollandaise sauce and enjoy immediately, sprinkled with a little more cayenne, if you like.

Fruity Nut & Oat
Morning Muffins

Preparation time: 15 minutes
Cooking time: 20 minutes
Makes 12

Some morning muffins feel too indulgent, some too worthy. These have the perfect balance: moist, sweet but not too sweet, and full of texture. They'll keep you going until lunch.

¾ cup (80 g) pecan nuts

½ cup packed plus 2 tbsp (120 g) light brown sugar

scant ½ cup (50 g) mixed seeds (try pumpkin, sesame, and sunflower seeds)

⅔ cup (65 g) rolled (porridge) oats

12 dried pitted dates, about ⅓ cup (50 g) prepared

scant ½ cup (50 g) golden raisins (sultanas)

2 cups (250 g) self-rising (raising) flour

½ tsp ground cinnamon

1 stick plus 1 tablespoon (125 g) unsalted butter

1 cup (250 g) plain (natural) yogurt

2 large (UK medium) eggs

1 large carrot

salt, if needed (see page 12)

1
Line a 12-hole muffin pan with paper baking cups and preheat the oven to 400°F/200°C/Gas Mark 6. Coarsely chop the pecan nuts. Mix 1 tablespoon each of the sugar, seeds, oats, and pecans together in a small bowl and set aside—this will make the topping.

2
Snip the dates into small pieces using kitchen scissors. In a large bowl, mix the dates and golden raisins (sultanas) with the remaining sugar, seeds, oats, and pecans, the flour, cinnamon, and a pinch of salt.

LUMPS IN THE SUGAR?
Because light brown sugar is stickier than other types, it can sometimes clump together. If you need to, rub the dry ingredients through your fingers a few times once the sugar has been added, squashing any lumps of sugar as you find them.

3
Melt the butter gently in a small saucepan. Take off the heat, and then, using a fork, beat in the yogurt, followed by the eggs.

4

Coarsely grate the carrot. Measure it after grating—you will need about 1⅓ cups (150 g). Add the butter mixture and grated carrot to the flour mixture. Using a spatula or metal spoon, stir everything together quickly, until just combined and still flecked with some dry flour. It's important not to overwork the mix, or the muffins may be chewy.

5

Scoop generous spoonfuls of the batter into the muffin cups until you've evenly filled each one. The easiest way to do this is to use 2 spoons. Scoop a big spoonful of batter from the bowl, then push it into the cup using the other spoon. Use all of the batter, and don't worry, the cups will be very full. Sprinkle with the topping.

6

Bake the muffins for 20 minutes, until risen, golden, and smelling delicious. Let cool for about 5 minutes, then lift the muffins out onto a wire rack. Eat warm or cold.

SURE THEY'RE READY?
Poke a toothpick or skewer into the middle of one of the muffins. It should come out dry. If the toothpick comes out coated in sticky batter, return the muffins to the oven for another 5 minutes.

STORING THE MUFFINS
They'll keep in an airtight container for 3–4 days.

Huevos Rancheros
(Mexican Spiced Beans
with Eggs)

Preparation time: 30 minutes
Cooking time: 10 minutes
Serves 2 (easily doubled)

Start the day with some spice with
this wonderfully healthy and filling
vegetarian breakfast dish. If you like
your eggs with cheese, sprinkle with
a handful of grated well-flavored
cheese (such as Cheddar or feta)
before broiling (grilling) at the end
of step 5.

---

1 onion

1 red bell pepper

½ green chile

1 large clove garlic

1 tbsp vegetable or sunflower oil

1 small bunch cilantro
    (coriander)

1 tsp ground cumin

1 (14-oz/400-g) can diced or
    chopped tomatoes

1 tsp chipotle paste

1 (14-oz/400-g) can pinto
    beans, drained

2 large (UK medium) eggs

salt and pepper

soft flour tortillas, to serve (optional)

1

Halve and slice the onion, then seed and chop the bell pepper into chunky pieces. Slice the chile (leave the seeds in if you like it hot) and crush the garlic. Heat a medium ovenproof skillet or frying pan over low heat, then add the oil. After 30 seconds, add the vegetables and stir well.

2

Cook the vegetables gently for 10 minutes or until softened.

3

While the vegetables soften, finely chop the stems from the cilantro (coriander). Stir the stems and the cumin into the pan, then cook for another 3 minutes, until it smells fragrant. Stir the tomatoes, chipotle paste, and pinto beans into the pan, then simmer for 5 minutes or until the tomato juices have thickened a little. Season with salt and pepper. Preheat the broiler (grill) to medium.

CHIPOTLE PASTE
Chipotle paste gives the beans a sweet, smoky, rounded flavor. If you can't find it, add 1 teaspoon tomato paste (puree), 1 teaspoon sugar, and ½ teaspoon paprika or smoked paprika instead.

PINTO BEANS
Pinto beans are traditionally used in Mexican cooking, but if you can't find them, try cranberry (borlotti) beans instead.

4

Crack an egg into a small cup. Use a spoon to make 2 hollows in the beans, then slide the egg into one of them. Repeat with the second egg.

5

Cover the pan with a lid, then cook gently for 5 minutes, until the eggs are cooked underneath but still a little wobbly on the top. To finish cooking the tops, put the pan under the broiler for 1–2 minutes, depending on how you like them.

6

To serve the dish, coarsely chop the cilantro leaves and sprinkle them over the pan. Good with warmed flour tortillas.

WARMING TORTILLAS
Soft-flour tortillas are available in most stores. To warm them, either give them a quick blast in the microwave, or wrap them in aluminum foil and heat in the oven at 350°F/180°C/Gas Mark 4 for 10 minutes.

Buttermilk Pancakes with Blueberries & Syrup

Preparation time: 10 minutes
Cooking time: 15 minutes
Serves 4 (makes 16 pancakes)

Who can resist a stack of light and fluffy pancakes? Piled high and drenched with maple syrup, they're very hard to refuse.

---

2 cups (250 g) all purpose (plain)
    flour
3 tbsp superfine (caster) sugar
1 tbsp baking powder
½ tsp salt
1 tbsp unsalted butter, plus extra
    to serve
½ cup (120 ml) milk
1 cup (250 g) buttermilk
1 tsp vanilla extract
2 large (UK medium) eggs
1 lemon, optional
2 tbsp vegetable or sunflower oil,
    for frying
1⅓ cups (200 g) blueberries
maple syrup, to serve

1
Put the flour, sugar, baking powder, and salt into a large bowl and whisk to combine. Make a well in the middle of the mixture.

2
Melt the butter in a small saucepan, then take off the heat. Whisk in the milk, buttermilk, vanilla, and finally the eggs. Finely grate the lemon zest, if using, and stir it in.

CAN'T FIND BUTTERMILK?
Buttermilk is slightly acidic, which helps the mix become extra fluffy and light. If you can't find buttermilk, you can use yogurt instead, or simply put 1 cup (240 ml) milk into a bowl or pitcher (jug) and add the juice from half a lemon. Let sit for a few minutes until the milk looks thick and lumpy, then use as above.

3

Pour the wet ingredients into the well in the dry ingredients.

4

Whisk to make a thick, smooth batter. Don't overwork it. If you plan to cook all the pancakes before eating them, preheat the oven to 275°F/140°C/Gas Mark 1.

5

Heat a large nonstick skillet or frying pan over a medium heat. Add 1 teaspoon of the oil, let it heat for a few seconds, then add 3 large spoonfuls of batter, helping each spoonful to spread out with the tip of the spoon. The mix should sizzle gently as the first spoonful hits the oil. Cook the pancakes for 1 minute, or until small bubbles start to pop on the surface and there's a tinge of gold around the edges.

6

Slide a spatula (fish slice) under a pancake and flip it over. Repeat with the remaining pancakes and cook for a minute on the second side, or until they are puffy and springy in the middle. Lift onto a plate. Eat immediately or keep warm in the preheated oven while you cook the rest of the pancakes. Add a little more oil to the pan for each batch.

7

Serve the pancakes hot, with a pat of butter, a drizzle of maple syrup, and a handful of blueberries.

TOO MUCH EFFORT FOR THE MORNING?

Although they're always best made fresh, you can make the pancakes the night before and reheat them in the morning. Either toast briefly, or preheat the oven to 350°F/180°C/ Gas Mark 4 and put the pancakes onto a heatproof dish. Cover with aluminum foil and reheat for 10 minutes, then serve.

Corn Cakes with Avocado Salsa & Bacon

Preparation time: 20 minutes
Cooking time: about 15 minutes
Serves 4 (makes 12 cakes)

Sizzling corn cakes with crisp bacon and a zingy salsa make a refreshing change from a traditional breakfast or brunch. For the puffiest, lightest corn cakes, cook the batter as soon as it's made.

---

2 ripe avocados

1 bunch scallions (spring onions)

1 mild red chile

2 limes

1⅔ cups (200 g) self-rising (raising) flour

½ tsp baking powder

¼ tsp salt, if needed (see page 12)

scant 1 cup (200 ml) milk

2 large (UK medium) eggs

2 (7-oz/200-g) cans corn kernels (sweet corn), drained

3 tbsp sunflower or vegetable oil

8 slices (rashers) dry-cured regular (streaky) bacon

salt and pepper

chili sauce, to serve (optional)

1
Make the salsa first. Cut each avocado in half. To do this, carefully push the blade of a knife into the avocado, until it stops against the pit (stone). Slide the knife all the way around the avocado, keeping the blade against the pit. Pull out the knife, then twist the two halves apart. Scoop out the pit with a spoon. Peel the skin away from the flesh, then cut the flesh into coarse cubes, or use a teaspoon to scoop the flesh into a bowl, if that's easier.

2
Thinly slice the scallions (spring onions) and seed and chop the chile. Mix half of the scallions and chile with the avocado and season with salt and pepper. Halve the limes and squeeze their juice over. Stir, then set the bowl aside.

TO SEED A CHILE
Cut the chile along its length, then use the tip of a teaspoon to scrape out the fiery seeds and white pith.

3
Make the corn cake batter. Mix the flour, baking powder, and salt in a large bowl, then add the milk and eggs. Whisk to a smooth, thick batter. Stir in the corn kernels (sweet corn) and remaining chile and scallions into the batter.

4

Preheat the broiler (grill) to high, ready to cook the bacon later. To cook the corn cakes, heat a large nonstick skillet or frying pan over medium-high heat. Add 2 teaspoons of the oil, and let it heat up for 30 seconds, then spoon in 3 large spoonfuls of the batter, well spaced apart. Let heat for 1 minute, or until the edges are golden and the batter starts to bubble on top.

5

Using a spatula (fish slice), turn the corn cakes over. Cook for another minute, or until the cakes look puffy and feel springy to the touch in the middle. Transfer to a plate and keep warm, either at the bottom of the broiler or in a low oven. Repeat with more oil and batter.

6

Put the bacon onto the rack of a broiler pan, then broil for 3 minutes on each side, or until crisp.

7

Serve the corn cakes on warmed plates with the salsa and bacon. A spot of chili sauce makes a very good addition.

Bircher Muesli

Preparation time: 5 minutes,
plus soaking
Serves 4–6

If you're looking for a healthy but
more exciting breakfast, try this
super-easy soaked muesli. I've used
raisins plus some apricots to add
sweetness and texture, but if you'd
rather use dates, dried apple, or
whatever dried fruit is available, then
feel free to throw them in. Finish it
off with fresh fruit and a drizzle of
honey or maple syrup.

---

2 apples (choose crisp apples with
    a good tangy flavor such as
    Braeburn, Fuji, or Pink Lady)
1⅔ cups (150 g) rolled (porridge)
    oats
1¼ cups (300 g) plain (natural)
    yogurt
½ cup (85 g) raisins or golden
    raisins (sultanas)
⅓ cup (50 g) ready-to-eat dried
    apricots or peaches
⅔ cup (150 ml) good-quality apple
    cider (cloudy apple juice)
¾ cup (80 g) slivered (flaked) toasted
    almonds
a splash of milk, if needed
1⅓ cups (7 oz/200 g) blueberries or
    other fresh fruit, to serve
maple syrup or honey, to serve
    (optional)

1
Coarsely grate the apples, without peeling first.

2
Put the apples, oats, yogurt, and raisins or golden raisins (sultanas) into a medium bowl. Snip in the dried apricots or peaches.

3
Add the apple juice, then stir well until evenly mixed. Cover the surface of the muesli with plastic wrap (clingfilm), then chill for at least 30 minutes or ideally overnight, which makes life easier in the morning.

4
Next day, give the muesli a stir. If it seems thick, loosen it with a splash of milk (or you can use more yogurt.) Stir in most of the toasted nuts.

Spoon the muesli into bowls or glasses, top with the rest of the nuts and the berries, then drizzle with honey or maple syrup to your taste.

Avocado & Chorizo Toast

Preparation time: 5 minutes
Cooking time: 5 minutes
Serves 4

Wake up your taste buds with this
big-flavored alternative to the bacon
sandwich: my perfect food for the
morning after the night before.
The quality of the bread will really
make all the difference here; you
want something with a good chewy
crust and character. If you can't find
sourdough, then halve
and toast some ciabatta or a
baguette instead.

---

9 oz (250 g) cooking chorizo
    sausages
2 ripe avocados
4 scallions (spring onions)
2 limes
a few shakes Tabasco sauce
1 tbsp extra virgin olive oil, plus
    extra for drizzling
4 thick slices good-quality bread,
    such as sourdough
1 clove garlic
1 handful fresh cilantro (coriander)
salt and pepper

1

Cut the sausages into bite-sized pieces. Heat a skillet or frying pan, add the sausages to the dry pan, then fry for 5 minutes, until golden and crisp around the edges. The sausages will release their own red oil as they cook.

CHORIZO
This spicy Spanish sausage is flavored with paprika and garlic, with a delicious smokiness. There are two types: cooking chorizo, which is soft like a regular sausage, and cured chorizo, which is firm and dry and eaten raw like a salami.

2

Meanwhile, cut each avocado in half, then use a spoon to scoop out the pits (stones) and the flesh. Coarsely slice or chop the flesh.

CHOOSING & STORING AVOCADOS
A ripe avocado will yield when gently pressed at the stem end. Don't buy anything that feels squashy, because it will be past its best. An underripe avocado will soon ripen up in the fruit bowl or in a paper bag with an apple (apples release a gas that speeds up ripening). Store the ripe fruit in the refrigerator.

3

Thinly slice the scallions (spring onions) and squeeze the juice from one lime. Add the juice and scallions to the avocados in a bowl. Shake in the Tabasco, add the oil, then season to taste with salt and pepper. Cut the remaining lime into wedges.

4

Preheat the broiler (grill) to high and spread out the bread on a baking pan (tray). Broil (grill) until golden on both sides. Cut the garlic in half and rub the cut side on the toast. Drizzle with a little extra virgin olive oil.

5

Top the toast with the avocado mixture, followed by the sizzling sausages and a spoonful of the cooking juices. Tear the cilantro (coriander) leaves over the top and serve with the extra lime wedges for squeezing.

Breakfast Blinis with Smoked Salmon

Preparation time: 15 minutes
Cook time: less than 10 minutes
Serves 4

Buckwheat flour gives a light nuttiness to these pancakes. A traditional blini would be made with yeast, but baking powder is a lot simpler and quicker to use. Have all your prep done before you cook the pancakes so you're free to eat them fresh from the pan and at their best.

1 bunch fresh dill
5 cups (100 g) wild arugula (rocket)
½ red onion
1 lemon
⅔ cup (150 g) crème fraîche or thick
    sour cream
2 tablespoons (25 g) unsalted butter
1⅔ cups (200 g) buckwheat flour
2 tsp baking powder
½ tsp fine salt
3 extra-large (UK large) eggs
1¼ cups (300 g) buttermilk or low-fat
    plain (natural) yogurt
2–3 tbsp vegetable or sunflower oil,
    for frying
1 tbsp capers in liquid (brine),
    drained
7 oz (200 g) smoked salmon
salt and pepper

1
Finely chop the dill and half of the arugula (rocket). Finely chop the onion.

2
Cut the lemon into wedges. Mix the crème fraîche or sour cream with a squeeze of lemon, then add half of the dill and season with salt and pepper.

3
Melt the butter in a saucepan or in a microwave-proof bowl.

4
Put the flour, baking powder, and salt into a large bowl. Crack the eggs into the bowl, then add the buttermilk and melted butter.

BUCKWHEAT FLOUR
Buckwheat isn't actually wheat, but a seed. The seeds are ground to make a nutty, grayish flour that is naturally gluten-free. Buckwheat grows well in harsh climates and soil too poor to sustain other cereal crops. It has been an important source of nutrition for centuries, used to make to make pancakes, noodles, pastas, and porridges. Find it in the baking or special diets area of larger stores. A mix of half and half whole-grain (wholemeal) and all purpose (plain) white flour makes a good substitute (but, of course, is no longer gluten free).

5

Using a balloon whisk, beat the ingredients until smooth and thick. Add the remaining chopped dill and chopped arugula.

6

When you're ready to cook, put the oven on low. Put a large nonstick skillet or frying pan over medium heat. Add a splash of the oil, then add three large spoonfuls of the batter. The batter should sizzle gently as it settles into the oil. Let the batter cook until you can see bubbles appear on the surface and a tinge of gold around the edge of each blini.

7

Flip the blinis carefully using a spatula (fish slice), then cook for another minute or so, until puffed up in the middle and golden on both sides. Keep the first few batches warm in the oven while you make the rest, adding a little more oil to the pan each time.

8

To serve, arrange the salmon on the blinis, spoon the dill cream on top, then sprinkle with the capers and onion. Serve with the remaining arugula leaves and a lemon wedge for squeezing.

Asparagus & Bacon Frittata

Preparation time: 5 minutes
Cooking time: about 15 minutes
Serves 4

Eggs, bacon, tomatoes—almost all
the elements of a classic traditional
English breakfast, but shaken up
with a fresh blast of basil pesto and
seasonal greens. Add a handful of
sliced mushrooms to the bacon,
if you like. If there are any leftovers
(I doubt it), pack them into lunch
boxes. Enjoy with good crusty bread.

---

6 slices (rashers) good regular
    (streaky) bacon (dry-cured is best)
5 oz (150 g) bunch asparagus
10 cherry tomatoes
8 large (UK medium) eggs
2 tbsp fresh store-bought pesto
extra virgin olive oil, for drizzling
salt and pepper
good-quality bread for serving
    (optional)

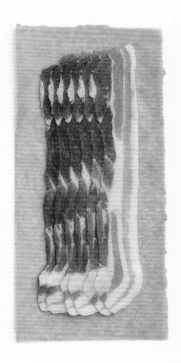
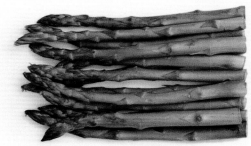

1
Snip the bacon into bite-sized pieces. Heat a 8-inch (20-cm) skillet or frying pan, then add the bacon and cook for 5 minutes or until golden and the fat has started to run.

2
Meanwhile, cut off the bottom 2 inches (5 cm) from each asparagus spear, because the ends can often be tough. Discard. Cut the spears into shorter lengths. Cut the cherry tomatoes in half.

3
Preheat the broiler (grill) to high. Lift the bacon onto a plate and spoon off the excess fat, leaving about 1 tablespoon behind in the pan. Add the asparagus to the pan and fry it for 3 minutes, or until bright green and just tender to the bite (try a bit if you're not sure, and remember it is going to cook more when the eggs are added).

WHY DRY-CURED BACON
Dry-cured bacon is processed without adding extra water to the pork. This means that it will release much less liquid, therefore shrinking less and crisping up more than other bacon.

4

Beat the eggs together. Season with pepper, but take it easy with the salt, because the bacon will add plenty. Return the bacon to the pan, then pour in the eggs. Turn the heat down to low.

5

Cook the frittata for 5 minutes, or until the eggs are nearly set. Stir the eggs around very gently a few times as they cook, letting the liquid egg fill the gaps that the spoon makes.

6

When the eggs are almost set, sprinkle with the cherry tomatoes, spoon over the pesto, then season with salt and pepper.

7

Put the pan under the broiler (grill) for just a few minutes, until the eggs are set and the top is turning golden. Serve cut into wedges, with a drizzle of extra virgin olive oil, and some good bread.

CHOOSING PESTOS
Fresh store-bought pesto has a better basil and Parmesan flavor than "ambient" pesto sold in a jar. It does cost more, but the flavor is worth it. Alternatively, you could add fresh chopped basil to jarred pesto, or make a batch yourself (see page 172).

Sticky Fig & Ricotta Toast

Preparation time: 5 minutes
Cooking time: 5 minutes
Serves 4, easily halved

Another great little breakfast that
looks stunning but is simplicity itself
to make. The maple and cinnamon
broiled (grilled) figs are also good
enjoyed as dessert, either warm
or cold, with thick yogurt.

8 ripe figs

1 handful whole almonds

2 tablespoons (25 g) unsalted butter

1 tsp ground cinnamon

4 tbsp maple syrup or honey

4 thick slices good-quality
   fruit bread

9 oz (250 g) ricotta cheese

1

2

1

Preheat the broiler (grill) to high. Trim the stems from the figs, if necessary, then cut a cross through each fig going almost all the way to the bottom. Open the fruit out a little, like a flower. Very coarsely chop the almonds.

2

Put the figs into a medium baking dish. Add a little dot of butter to the middle of each fig, then sprinkle with cinnamon and drizzle with the maple syrup or honey.

CHOOSING FIGS

Ripe figs will be soft, but not squashy, and smell honeyish. Some are deep purple when ripe, some more greenish. My favorites are deep ruby pink inside and not too dry. If you are shopping at the market, ask to see/try one before you buy. Store them in the refrigerator when ripe and enjoy them at room temperature.

3

Broil (grill) the figs for about
5 minutes, or until softened but not
collapsed and surrounded with a
delicious cinnamon butter syrup.

4

Let the figs cool for a few minutes.
While you wait, spread out the bread
on a baking pan and toast under the
broiler. Add the nuts to the baking
sheet when you toast the second
side of the bread.

5

Spread the ricotta over the toast,
then top with the figs, nuts, and
spoonfuls of the warm syrup.

Soups &
Salads

Greek Salad

Preparation time: 20 minutes
Serves 4

Save this classic salad for summer, when tomatoes are at their best. For a light meal, all that's needed is some crusty bread on the side. For a more filling option, drain and rinse a can of lima (butter) beans and stir through at the end of step 3. It's also good as a side dish for barbecued lamb or chicken.

---

8 medium or 4 large ripe tomatoes

1 small red onion

1 tbsp red wine vinegar

⅓ cup (80 ml) extra virgin olive oil

2 tsp dried oregano

1 cucumber

½ red bell pepper

1 handful fresh flat-leaf parsley

¾ cup (80 g) pitted kalamata or
    black olives

7 oz (200 g) feta cheese

salt and pepper

crusty bread, to serve (optional)

1
Cut each tomato into 6 wedges and finely slice the red onion. Put into a large mixing bowl. Splash over the vinegar and 3 tablespoons of the oil, then add 1 teaspoon of the oregano, and season with salt and pepper. Set aside for 10 minutes. This will soften the onion a little and draw some of the juices out of the tomatoes, which will help make a tasty dressing.

CHOOSING TOMATOES
A perfectly ripe tomato will be deep ruby red, yield a little to the touch, and smell aromatic. Unless they're a special variety, avoid tomatoes that are still green around the top or a pale orange-red, because their flavor will be disappointing.

2
Meanwhile, cut the cucumber in half, then halve each piece along its length. Peel off the skin using a peeler. Scoop out the seeds using a teaspoon, then discard them. This will stop the cucumber from becoming soggy. Cut the cucumber into half-moon slices.

3
Remove the seeds from the bell pepper, then finely slice it. Coarsely chop the parsley and add this to the bowl along with the bell pepper, cucumber, and olives. Stir.

Spoon the salad onto plates or shallow bowls, then crumble the cheese into each bowl. sprinkle the remaining oregano over the cheese and drizzle the remaining oil over and around. Serve with crusty bread.

Grilled Halloumi with Pomegranate Tabbouleh

Preparation time: 15 minutes
Cooking time: 5 minutes
Serves 4, easily doubled or more

Tabbouleh is a fresh, lively Middle Eastern salad of chopped herbs with plenty of lemon and bulgur wheat, and here I've added chickpeas to make it extra sustaining. The salad is also delicious with goat cheese, fish, grilled meat, and hummus, among other things.

⅔ cup (120 g) bulgur wheat
1⅔ cups (400 ml) vegetable broth (stock)
2 lemons
3 tbsp extra virgin olive oil, plus extra to drizzle (optional)
1 large bunch fresh flat-leaf parsley
1 large bunch fresh mint
1 bunch scallions (spring onions)
1 (14-oz/400 g) can chickpeas, drained
½ cup (100 g) pomegranate seeds
1 lb 2 oz (500 g) halloumi cheese
salt and pepper

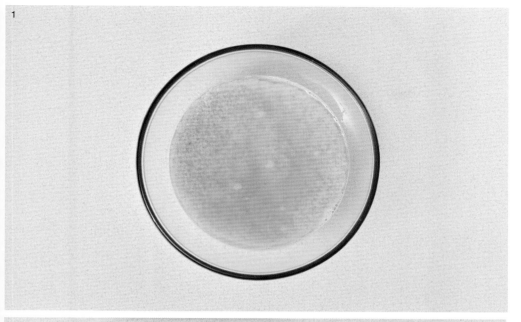

1
Put the bulgur wheat into a large bowl. Bring the broth (stock) to a boil in a saucepan. Pour it over the bulgur, then cover the bowl and let stand for 15 minutes or until tender.

2
While you wait, finely grate the zest from the lemons, then squeeze the juice from 1 (about 3 tablespoons). Whisk the zest and juice with the olive oil and some salt and pepper.

3
Pick the parsley and mint leaves, then finely chop. Trim and thinly slice the scallions (spring onions).

BULGUR WHEAT
Bulgur wheat is part-ground, part-cooked wheat that's really healthy and quick to use and has a more interesting texture than couscous. If you can't find bulgur, use couscous instead, adding enough hot broth (stock) to just cover the surface. Alternatively, the salad could easily be made with cooked quinoa, rice, or any other of your favorite grains.

4

Drain the bulgur in a sieve, then return to the bowl. Add the dressing, herbs, scallions, chickpeas, and most of the pomegranate seeds. Stir well and season to taste with salt and pepper.

5

When you're ready to serve, heat a ridged grill (griddle) pan. Cut the halloumi into slices about ½ inch (1 cm) thick. Cook the cheese for 2 minutes on each side, or until it comes away easily from the ridges of the pan. A spatula (fish slice) will be handy to lift and turn the cheese. If you don't have a grill pan, just fry the halloumi in a dry skillet or frying pan instead.

6

Spoon the salad onto serving plates, top with the cheese, then sprinkle with the rest of the pomegranate seeds. Serve with a wedge of lemon and a drizzle more oil, if you like.

Peach & Mozzarella Platter

Preparation time: less than 10 minutes
Serves 2, easily doubled or more

When fuzzy peaches are at their aromatic best, why save them for dessert? Served with salty cured ham, creamy cheese, and balsamic vinegar, they make one of the best lazy suppers going. Let the fruit come up to room temperature before preparing—the flavor will be more rounded and the texture softer.

---

2 ripe peaches or nectarines

4 slices prosciutto, Serrano, or
    other tasty cured ham

1 (8-oz/225-g) ball buffalo
    mozzarella, drained

1 handful fresh basil

2 tsp balsamic vinegar, or more
    to taste

a little extra virgin olive oil

salt and pepper

good crusty bread, to serve

1

Run your knife around each peach, then twist in half and remove the pits (stones). Cut the flesh into wedges.

PREPARING STONE FRUIT
Sometimes removing pits (stones) from peaches and other stone fruit (plums, cherries) is a cinch, sometimes not. It depends on whether the fruit is "clingstone" or "freestone." As you'd expect, clingstone peaches have flesh that clings to the pit and freestone fruit comes away easily. There's no real way to tell them apart when buying, but if you end up with clingstones, then don't worry—just cut the fruit away in large pieces instead.

2

Spread the peaches over a large plate. Tear the ham a little, then arrange it around and over the fruit.

3

Tear the mozzarella over the peaches and ham in coarse chunks or ribbons.

CHOOSING MOZZARELLA
Because this cheese will be eaten more or less unadulterated, quality is all-important. Save the cheaper cow milk mozzarella for topping pizzas or pasta casseroles.

4

Sprinkle with the leaves from the basil, the balsamic vinegar, and a little oil, then season with a little salt and plenty of black pepper. Enjoy the salad as soon as you have dressed it, with good crusty bread.

Cobb Salad with Honey Mustard Dressing

Preparation time: 20 minutes
Serves 4, or 6 as part of a meal

This useful salad will accommodate more or less anything you put in it. It's ideal for a picnic, just make sure that you layer up the ingredients in a sensible order: heavier things at the bottom and delicate at the top, and keep the buttermilk dressing separate until the final moment.

---

8 slices (rashers) smoked regular (streaky) bacon (dry-cured is best)

3–4 large (UK medium) eggs

1 (2¼-lb/1-kg) ready-cooked chicken

2 ripe avocados

2 tsp red or white wine vinegar

1 crisp, leafy lettuce such as Romaine or Cos

⅔ cup (150 g) buttermilk or plain (natural) low-fat natural yogurt

1 small clove garlic

1 tbsp honey

1 tbsp whole-grain mustard

1 handful chives or scallions (spring onions)

salt and pepper

1

Heat a nonstick skillet or frying pan over medium heat. Snip or cut the bacon into bite-size pieces, then add to the pan. Fry over medium heat for 5 minutes, or until crisp and the fat has run out of the meat. Set the bacon aside on paper towels, letting the excess fat drain away.

2

Meanwhile, put the eggs into a pan of cold water, then bring to a boil. Start a kitchen timer when big bubbles start to rise every few seconds. Boil the eggs for 7 minutes for yolks that are firm, but not totally dry in the middle.

3

Cool the eggs under cold running water for a few minutes, then peel and cut into quarters.

4

Tear the chicken into bite-size pieces, discarding the skin and the bones. If the chicken was hot when you bought it, and you're not eating the salad immediately, then let it cool thoroughly at this point.

5

Cut the avocado in half, then remove the pit (stone). Slice crisscrossed lines in the flesh, cutting down to, but not through, the skin. Scoop out the pieces of avocado with a spoon and drop into the bowl. Toss with 1 teaspoon of the vinegar to prevent the flesh from turning brown.

6

Shred the lettuce and use it to cover the chicken. Top with the avocado, then the bacon and eggs and sprinkle with a little salt and pepper.

7

Put the buttermilk or yogurt into a jar or small bowl. Crush the garlic, add to the jar with the remaining vinegar, then the honey and mustard, plus some salt and pepper. Snip in the chives using kitchen scissors. Seal the jar and shake or whisk with a fork to combine.

8

Serve the salad with the dressing to spoon over each serving. Make sure you dig down well so everyone gets a bit of everything.

Vietnamese Herb & Noodle Salad with Shrimp

Preparation time: 10 minutes
Serves 2, easily doubled

Fresh Vietnamese summer rolls are ideal summer food but, unless you live near a specialty grocery store or deli, the wrappers can be very hard to find. This recipe uses all the same flavors but has rice noodles instead of the wrappers. The salad goes wonderfully with shredded cooked chicken and pork, too.

2 oz (50 g) thin rice noodles

½ cucumber

2 carrots

1 handful fresh mint

1 handful fresh cilantro (coriander)

1 lime

1 tbsp nam pla (Thai fish sauce)

1 tbsp light brown sugar

1 small hot red or green chile

1 clove garlic

½ small iceberg lettuce

5 oz (150 g) whole cooked
   large shrimp (prawns)

1

Boil a saucepan or kettle of water. Put the noodles into a large heatproof bowl and pour plenty of just-boiled water over them to cover. Let stand for 5 minutes, until softened and just tender. Thicker noodles take more time to soak than thinner ones so check the package instructions.

2

Prepare the vegetables and herbs while you wait. Thinly slice the cucumber, then cut into sticks. Coarsely grate or shred the carrots. Pick the leaves from the mint and the cilantro (coriander). Tear any larger mint leaves.

RICE NOODLES

Rice noodles are all about texture. Made with rice flour, these slippery white noodles have a light, barely there flavor that will easily take on most Asian sauces and dressings and can also be used in soups. They vary from fine threads to wide ribbons and most just need a quick soaking or can be added at the end of cooking (check the package first). To prepare ahead, drain, rinse and drain again, then run a little oil through the strands to keep them separated.

3

Squeeze the lime juice and mix with the nam pla (Thai fish sauce) and sugar. Thinly slice the chile and crush the garlic, then add to the mixture.

4

Thinly shred the lettuce.

5

Drain the noodles in a sieve. If you are concerned that they might be starting to stick together, rinse under cold running water and let drain.

6

Toss the vegetables, noodles, herbs, and shrimp (prawns) together, then drizzle with the dressing to serve.

Steak Tagliata with Artichokes

Preparation time: 10 minutes,
plus marinating and resting
Cook time: 5 minutes
Serves 2, easily doubled or more

Italians love to eat tagliata (which
translates as "cut"), a classic
combination of chargrilled steak, peppery
leaves, and shaved Parmesan. I think it's
the perfect alternative to good old steak
and fries when the weather is hot. The
steak in the photographs is strip steak
(sirloin), but you can choose from other
cuts, too.

---

1 (9-oz/250-g) New York strip steak
   (sirloin), trimmed of excess fat
2 sprigs fresh rosemary
1–2 tbsp extra virgin olive oil
2½ cups (50 g) wild arugula (rocket)
3 oz (80 g) chargrilled artichoke
   hearts preserved in oil, drained
chunk of Parmesan cheese,
   for shaving
2 tsp capers in liquid (brine), drained
2 tsp balsamic vinegar
salt and pepper

1

Put the steak onto a plate. Finely chop the rosemary needles, then rub them all over the steak with 1 teaspoon oil. Cover and let marinate for at least 30 minutes at room temperature or up to 24 hours in the refrigerator.

STEAK TEMPERATURE
Cold meat is more likely to overcook because it takes longer for heat to reach the center of the steak or roast. Either marinate the steak ahead of time, then remove from the refrigerator 30 minutes before cooking, or take the steak from the refrigerator, rub with the marinade, and set aside for at least 30 minutes.

2

Heat a ridged grill (griddle) pan until very hot. Season the steak generously. Add the steak to the pan, then let it cook, without moving it, for 2 minutes (or 2½ minutes if it's particularly thick). Press the steak a few times with your tongs or a spatula to encourage a deep, golden crust underneath.

GRILLING MEAT
It's better to oil the meat than to add oil to the pan, because this will reduce the amount of smoke that will come from the pan. If the steak doesn't make a loud sizzle as soon as it hits the pan, then the pan isn't hot enough—take the steak out. Keeping the heat high encourages the meat to develop a brown crust and good flavor.

3

After 2 minutes, turn the steak over and fry for another 2 minutes. If the steak has fat around the edge, hold the steak fat edge down against the pan and cook for about 30 seconds, until golden. This will cook your steak to medium-rare. Adjust the timing accordingly to your taste.

4

Transfer the steak to a plate, cover loosely, and let rest for 2 minutes, or until surrounded with juices.

WHICH STEAK?
It's up to you what kind of steak you choose: filet mignon (fillet) is the most tender but also the costliest cut. Because filet has little fat throughout the meat, it's best cooked on the rarer side. Strip or tenderloin steak (sirloin) is a good all-round choice, with a fair marbling of fat but still very tender.

5

While the steak rests, sprinkle the arugula (rocket) and artichokes over a platter. Use a vegetable peeler to shave the Parmesan, or just grate it coarsely. You'll need a small handful.

6

Using a sharp knife, cut the steak into thick slices.

7

Nestle the steak into the salad, then pour over the resting juices. Sprinkle the salad with the Parmesan, capers, then the oil and vinegar. Serve immediately.

Chicken Noodle Soup

Preparation time: 15 minutes
Cooking time: 25 minutes
Serves 4

Reviving and low in fat, this chicken soup is much better than anything you can buy in a package, and it doesn't take much longer to prepare. Poaching the chicken in the soup means that all its flavor is trapped in the liquid and the meat won't dry out.

---

2 stalks celery

2 carrots

2 tablespoons (25 g) butter

½ tsp salt

1 sprig fresh thyme

1 bay leaf

2 skinless, boneless chicken breasts

5 cups (1.2 liters) chicken broth (stock)

1 nest thin egg noodles, about 2¼ oz (65 g)

1 small handful fresh flat-leaf parsley

½ lemon

salt and pepper

crusty bread, to serve (optional)

1

Finely chop the celery and carrots. Heat a medium saucepan over low heat, then add the butter. Once it's foaming, add the celery and carrots, ½ teaspoon salt, a few grinds of pepper, the thyme leaves, and bay leaf. Cover with a lid and cook gently for 10 minutes or until the vegetables are starting to soften, stirring occasionally.

2

Place the chicken breasts on top of the vegetables, then pour in the broth (stock).

3
Bring the pan to a boil, then
reduce the heat to a simmer. Cover,
then cook for 10 minutes, until the
chicken is cooked through and
the vegetables are tender. Lift the
chicken out of the pan and onto
a board. Shred the meat into small
pieces using 2 forks, or just chop
it into small pieces with a knife, then
return it to the pan.

IS THE CHICKEN COOKED?
After 10 minutes, the chicken will
have turned from pink to white. If in
doubt, lift a piece out, then slice it
through its thickest part. The meat
should be white all the way through.
If not, return it to the pan for another
couple of minutes.

4
Crumble the nest of noodles into the
pan with your hands, then simmer
for 4 minutes, until the noodles are
tender. Coarsely chop the parsley
and stir it through. Squeeze in a little
lemon juice, taste the soup, then
season with salt and pepper.

5
Enjoy the soup on its own, or with
crusty bread and butter.

GETTING AHEAD
If you're making this soup in
advance, prepare it to the end of
step 3, then stop. Once cool, chill
it in the refrigerator. When ready
to serve, bring the soup back to a
simmer, then add the noodles and
carry on as above.

Tomato & Thyme Soup

Preparation time: 5 minutes
Cooking time: 20 minutes
Serves 4

It's best to choose canned tomatoes over fresh for a soup like this, because they're packed with the intense flavor it needs.

---

1 carrot

1 onion

2 tablespoons (25 g) butter

1 sprig fresh thyme

1 large clove garlic

2 tbsp sun-dried tomato
   paste (puree)

3 (14-oz/400-g) cans diced or
   chopped tomatoes

2½ cups (600 ml) hot chicken or
   vegetable broth (stock)

3 tbsp light (single) or heavy (double)
   cream, plus a little more to serve

salt and pepper

crusty bread, to serve (optional)

1

Coarsely grate the carrot and coarsely chop the onion. Melt the butter in a medium saucepan, then add the onion, carrot, and almost all of the thyme leaves. Season with salt and pepper, then cover the pan.

2

Keeping the heat low, cook the vegetables for 15 minutes, until soft and sweet, but not colored. Stir them twice during cooking. Thinly slice or crush the garlic and add to the pan during this time.

3

Stir in the sun-dried tomato paste (puree), tomatoes, and broth (stock), then simmer gently for 5 minutes or until the vegetables are tender.

SUN-DRIED TOMATO PASTE
Sun-dried tomato paste is a little sweeter than ordinary tomato paste and contains oil, which adds to the texture of the soup. If you can't find it, use ordinary tomato paste, then and add a pinch of sugar and 2 teaspoons of olive oil.

4

Add the cream, then put an immersion (stick) blender into the pan and blend the soup until smooth. Alternatively, use a jug blender. Season to taste.

5

Ladle the soup into bowls, swirl in a little more cream, sprinkle with the remaining thyme, then serve, with crusty bread, if you like.

VARIATION
To serve this soup as an appetizer, it's good to give it a slightly silkier, smoother texture. After blending, pass the soup through a sieve into another pan. Be careful not to boil the soup when reheating it, because this will affect the texture.

Shrimp & Mushroom Laksa

Preparation time: 10 minutes
Cooking time: 10 minutes
Serves 4 (easily halved)

Spicy noodle soups like this one are staple quick dishes across southeast Asia. If laksa paste is hard to find, use a good-quality red or green Thai curry paste instead. Authentic Thai brands will have the best flavor. Laksa paste itself tends not to be spicy, so if you like your food hotter, add a little chopped chile during step 2.

3½ oz (100 g) rice noodles,
    either thick or thin
5 oz (150 g) shiitake or oyster
    mushrooms
1 bunch scallions (spring onions)
2 tsp vegetable or sunflower oil
2 tbsp laksa paste or Thai curry
    paste (red or green)
1⅔ cups (400 ml) coconut milk
    (use reduced fat, if you like)
1⅔ cups (400 ml) fish or chicken
    broth (stock)
7 oz (200 g) large, raw shrimp
    (prawns)
1 lime
1½ cups (5 oz/150 g) bean sprouts
1–2 tbsp nam pla (Thai fish sauce),
    to taste
½ tsp sugar
1 handful fresh cilantro (coriander),
    to serve

1
Boil a saucepan or kettle of water. Put the noodles into a large heatproof bowl, then pour over enough boiling water to cover. Let soak while you prepare the rest of the recipe. Stir the noodles a few times to separate any that have stuck together.

2
Meanwhile, slice the mushrooms thickly, and thinly slice the scallions (spring onions). Heat 1 teaspoon of the oil in a saucepan over high heat. Add the mushrooms and scallions and fry for 2 minutes, until just softened. Transfer to a plate.

3

Lower the heat, then add the remaining oil to the pan. Sizzle the laksa or Thai curry paste in the oil for 3 minutes, stirring frequently, until fragrant.

4

Stir in the coconut milk and broth (stock), then simmer for 2 minutes. Add the shrimp (prawns) to the pan, then simmer for 3 minutes or until the shrimp have turned from gray to pink all over. Squeeze the lime while you wait.

CHOOSING SHRIMP
Frozen shrimp (prawns) are just as good, if not better, than chilled shrimp, because they are frozen at sea when fresh. To defrost frozen raw shrimp quickly, put them into a bowl and cover with cold water. Change the water a couple of times over a 10-minute period, after which time the shrimp will be defrosted. Drain well.

5

Stir in the bean sprouts and return the scallions and mushrooms to the pan. Season the soup with the nam pla (Thai fish sauce), lime juice, and sugar, then take it off the heat. The bean sprouts should still have plenty of texture.

6

Drain the noodles in a colander, then divide among 4 serving bowls. Ladle over the soup, then tear over the cilantro (coriander) to serve.

Tuna Salad Niçoise

Preparation time: 10 minutes
Cooking time: 20 minutes
Serves 2 as a main course
(easily doubled)

Far more than just a salad, a proper tuna Niçoise is a filling, colorful meal packed with the classic punchy flavors of southern France. Quality of ingredients is important in this kind of cooking. If you start with good basics, you'll be rewarded with a dish you'll want to make again and again.

1 tsp salt

7 oz (200 g) new (salad) potatoes, about the size of small eggs

2 large (UK medium) eggs, at room temperature

3½ oz (100 g) fine green beans

1 small clove garlic

1 (5½-oz/160-g) can or jar of tuna in olive oil

1 tbsp red wine vinegar

½ small red onion

3½ oz (100 g) cherry tomatoes

4 anchovy fillets in oil, drained

½ cup (50 g) pitted Niçoise or other black olives

salt and pepper

1
Fill a medium saucepan with water, add 1 teaspoon salt, and bring to a boil. Add the potatoes, then boil for 20 minutes or until tender. With 7 minutes to go, add the eggs to the pan. Trim the stem end of the beans, then with 5 minutes left, add them to the pan.

2
Make the dressing while you wait. First slice the garlic and chop it finely. Sprinkle with some salt, then, holding the knife at an exaggerated slant, scrape and mash the garlic and salt together against the board until the garlic turns into a paste. Work on a little of the garlic at a time until all of the garlic is crushed.

GOT A GARLIC CRUSHER?
There's nothing wrong with using a garlic crusher if you find it easier than crushing with a knife. However, crushing the garlic to a paste with a knife helps to release more of the aromatic oils from within the clove.

3
Drain 3 tablespoons of the oil from the can of tuna into a small bowl. Whisk the vinegar and garlic into the oil, plus some salt and pepper.

4
Drain the eggs, potatoes, and beans into a colander. Rinse under cold running water for 1 minute to cool everything quickly, then set aside.

5

Finely slice the onion into half moons. Cut the tomatoes and potatoes in half. Put into a large bowl and add the beans and olives.

6

Crack the egg shells all over by knocking them gently on the work surface. Peel the shells away from the whites. If they're being resistant, peeling the eggs under cold water will help. Cut each egg in half. Season the cut side of each egg with salt and pepper.

7

Slice the anchovies in half lengthwise, or just chop. Toss most of the dressing with the vegetables.

8

Spoon the salad onto plates. Top each pile of salad with 2 halves of egg, some tuna, and some pieces of anchovy. Drizzle the rest of the dressing around, then serve.

SHOPPING TIPS
If you've already got salted anchovies in the cupboard, rinse them in plenty of water before use and substitute them for the anchovies in oil. Be sparing with the salt when seasoning the dressing.

Traditionally, this recipe would use the small, sourish black Niçoise olives of its region of origin. Kalamata olives make a good alternative.

Salad potatoes have a creamy, firm texture when cooked. Any small, waxy potato will work; try baby red or fingerling potatoes in the US, or Charlotte or Nicola in the UK. A salad potato is cooked when a knife slips easily through the flesh.

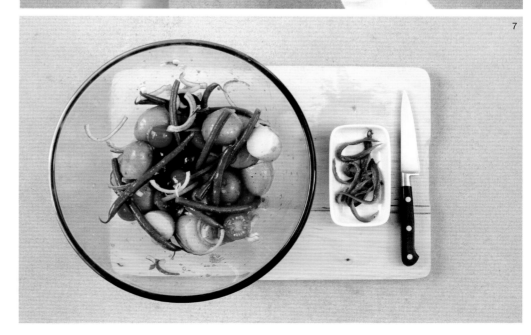

Made for Sharing

Crispy Duck Pancakes

Preparation time: 20 minutes
Cooking time: 1½ hours
Serves 6 (easily doubled)

There's no secret to making this classic Chinese dish—all that's needed is the patience to wait while the duck slowly cooks to crisp, melting perfection.

2 tsp Chinese five-spice powder

2 tsp salt

½ teaspoon black pepper

4 duck legs

1 large cucumber

2 bunches scallions (spring onions)

24 Chinese pancakes

½ cup (120 ml) hoisin sauce

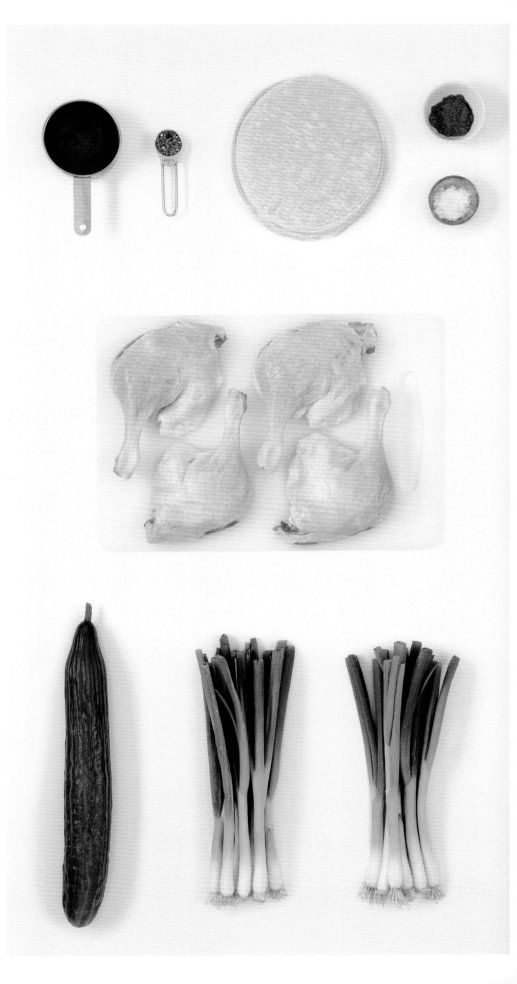

1

Preheat the oven to 325°F/160°C/ Gas Mark 3. Mix the five-spice powder with the salt and pepper. Put the duck legs into a roasting pan. Rub the duck legs all over with the salty spice.

2

Roast the duck for 1½ hours, or until the skin is dark golden and crisp and the meat is tender. The fat will have run out of the skin. A convection or fan-assisted oven will give a really crisp result, so if you have the option, use a convection oven, not forgetting to reduce the temperature by 25°F/20°C.

3

Meanwhile, cut the cucumber into thin sticks and trim, then finely shred the scallions (spring onions). Cutting the scallions into thin strips can be difficult, so slice into rounds if preferred.

4

When the duck is cooked, cover the pancakes with aluminum foil and put into the oven for 10 minutes to warm through (or follow the package instructions). Use 2 forks to pull the duck flesh and skin away from the bones. They should come away from the bones very easily. Keep the duck warm on a plate in the oven. Don't cover it with foil, or the skin will lose its crispness.

5

Spoon the hoisin sauce into a serving dish. Serve the sauce, shredded duck, sliced cucumber, scallions, and pancakes separately and let everyone assemble their own. To assemble, spoon about 1 teaspoon of hoisin sauce onto a pancake, then spread it out with the back of the spoon. Arrange a couple of sticks of cucumber, a few shreds of scallion, and a little duck in a line across the middle of the pancake. To roll, tuck the bottom of the pancake up, then roll the sides over, leaving the top open.

CHINESE PANCAKES
If you can't find thin Chinese pancakes in the store, try flour tortillas instead. Chinese pancakes are also made with flour, so the flavor is similar. If the tortillas are larger, cut them in half and wrap around the filling in a cone shape instead of a roll.

Spinach Ricotta Pockets with Roasted Pepper Dip

Preparation time: 30 minutes, plus cooling
Cooking time: 20 minutes
Makes about 18 pasties

Bring these along to a picnic or party as a veggie-friendly option, with plenty of flavor, texture, and color. I especially like to use Spanish piquillo peppers for the dip, which have a deep smoky edge to them and a vibrant red color.

---

14 oz (400 g) spinach

9 oz (250 g) crimini (chestnut)
    mushrooms

2 tbsp extra virgin olive oil

6 tbsp (80 g) unsalted butter

whole nutmeg, for grating

9 oz (250 g) ricotta cheese (drained
    of any liquid)

1 extra large (UK large) egg

12 large sheets phyllo (filo) pastry,
    thawed if frozen

1 jar roasted red peppers,
    1 cup (175 g) drained

1 clove garlic

salt and pepper

1
Boil a saucepan or full kettle of water. Put the spinach into a colander in the sink.

2
Pour the just-boiled water slowly and evenly over the spinach until it has wilted right down. Cool the spinach under cold running water, then squeeze out all the water with your hands (or put it in a clean dish towel/tea towel and wring it dry).

3
Slice the mushrooms. Heat 1 tablespoon of oil and 1 teaspoon of the butter in a skillet or frying pan. When the butter foams, add the mushrooms and fry for 5 minutes or until golden and the pan is dry.

4
Add the spinach to the pan with the mushrooms and cook for a couple of minutes to drive off any remaining liquid (this will keep the pastry crisp later). Season with plenty of salt and pepper, and about ¼ teaspoon finely grated nutmeg. Tip into a bowl and cool.

5
When the vegetables are cold or nearly cold, add the ricotta, break in the egg, and mix well to combine. Season to taste with salt and pepper. The filling can be made and chilled a day ahead, if you like.

6

Preheat the oven to 400°F/200°C/ Gas Mark 6. Melt the remaining butter in a small saucepan. Unwrap the pastry, take out 2 sheets, then cover the rest with plastic wrap (clingfilm) or a slightly damp dish towel to prevent it from drying out. With the long edge facing you, cut the pastry into three equal strips. The pastry used in the photos was 9½ inches x 11 inches (24 cm x 28 cm), but different brands vary, so adjust as necessary. Brush the top pieces with melted butter.

7

Spoon a heaping tablespoon of the filling at the bottom of one of the strips, then fold the corner over to make a triangle shape. Keep folding the triangle over and over until you have made a neat triangle. Brush the outside with a little butter, then set on a baking sheet. The pockets can be chilled at this point and baked next day, if you like.

8

To make the dip, put the roasted peppers, peeled garlic, and remaining oil into a pitcher (jug) and blend until smooth using an immersion (stick) blender. You could use a food processor instead, or just chop the roasted peppers finely and mix with the crushed garlic and oil. Season to taste.

9

Bake the pockets for 20 minutes, or until crisp, puffed, and golden. Let cool, then serve with the red pepper dip.

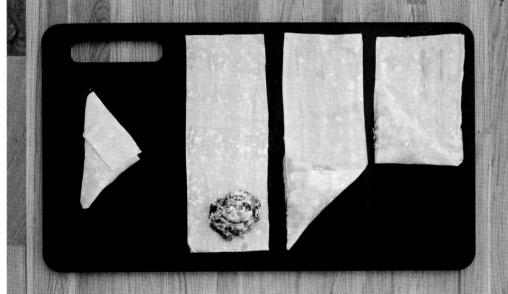

10

Chicken Satay
with Peanut Sauce

Preparation time: 20 minutes,
plus 30 minutes for marinating
Cooking time: 7 minutes
Serves 6

It's doubtful many Thai street food
sellers use peanut butter in their
satay, but it's a great shortcut
ingredient for us and tastes pretty
authentic. For the juiciest, most
flavorful satay, let the chicken
marinate for at least a couple
of hours.

4 large, skinless boneless
   chicken breasts
1 thumb-sized piece fresh ginger
1 tsp ground turmeric
1 tsp ground coriander
2 tbsp nam pla (Thai fish sauce)
2 tbsp sugar
1½ tsp ground cumin
4 tbsp coconut cream or
   coconut milk
1 large green chile
1 onion
2 cloves garlic
1 stalk lemongrass
2 tbsp vegetable or sunflower oil
4 heaping tbsp crunchy
   peanut butter
1 handful fresh cilantro (coriander),
   to serve
20 wooden or metal skewers

1
Cut each chicken breast into 5 long strips along its length.

2
Finely grate the ginger and put it into a large bowl. Mix in the turmeric, ground coriander, 1 tablespoon nam pla (Thai fish sauce), 1 tablespoon sugar, 1 teaspoon cumin, and 1 tablespoon coconut cream or milk. Add the chicken, stir, then cover and marinate for 30 minutes at room temperature, or up to 24 hours in the refrigerator.

COCONUT CREAM
Coconut cream is thicker and more creamy than coconut milk. It rises to the top of nonhomogenized coconut milk sold in a can, much like cream does on whole milk. Leftover coconut cream and coconut milk both freeze well. Freeze in an ice cube tray, then transfer the cubes into bags.

3
If you're using wooden skewers, soak them in cold water while you wait for the chicken to marinate. This will stop them from burning too much under the broiler (grill). Next, make the peanut dip. Seed and very coarsely chop the chile. Coarsely chop the onion, garlic, and lemongrass. Put into the bowl of a food processor with the remaining cumin, sugar, 1 tablespoon of the oil, and 2 tablespoons water.

4

Blend the ingredients together to make a smooth paste. Heat the remaining oil in a saucepan, add the paste, then fry over high heat for 4 minutes, until fragrant. Stir it as it cooks.

5

Tip the peanut butter and a scant ½ cup (100 ml) water into the pan and stir. The sauce will boil and thicken quickly. Season with the remaining nam pla. Set aside while you cook the chicken; add a splash of hot water if it starts to thicken up.

6

After the marinating time, thread each piece of chicken onto a skewer. Put the skewers into large baking pans, well spaced apart. Preheat the broiler to high.

7

Broil (grill) the chicken for about 7 minutes, turning the skewers half way through cooking, until turning golden and cooked through. Spoon a little of the remaining coconut cream or coconut milk over the chicken as it cooks. Serve drizzled with more of the coconut cream or milk, sprinkled with the cilantro (coriander) leaves and with the peanut sauce ready for dipping.

GETTING AHEAD
Marinating the chicken overnight? You can make the sauce in advance, too. Cool, then keep it covered in the refrigerator. Reheat gently in a saucepan, adding a little water to loosen.

Chicken Wings & Blue Cheese Dip

Preparation time: 15 minutes
Cooking time: 40 minutes
Serves 6 (easily doubled)

Chicken wings are much overlooked, but they're cheap to buy and have loads of flavor. In this recipe, the crisp wings are tossed with chili sauce, then served with a creamy blue- cheese dip and crisp celery. It's an unlikely combination, perhaps, but an irresistible one.

2¼ lb (1 kg) chicken wings

¼ tsp salt, plus extra to taste

¼ tsp black pepper, plus extra
    to taste

¼ tsp cayenne pepper

2¾ oz (70 g) strong blue cheese,
    such as Stilton, St. Agur,
    or Gorgonzola

5 tbsp plain (natural) yogurt

4 tbsp good-quality mayonnaise

1 bunch celery

scant ½ cup (100 ml) chili sauce
    (such as Frank's)

1
Preheat the oven to 400°F/200°C/ Gas Mark 6. If the tips of the chicken wings haven't already been removed, cut them off with kitchen scissors, then cut each wing into 2 pieces through the joint using a sharp knife.

2
Put the wings into a large roasting pan, then add the salt, pepper, and cayenne. Rub the seasonings all over the chicken using your hands.

3
Put the chicken into the oven and roast for 40 minutes or until crisp and golden, turning once. Meanwhile, make the blue cheese dip. Put the blue cheese into a large bowl, then mash with a fork. Add the yogurt and mayonnaise and season with salt and pepper. Mix well and chill in the refrigerator until needed.

4

Trim the base off the bunch of celery, then separate out the stalks. Trim off any leaves. Cut the celery into finger-length sticks.

5

When the chicken wings are crisp all over and tender, pour the chili sauce over them and stir well to coat.

6

Serve the chicken with the dip and celery sticks, with plenty of napkins for sticky fingers.

Easy Ciabatta Pizzas

Preparation time: 5 minutes
Cooking time: 10 minutes
Serves 2–4, easily doubled

This is more of a suggestion than a recipe really—if you don't have goat cheese or would rather use mozzarella, then fine. Ham instead of salami, mushrooms instead of tomatoes, red onions instead of olives … just use your favorite ingredients. No need to buy a special pizza topping sauce either—just use tomato sauce and dried herbs.

3 tbsp tomato paste (puree)
2 tsp dried oregano or mixed
   dried herbs
2 tbsp extra virgin olive oil, plus
   extra for drizzling
1 large clove garlic
1 large ciabatta loaf
1 (4-oz/120-g) log of goat cheese
2–3 tomatoes
10 slices spicy salami or pepperoni
½ cup (50 g) black or green
   pitted olives
1 handful arugula (rocket) or fresh
   flat-leaf parsley
salt and pepper

1

Mix the tomato paste (puree), most of the oregano, the olive oil, and some salt and pepper in a bowl. Crush the garlic and stir into the mixture.

2

Preheat the broiler (grill) to medium–high. Cut the bread in half lengthwise, then put onto a baking sheet, cut side up. Put under the broiler for 2 minutes or until pale golden. Spread the sauce over the bread, making sure that it goes all the way to the edges.

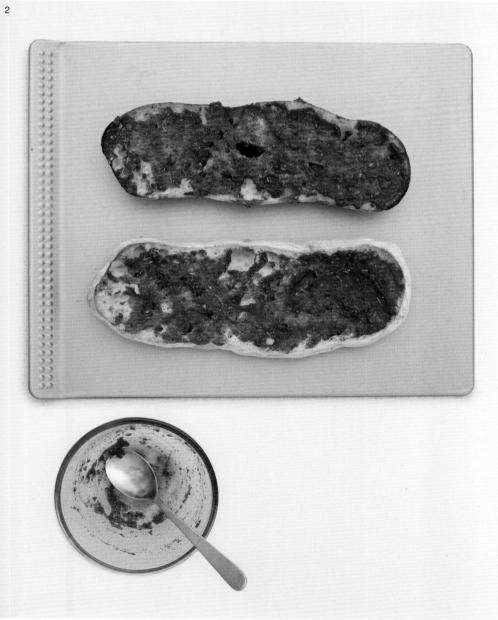

3

Slice or crumble the goat cheese and slice the tomatoes.

4

Arrange the cheese, tomatoes, salami, and olives over the bread without overlapping too much—that way everything will get a good blast from the heat of the broiler. Try to cover the edges of the bread, too, so that they don't burn. Sprinkle with a little more oregano and some black pepper, then drizzle with oil to help everything meld together.

5

Broil (grill) the pizzas for about 10 minutes, or until the cheese, tomatoes, and salami are starting to turn golden. Serve with a sprinkling of arugula (rocket) or parsley leaves and a fresh salad, if you like.

Cheese Nachos with Guacamole

Preparation time: 30 minutes
Cooking time: 7 minutes
Serves 6

Crisp nachos are always popular, and they make a great choice of snack if you're not sure who does or doesn't eat meat. Layering the sauce, tortillas, and beans means that every tortilla should have something tasty on it, right down to the bottom of the dish.

1 clove garlic

3 tbsp extra virgin or mild olive oil

1 (14-oz/400-g) can diced or chopped tomatoes

3 ripe avocados

1 small bunch fresh cilantro (coriander)

1 red onion

1 ripe tomato

2 limes

8 oz (200 g) tasty melting cheese, such as Cheddar

14 oz (400 g) tortilla chips, lightly salted or "original" flavor

1 (14-oz/400-g) can black beans, drained

1 handful sliced jalapeño chilies from a jar, drained

1 cup (250 g) sour cream

salt and pepper

1

Make the tomato sauce for the nachos first. Thinly slice the garlic. Put a saucepan over low heat and add 2 tablespoons of oil. After about 30 seconds, add the garlic and let it sizzle gently for 2 minutes. Don't let it color.

2

Turn up the heat, then add the canned tomatoes. Simmer, uncovered, for 15 minutes, until the mix is thickened and reduced by about a third. Season with salt and pepper, then cool. The sauce can be made well in advance and frozen.

3

For the guacamole, cut each avocado in half. Scoop out the pit (stone) with a spoon, then spoon the flesh into a large bowl.

CHOOSING AND
PREPARING AVOCADOS
See the note on page 43.

4

Mash the avocado against the side of the bowl using a fork. Finely chop the cilantro (coriander) stems (stalks) and coarsely chop most of the leaves. Finely chop the onion and coarsely chop the ripe tomato. Stir into the avocado with the remaining olive oil. Squeeze the juice from the limes and stir it in. Season with salt and pepper. You can keep the guacamole chilled and covered tightly with plastic wrap (clingfilm) for up to 24 hours.

5

Preheat the oven to 400°F/200°C/ Gas Mark 6. Grate the cheese. Put half the tortilla chips into 2 large ovenproof dishes. Haphazardly spoon over half of the tomato sauce, then spread over half the beans and sprinkle with a few jalapeños and a little of the cheese. Repeat to make more layers, ending with cheese.

6

Bake the nachos for about 7 minutes, or until the cheese has melted. Sprinkle with more jalapeños and the remaining cilantro leaves. Spoon some of the guacamole and sour cream on top and serve the rest on the side.

Sticky Soy Ribs with Asian Slaw

Preparation time: 20 minutes,
plus marinating
Cooking time: About 3 hours
Serves 6, easily doubled

Satisfy the caveman (or woman) in you with these tender ribs, cooked until melting in the oven, then grilled to crisp and dark on the barbecue. Whether buying whole racks of pork ribs, or baby back beef ribs, ask for the membrane (from the back of the rack) to be removed for you.

1 finger-length piece fresh
  ginger
3 cloves garlic
4½ lb (2 kg) pork spare ribs
½ cup (100 g) sugar
1 tbsp Chinese five-spice powder
⅔ cup (150 ml) light soy sauce
2 tbsp sesame oil
1 large or 2 smaller heads
  Napa cabbage (Chinese leaf))
1 bunch scallions (spring onions)
1 red chile
scant ½ cup (100 ml) rice vinegar
2 tbsp sesame seeds
salt and pepper

1

Finely grate the ginger and garlic, then rub all over the ribs.

2

Put 5 tablespoons of the sugar, the five-spice powder, then the soy sauce and 1 tablespoon sesame oil into a nonmetallic container or a large plastic food bag. Mix together, then add the ribs. Massage the marinade around the meat, then let marinate in the refrigerator for at least 2 hours or up to 24 hours. The longer the better.

3

Preheat the oven to 325°F/160°C/Gas Mark 3. Lift the ribs from the marinade, then put them into a large roasting pan. Keep the marinade. Splash a cup of water in the bottom of the pan, then cover the whole thing with a tent of aluminum foil—the ribs will be steaming until tender.

4

Bake the ribs for 2½ hours, then have a look and see how they are doing. The meat should be tender and easy to pull away from the bones. If not, spoon some of the juices over the ribs (or add more water if the pan looks dry), then cover the meat again and return to the oven for another 30 minutes before testing again. Smaller racks will take less time and vice versa. The ribs can be cooked and chilled in advance, ready to be grilled (barbecued) the next day.

USING BEEF RIBS
Beef ribs are delicious cooked this way, too. they will need 3–4 hours in the oven, depending on their size.

5

To prepare the slaw, finely shred the Napa cabbage (Chinese leaf) and thinly slice the scallions (spring onions). Put into a large bowl, then cover and chill until needed.

6

To make the dressing, seed and finely chop the chile, then put it into a small bowl. Mix in the vinegar, remaining sugar (this will be about 3 tablespoons), and sesame oil, then season with a pinch of salt. Cook the sesame seeds in a saucepan over medium heat for a few minutes until golden and smelling toasty, stirring often.

7

Skim the excess fat from the juices in the roasting pan (beef ribs will release a lot), then put the juices and remaining marinade into a saucepan and boil for about 10 minutes until syrupy.

8

Before you begin the final cooking, check that the barbecue coals are glowing white hot, or your gas barbecue is preheated to 400°F/200°C. Toss the salad dressing through the salad and set aside (you want this one to absorb plenty of the dressing). Cook the ribs for about 5 minutes on each side, until sizzling and dark golden. If you are cooking the ribs from cold, give them a little longer to be sure they're heated through. Transfer to a board and cut into individual ribs, or portions of several. Spoon the syrupy sauce over the ribs and sprinkle with the sesame seeds, then serve with the salad.

IF IT RAINS
Cook the ribs under a hot broiler (grill) until sizzling.

Sticky BBQ Chicken & Slaw

Preparation time: 40 minutes,
plus marinating time
Cooking time: 40 minutes
Serves 6, easily doubled

For chicken pieces that are tender right through, I always cook them in advance in the oven, then finish them on the grill (barbecue). That way the coals can impart that chargrilled flavor, and the chicken will fall off the bone. It also means you'll have more room on the grill. The sauce is ideal for dipping sausages and wings and is irresistible.

---

12 chicken pieces, preferrably thighs
   and drumsticks, skin on

2 tbsp paprika

1 handful fresh thyme

2 tsp salt

½ tsp freshly ground black pepper

1 tsp chili powder

½ packed cup plus 2 tbsp (120 g)
   dark brown sugar

⅔ cup (150 ml) ketchup

1 tsp Tabasco sauce

2 tbsp Worcestershire sauce

1 small red cabbage

1 onion

2 crisp, well-flavored apples

⅔ cup (150 g) mayonnaise

2 tbsp apple cider vinegar

1 generous tsp black onion
   (kalonji) seeds

salt and pepper

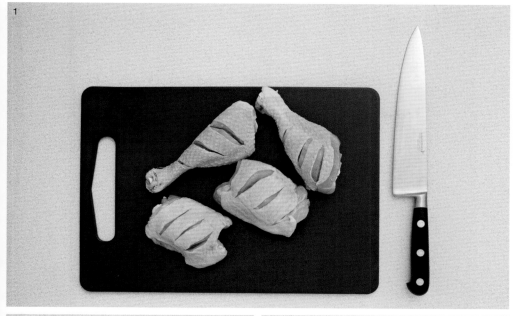

1

Slash the chicken pieces with a sharp knife, going right down to the bone. This will help the smoky taste to sink into the chicken and will also help the heat get into the meat as it cooks.

2

Mix the paprika, thyme, salt, pepper, chili powder, and 3 tablespoons of the sugar in a large bowl or food bag, then add the chicken and rub well. Let the chicken marinate in the rub for at least 1 hour—ideally up to 12 hours in the refrigerator.

3

Preheat the oven to 350°F/180°C/ Gas Mark 4. Make the barbecue sauce. Mix the remaining sugar, ketchup, Tabasco, and Worcestershire sauce until smooth. This can be made several days in advance and will keep in the refrigerator for at least 2 weeks.

4

Spread out the chicken on a large roasting pan. Roast the chicken for 30 minutes, until cooked all the way through (make a cut with a sharp knife to check—the meat may still be a little pink because it is darker leg meat, however, it should not be bloody). This can be done several hours ahead, if it helps—cool the chicken and put into the refrigerator as soon as possible.

5
For the slaw, cut the cabbage into wedges, remove any hard pieces from the central core, then thinly slice.

6
Thinly slice the onion and the apples (no need to peel the apples first), and add to the cabbage in a large bowl.

7
Mix the mayonnaise and vinegar together to make the dressing.

8
Toss the dressing into the slaw, season with salt and pepper to taste, then sprinkle with the onion seeds. The slaw can be made up to a day in advance.

9
Before you begin the final cooking, check that your charcoal is glowing white hot, or your gas barbecue is preheated to 400°F/200°C. Add the chicken and cook for 10 minutes, turning regularly, until charred and sizzling and hot through to the middle. This may take a few more minutes if you roasted the chicken ahead and chilled it. Spoon or brush over some of the sauce, then serve the chicken with the slaw and the rest of the sauce for spooning.

IF IT RAINS
Turn the oven up to 425°F/220°C/ Gas Mark 7. Roast the chicken for another 10 minutes in the oven, until sizzling and dark, then finish with the sauce as before.

Cheese & Onion Tart

Preparation time: 1 hour 15 minutes,
plus 50 minutes for chilling
Cooking time: 30 minutes
Serves 8–10 (makes 10 slices)

A delicate, slightly wobbly homemade tart is a simple pleasure to cook and eat, and a great option for lunches, buffets, and picnics, because it can be transported in its pan. If you don't want to make your own pastry, use a package of store-bought shortcrust pastry instead. To turn this into a Quiche Lorraine, see the instructions on page 130.

4 large (UK medium) eggs

1¾ cups (220 g) all-purpose (plain) flour, plus extra for rolling

¼ tsp salt

1 stick plus 1 tbsp (125 g) cold, unsalted butter

3 large onions

1 tbsp mild olive oil

5 oz (150 g) Gruyère or Cheddar cheese

1¼ cups (300 ml) heavy (double) cream

scant ½ cup (100 ml) milk

salt and pepper

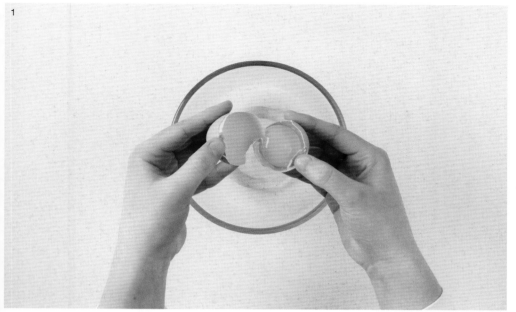

1
Make the pastry dough first.
Separate 1 egg yolk and white by
gently cracking the shell against the
side of a small bowl. Slowly pull the
shell apart as cleanly as possible
along the crack, tipping the yolk
into 1 half of the shell. Let the white
drain away into a bowl below. Drop
the yolk into another small bowl.

2
Add 2 tablespoons ice-cold water
to the yolk, then beat together with
a fork. Put the flour into a large bowl
and add the salt. Cut 7 tablespoons
(100 g) of the butter into cubes, then
sprinkle them over the flour.

3
Rub the ingredients together. To do
this, use both hands to lift the butter
and flour from the bowl, then gently
pass them between your fingers
and thumbs as they drop back into
the bowl. As you repeat the action,
the butter will gradually work its
way into the flour. Lift the mixture
up as you go to keep it cool and
aerated. The mix will end up looking
like fine bread crumbs.

MAKING PASTRY DOUGH WITH
A FOOD PROCESSOR
If you'd prefer to use a food
processor, blend the butter and
flour together for about 10 seconds,
until the mix resembles fine bread
crumbs and no flecks of butter
remain. Add the egg mix and pulse
a few more times, until balls of
dough come together in the bowl.

4
Add the yolk mix to the bowl, then, using a table knife, quickly stir it into the rubbed-in crumbs to make a coarse-looking dough.

5
Press the clumps of dough firmly against the bowl to make a ball, then tip it onto the work surface and shape it into a flat disk, paying particular attention to the edge, pinching any cracks together to keep the dough in a smooth round. Wrap in plastic wrap (clingfilm), then chill in the refrigerator for at least 30 minutes, until firm but not rock hard.

6
While the dough chills, make the filling. Thinly slice the onions. Put a skillet or frying pan over low heat, then add the remaining butter and the oil. When the butter starts to foam, add the onions.

7
Cook the onions for 10 minutes, until soft, then turn up the heat a little and cook for 10 more minutes, until they take on a tinge of gold. Stir the onions often to prevent them from catching on the bottom of the pan. Meanwhile, break the remaining eggs into a large pitcher (jug) and beat with a fork. Grate the cheese. Add the cream, milk, and 1 cup (120 g) of the cheese to the eggs, then season with salt and pepper.

TO MAKE A QUICHE LORRAINE
Turn your tart into a quiche lorraine by frying 6 chopped slices (rashers) of bacon until golden and adding them to the filling with the cheese. Alternatively, just add 4 large slices of torn, cooked ham. Omit the onions.

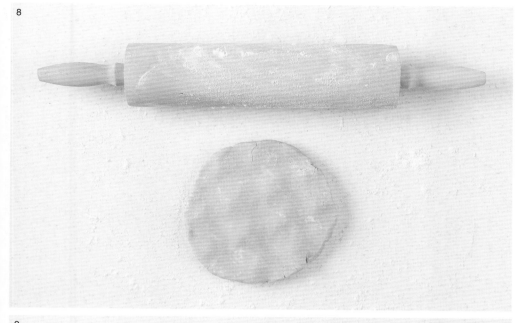

8

Dust the work surface and a rolling pin with flour. Have ready a 9-inch (23-cm) loose-bottomed tart pan. Using a rolling pin, press shallow ridges evenly across the dough, then rotate it by a quarter turn. Repeat this until the dough is about ½ inch (1 cm) thick. This will help the dough to stretch without becoming tough.

9

Now roll out the dough. Push the rolling pin in only one direction, turning the dough by a quarter turn every few rolls, until it's about 4-mm (⅛-inch) thick. Using a rolling pin to help, lift the dough over the pan.

10

Ease the dough gently into the pan, then press it gently into the fluted edge, using your knuckles and fingertips.

ANY HOLES?

If your dough has ripped or small holes have appeared, don't panic. Dampen a little of the leftover dough and stick it down well to seal the gap.

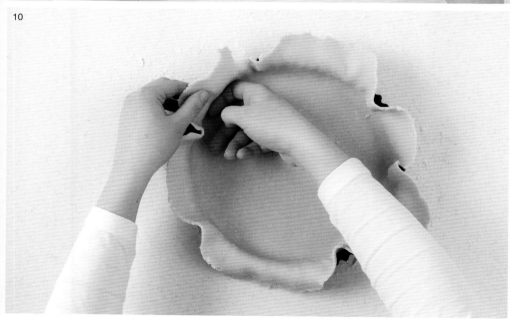

11

Trim the top of the dough with a pair of scissors so that it just overhangs the pan. Lift the pan onto a baking sheet, then chill in the refrigerator for 20 minutes, until firm. Put an oven shelf in the middle of the oven and preheat it to 400°F/200°C/Gas Mark 6.

12

Tear a sheet of parchment (baking) paper large enough to completely cover the pan and overhang the dough. Scrunch up the paper, then use it to cover the dough. Cover the paper with a layer of pie weights (baking beans), mounding them up at the edges, then bake, still on its sheet, for 20 minutes.

PIE WEIGHTS (BAKING BEANS)
These are actually small ceramic balls, used to weigh down the dough as it cooks, which helps it to keep its shape. Ceramic weights are the most effective, but dried chickpeas or rice can be used instead. Cool and reuse them only for baking.

13

Remove the paper and pie weights. The pastry should be pale but feel dry and be turning gold at the edges. Return to the oven and cook for another 10 minutes or until the bottom is starting to brown. Remove from the oven. Turn the oven down to 325°F/160°C/Gas Mark 3.

14

Sprinkle the onions over the bottom of the tart, then pour over the creamy filling. Make sure that the cheese is evenly distributed. Sprinkle the remainder over the top.

15

Bake for 30 minutes or until the filling is set with just a slight wobble in the middle. Once cooled, remove the tart from the pan, then cut into wedges to serve.

Lamb Kofte with Tzatziki

Preparation time: 40 minutes,
plus chilling
Cooking time: 10–15 minutes
Serves 6, easily doubled

Kofte, classic lamb meatballs served all over the Middle East, make a great alternative to burgers and are simple to cook. This mix is highly spiced—in an aromatic rather than hot way—and tempered beautifully with a scoop of cooling cucumber yogurt sauce. Add a crushed garlic clove to it for extra bite, if you like.

2 onions

2 cloves garlic

¼ cup (50 g) dried, ready-to-eat apricots

1 bunch fresh mint

1¾ lb (800 g) good-quality
ground (minced) lamb

1 tbsp ground cumin

1 tsp chili powder

1 tbsp dried thyme

1 large (UK medium) egg

½ tsp salt, plus extra to taste

½ tsp pepper, plus extra to taste

2 cucumbers

1½ cups (375 g) plain (natural)
yogurt

6 flatbreads (see page 298),
or use store-bought pita bread,
to serve

1
Finely chop the onions and crush the garlic, then finely chop the apricots and half of the mint.

2
Put the ground (minced) lamb into a large bowl with the onions, garlic, chopped apricots, mint, cumin, chili, thyme, and egg. Season generously with ½ teaspoon each salt and pepper.

3
Mix everything together with your hands until evenly combined. If you want to check the seasoning and flavor of the kofte, you can fry a little piece of the mixture and add more to your taste. With slightly damp hands, shape the kofte mixture into 25–30 walnut-sized balls. Cover and chill for at least 30 minutes or for up to 2 days.

4

To make the tzatziki, peel the cucumbers, then scoop out the seeds using a teaspoon. Leaving the seeds in will lead to a watery sauce. Thinly slice or grate the flesh.

5

Mix the cucumber with the yogurt. Tear in the remaining mint leaves, then season to taste with salt and pepper.

6

Fry the kofte in a large skillet or frying pan for about 10 minutes or until golden and hot through to the middle—you may need to do this in two batches. Alternatively, cook on a rack under a hot broiler (grill) or grill (barbecue) outdoors. When ready, serve the kofte with the tzatziki and flatbreads.

Spicy Pulled Pork

Preparation time: 30 minutes,
plus steeping time
Cooking time: about 2 hours
Serves 4–6, easily doubled

Here's my version of pork carnitas,
a fun and tasty Mexican meal to
share with relaxed company and a
few beers. It's aromatic spicy more
than hot spicy, so add fresh chile to
the salsa if you like things with a bit
more kick.

2 tbsp extra virgin olive oil
2¼ lb (1 kg) pork shoulder, boned
   and cut into large chunks
   (ask your butcher to do this)
2 red onions
2 cloves garlic
1 tbsp ground cumin
1 tbsp ground coriander
1 tsp hot paprika (or add
   ½ teaspoon chili powder to
   normal paprika)
1 tsp ground cinnamon
1 tbsp dried oregano
4 tbsp apple cider or white
   wine vinegar
1 tbsp tomato paste (puree)
2 limes
1 (14-oz/400-g) can black beans,
   drained (or use pinto or red
   kidney beans)
2 ripe avocados
1 bunch fresh cilantro (coriander)
salt and pepper
flour or corn tortillas, to serve

1

Preheat the oven to 325°F/160°C/ Gas Mark 3. Put a flameproof casserole over medium-high heat and add a spoonful of the oil. Season the pork with salt and pepper, then add half the meat to the pan, spacing it out well. Turn the meat every few minutes, until deep golden all over. If the meat doesn't release itself from the pan immediately, then leave it and try again in a minute or so. Set the first batch aside on a plate, then fry the second, adding more oil, if needed.

2

While the pork browns, thinly slice both onions and crush the garlic.

3

Lift the second batch of meat from the pan. Turn the heat down, add half of the onion and all of the garlic, then soften in the remaining fat for 5 minutes.

4

Stir in the spices and oregano until fragrant, then add the vinegar and tomato paste (puree) and return the meat to the pan. It will smell pretty vinegary at this point, but stick with it. Pour in 2 cups (450 ml) water or enough to come halfway up the top pieces of meat. Cover the pan, leaving a small gap for the steam to escape, then put into the oven and cook for 2 hours.

GET AHEAD

Cook the pork up to 2 days in advance, if you like, and keep chilled. The flavors will improve and it will also be easy to lift off the excess fat.

5

While the pork cooks, prepare the accompaniments. Put the remaining sliced onion into a bowl. Add the juice of 1 lime and a pinch of salt, mix, then let marinate in the refrigerator. The onion will become more and more pink.

6

For the salsa, tip the beans into a bowl. Cut the avocados in half, then remove the pits (stones). Slice crisscrossed lines in the flesh, cutting down to, but not through, the skin, then scoop into the bowl. Squeeze in the rest of the lime juice, stir, then season with salt and pepper. Coarsely chop the cilantro (coriander) and sprinkle it over the top, ready to stir in later. Chill until needed.

7

When the pork is ready, it will be tender and soft enough to cut easily with a spoon. If it isn't ready, return to the oven and cook for another 30 minutes. Transfer the meat to a board or plate. Spoon off any excess fat from the pan, then simmer the sauce down until thick and tasty. Taste it for seasoning, then spoon into another bowl.

8

Warm the tortillas according to the package instructions. Shred the pork using 2 forks, then put it into a serving dish. You can either mix it with the sauce or serve the sauce separately. Pile the meat and sauce onto the tortillas with some salsa and onions, then wrap and enjoy immediately.

Simple
Dinners

Salmon with Garlic, Ginger, Greens & Rice

Preparation time: 15 minutes
Cooking time: 15 minutes
Serves 2 (easily halved)

Here's a quick, energizing supper for weary souls. The recipe involves steaming the fish and vegetables, but don't worry if you haven't got a steamer: the method gives a clever alternative using a plate and a skillet or frying pan as well.

¾ cup (150 g) basmati rice
1 mild red chile
1 large clove garlic
1 thumb-sized piece fresh
   ginger
2 heads bok choy
2 fillets salmon, skinless if possible
2 tbsp soy sauce, plus more
   to serve, if liked
1 tsp toasted sesame oil
salt

1

First, prepare the rice. Put the rice into a medium saucepan, then cover with cold water. Swish the rice around in the water a few times; the water will become cloudy. Carefully drain the water away from the rice, then repeat this several times until the water runs clear.

WHY RINSE RICE?
Rice is naturally surrounded by starchy molecules, which expand when they're boiled and can make rice sticky and stodgy. In some cases, such as risotto, it's important to keep the starch. But for fluffy basmati, rinsing is essential.

2

Cover the rice with double its volume of water, or just enough to cover the rice by a fingertip. Season with salt, then put the pan over high heat and bring to a boil. Once boiling, turn the heat to a simmer, stir the rice, then cover it with a tight-fitting lid. Cook the rice for 10 minutes. Meanwhile, start the vegetables.

NEED TO INCREASE
THE QUANTITY?
It's easy to increase these quantities if you're cooking for more than two. Allow scant ½ cup (75 g) rice per person and cover it with double the quantity of water of rice, or enough to cover it by a fingertip's depth. The cooking time will be the same, even for a large panful.

3

Halve and seed the chile, then thinly slice it. Thinly slice the garlic and finely grate the ginger. Cut the leafy parts of the bok choy away from the fleshy bases, then cut the bases in half lengthwise.

4

If you have a steamer, put a plate into its base. Half-fill a saucepan the same size as the steamer with water, then sit the steamer on top. Alternatively, put a dinner plate into a large skillet or frying pan, then add enough water to come halfway up the outside of the plate. Bring the water to the boil. Put the salmon and bok choy onto the plate, then sprinkle with the chile, garlic, and ginger. Spoon the soy sauce over and around the fish and greens.

Cover the steamer or frying pan, then steam for 5 minutes. Nestle the bok choy leaves alongside the fish and replace the lid. Steam for another 5 minutes.

5

Meanwhile, check the rice. When it has finished cooking, take it off the heat and let it sit with the lid on for 10 minutes (or longer, it won't spoil). The rice will be cooked and fluffy.

6

The salmon and greens are cooked when the bok choy leaves are wilted, the stems are tender, and the salmon flakes easily in the middle. Drizzle with the sesame oil.

7

Lift the salmon and greens onto warmed plates, then spoon over some of the tasty cooking juices. Splash with more soy sauce to taste. Fluff up the rice with a fork and serve alongside the fish.

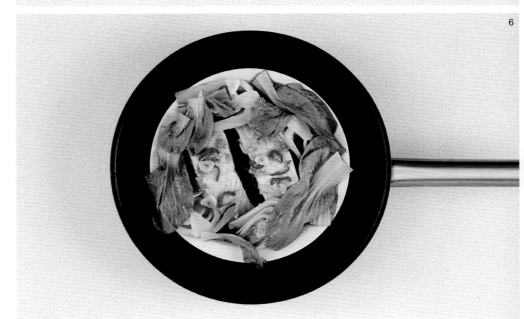

Chicken & Ham Parmesan

Preparation time: 15 minutes
Cooking time: 15–20 minutes
Serves 4

The whole family will enjoy sharing this good old classic. Instead of coating the chicken in crumbs and frying it, I just top it with cheesy crumbs and bake. The tomato sauce is rich, thick, and super simple to make. Use it on pasta or to serve with simple grilled steak, chicken, or chops.

2 cloves garlic

11 oz (300 g) ripe tomatoes

1 bunch fresh basil

3 tbsp extra virgin olive oil

2 tbsp tomato paste (puree)

1 tsp sugar

½ cup (25 g) fresh white bread
  crumbs

1 oz (25 g) chunk Parmesan or other
  tasty, mature hard cheese

1 (4-oz/120-g) ball buffalo
  mozzarella cheese, drained

4 skinless, boneless chicken breasts

4 slices smoked ham, not too thick

salt and pepper

green salad and crusty bread, to
  serve (optional)

1

Start the tomato sauce first. Crush or finely slice the garlic and coarsely chop the tomatoes and most of the basil leaves.

2

Heat 2 tablespoons of the oil in a skillet (frying pan), then add the garlic. Cook for 1 minute, until softened but not golden, then add the tomatoes and chopped basil. Stir in the tomato paste (puree) and sugar.

3

Simmer the sauce for a couple of minutes until the tomatoes are softened and the sauce is rich and thick. Season to taste with salt and pepper.

4

Preheat the oven to 375°F/190°C/
Gas Mark 5. Grate the Parmesan.
Mix the crumbs, Parmesan, and the
rest of the oil. Cut the mozzarella
into 8 slices.

5

Slice the chicken through the side
of each breast, cutting almost all
the way through but not quite, then
open out to make a heart shape.
Season the chicken with pepper,
place a ruffled slice of ham on the
right hand side of each breast,
then top with a piece of mozzarella.
Fold over the left hand side of the
chicken to close.

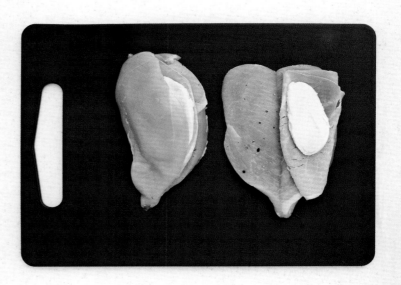

6

Spoon the sauce into a baking dish,
then sit the chicken in the tomato
sauce. Top the chicken with the
remaining mozzarella and sprinkle
with the cheesy crumbs. The whole
dish can be covered and chilled
for up to a day, if you want to get
ahead.

7

Bake the chicken for 20–30
minutes (longer if was chilled in the
refrigerator) or until golden on top,
the cheese is melting in the middle,
and the chicken is cooked through.
Let the dish sit for a few minutes
to let the chicken rest a little, then
sprinkle with the remaining basil
leaves and serve with a salad
and crusty bread.

Mushroom Risotto

Preparation time: 25 minutes
Cooking time: 20 minutes
Serves 4

A bowl of risotto is one of those wonderful meals that takes no real effort to make, but feels like special a treat. Even better, all the ingredients are from the pantry or cupboard, apart from the fresh mushrooms, of course. Choose a mixture of wild mushrooms, if you're lucky enough to see them at the grocery store.

1 oz (30 g) dried porcini

1 onion

2 cloves garlic

1 tbsp mild olive oil

6 tbsp (80 g) butter

5 cups (1.2 litres) chicken broth (stock)

2 cups (350 g) risotto rice, preferably Aborio or Carnaroli (see page 154)

scant ½ cup (100 ml) dry white wine

2 oz (50 g) Parmesan cheese (⅔ cup grated)

9 oz (250 g) chestnut mushrooms, or a mix of chestnut and wild, or cultivated mushrooms such as oyster and enoki

salt and pepper

1

Boil a saucepan or kettle of water, then measure ⅔ cup (150 ml) boiling water into a heatproof liquid measuring cup (jug). Stir in the dried porcini and push them under the water level. Let stand for 15 minutes. The mushrooms will start to swell.

WHAT ARE PORCINI?
Porcini (also known as ceps) are highly flavored mushrooms often used in Italian cooking. Fresh porcini are seasonal and expensive; dried are more economical and have the same flavor. They must be soaked, after which they can be added to sauces, pasta, and meat dishes.

2

Meanwhile, finely chop the onion and crush the garlic. Heat a skillet, frying pan, or shallow flameproof casserole over low heat, then add the olive oil and 3½ tablespoons (50 g) butter. Add the onion and garlic and cook for 10 minutes, stirring occasionally, until the onions are soft and translucent.

3

Scoop the mushrooms out of their soaking liquid with your hands, and put them onto a cutting (chopping) board. Pour the soaking liquid from the mushrooms into another pan. Leave the last few drops of the liquid behind in the pitcher, because these can be gritty. Add the broth (stock) to the pan, set it over medium heat, and keep it at a simmer.

4

Coarsely chop the mushrooms and add them to the pan with the onions. Stir in the rice. Cook for 2 minutes, stirring, until the rice is well coated in the butter and turning a little translucent. Pour in the wine, then let it bubble until mostly evaporated. This will happen quite quickly.

5
Add one ladle of the mushroom-flavored broth (stock) to the pan, then stir until the rice has absorbed it. Don't have the heat too high under the rice, or the liquid will bubble and evaporate instead of being absorbed into the rice.

6
Continue adding the broth little by little, stirring all the time, until the rice becomes plump and just tender and surrounded by a creamy sauce. Taste the rice—it should be just soft, without any chalkiness in the middle. Try not to rush it; the whole process should take no less than 20 minutes.

7
Once all the broth has been added, take the pan off the heat. Grate the Parmesan, then stir half of it into the rice. Season with salt and pepper. Dot half the remaining butter over the rice.

8
Cover the pan and set aside for 5 minutes. While the risotto rests, thickly slice the fresh mushrooms, if large. Melt the last of the butter in another skillet over high heat. Add the mushrooms and fry them for 2–3 minutes, stirring frequently, until golden.

9
Serve the risotto in shallow bowls, topped with a spoonful of hot, buttery mushrooms and a little of the remaining Parmesan.

RISOTTO RICE
There are three main types of risotto rice, all of which have a small, round grain: Arborio, Carnaroli, and Vialone Nano. For the beginner cook, Carnaroli is a good choice. Arborio is the most commonly found but it's easy to overcook. Vialone Nano takes longer to cook and is a little harder to track down.

Shrimp Pad Thai

Preparation time: 15 minutes
Cooking time: 10 minutes
Serves 4

Give tofu a try in this quick Thai café classic. Leftover cold roast chicken could be added to the noodles, too.

14 oz (400 g) wide rice noodles

1 (9-oz/250-g) pack firm tofu, drained

3 cloves garlic, crushed

1 bunch scallions (spring onions)

1 small bunch fresh cilantro (coriander)

1 tbsp vegetable or sunflower oil

3 tbsp tamarind paste (optional)

3 tbsp sweet chili sauce

3 tbsp nam pla (Thai fish sauce)

1½ tbsp sugar

1 handful roasted peanuts (optional)

4 large (UK medium) eggs

200 g (7 oz) uncooked large shrimp (prawns), shelled and deveined

½ tsp dried chili flakes (or more if you like)

2 limes

1 cup (100 g) bean sprouts

1

Boil a saucepan or kettle of water. Put the noodles into a large heatproof bowl, then pour over enough just-boiled water to cover. Stir gently and let soak until you get to step 8.

WHAT TO DO IF YOUR NOODLES STICK TOGETHER
Sometimes rice noodles just want to stick together as they soak. If this happens, rinse the noodles in a colander under cold running water and separate the strands with your fingers.

2

While you wait, cut the tofu into cubes about ¾ inch (2 cm) across. Crush the garlic and thinly slice the scallions (spring onions). Pick the leaves from the cilantro (coriander).

3

Put a large nonstick skillet, frying pan, or wok over medium-high heat. Add the oil, then the tofu. Fry for 6 minutes, stirring frequently, or until the tofu is golden all over. Lift the tofu onto paper (kitchen) towels using a slotted spoon. This will absorb any excess oil.

4

Meanwhile, put the tamarind paste, chili sauce, nam pla (Thai fish sauce), and sugar into a small pitcher (jug) and stir together. Coarsely chop the peanuts, if using. Crack the eggs into a bowl and loosely beat them with a fork.

TAMARIND PASTE
This runny brown paste is made from the tamarind pod. Tamarind has a uniquely sourish taste and adds piquancy to many Asian recipes. It's stocked in most larger stores, but if you can't find it, be more generous with the lime juice.

5

Put the pan back over high heat. It shouldn't need more oil. Add the shrimp (prawns) and fry for 2 minutes, until they turn completely pink. Now add the garlic, chili flakes, and half the scallions. Cook for a few seconds, stirring, until the garlic and scallions smell fragrant.

6

Transfer the shrimp to a plate, then add the beaten eggs to the pan. Cook for 30 seconds to 1 minute, moving the eggs around the pan a little with a wooden spoon until just set, like an omelet.

7

Lift the omelet out of the pan and transfer it to a cutting board. Roll it up like a pancake, then cut across the roll to make long thin strips. Take the pan off the heat if you feel you need to concentrate on this part.

8

Return the pan to the heat, drain the noodles, and add them to the pan. Add the sauce, most of the cilantro leaves, the shredded egg, tofu, shrimp, the remaining scallions, and a squeeze of lime juice, then toss well.

GETTING A GRIP
A pair of tongs is a great tool here, because they will help you to turn and toss the noodles in the sauce. If you haven't got tongs, try using 2 wooden spoons—holding them as you would salad servers.

9

For an authentic look, serve the peanuts and bean sprouts in little piles alongside the noodles, then sprinkle with the rest of the cilantro. Cut the remaining lime into wedges and put a wedge on each plate.

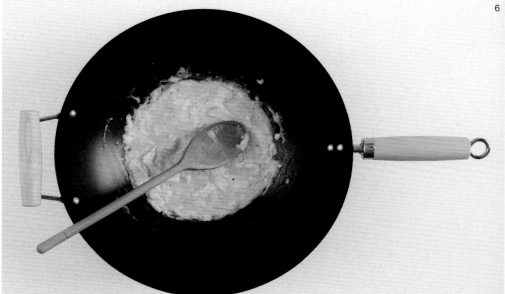

Butternut Curry with Spinach & Cashews

Preparation time: 25 minutes
Cooking time: 35 minutes
Serves 4 (easily halved)

Colorful, fragrant, and full of texture, this dish shows you don't need meat to make a good curry. Lentils, chickpeas, and nuts add protein to the melting pot of vegetables and spices for a healthy, balanced meal. It would also make a great side dish to go with the Lamb & Potato Curry (page 224).

---

medium butternut squash, about
   2¼ lb (1 kg)
1 onion
4 tbsp vegetable or sunflower oil
1 tbsp butter
2 cloves garlic
1 thumb-sized piece fresh
   ginger
1 small hot green chile (see note)
1 tsp ground turmeric
1 tsp cumin seeds
1 tsp ground coriander
2 cinnamon sticks
1 tbsp freeze-dried curry
   leaves (optional)
½ cup (100 g) red lentils
3 or 4 ripe tomatoes
1 (14-oz/400-g) can chickpeas,
   drained
¾ cup (100 g) cashew nuts
2 large handfuls baby leaf spinach
salt and pepper
chapatis, naan breads, or rice
   (see page 145), to serve (optional)
 relish or chutney, to serve (optional)

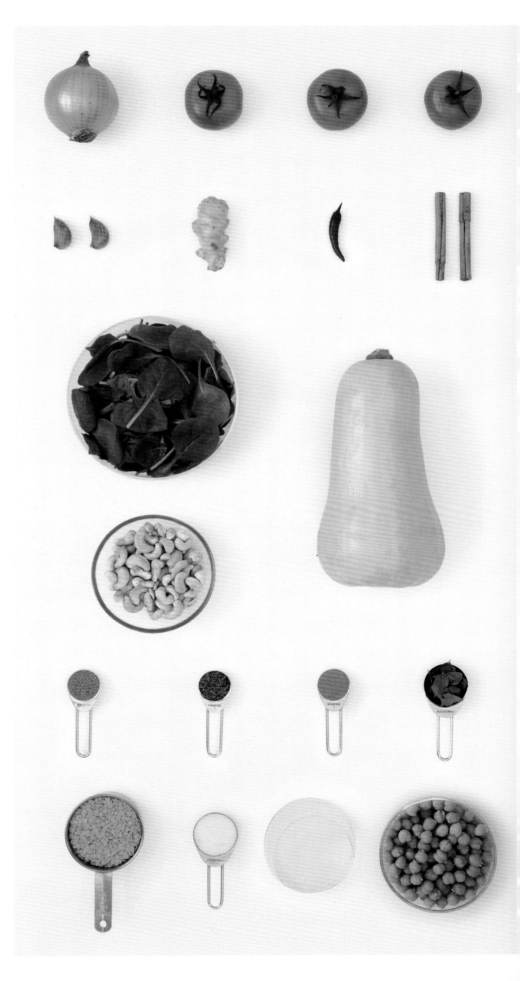

1

Peel the squash using a good peeler or a small sharp knife. Be careful, because the skin is tough. Cut into 4 pieces. Scoop out the seeds using a tablespoon. Cut the flesh into large cubes about 1¼ inches (3 cm) across.

2

Halve and slice the onion. Put a large skillet, frying pan, or wok over medium-high heat. Add the oil and butter, wait for 30 seconds, then add the squash and onions, and season with salt and pepper. Cook for 5 minutes, stirring often, until the vegetables are starting to soften.

3

While the vegetables cook, thinly slice the garlic and finely grate the ginger. Slit the chile, without cutting through the stem (stalk) end. If using a larger, milder chile, seed and finely chop it, then add the flesh to the pan.

HOW HOT IS THE CHILE?
Fat chilies tend to be be milder. Smaller chilies, whether thin, finger length, or small and squat, are usually much hotter. In this recipe, a hot chile is simply split, but not chopped. This is a good way to add some heat and the flavor from a hot chile, without having to chop it or remove the seeds. Remember, all chilies vary. So, before you start chopping, slice a little from the end of the chile, touch the cut end with your finger, then touch the tip of your tongue. If it's hotter than you'd like, go easy—if it's milder, use more, or add the seeds, too.

4

Boil a saucepan or kettle of water. Stir the garlic, ginger, chile, spices, and curry leaves, if using, into the pan and cook for 2 minutes, until fragrant and the vegetables are coated in spice.

5

Stir in the lentils, then pour in 1¾ cups (400 ml) boiling water. Stir, then cover and simmer for 10 minutes, stirring a few times. While you wait, preheat the oven to 350°F/180°C/Gas Mark 4 and coarsely chop the tomatoes.

6

Stir the tomatoes in with the chickpeas, cover the pan again, then simmer for another 10 minutes, stirring once or twice. The lentils should be plump and tender. Squash one against the side of the pan to be sure. Season the curry with salt and pepper.

7

Next, toast the nuts. Sprinkle the nuts over a baking sheet and roast them in the oven for 5 minutes, or until golden.

8

To finish the dish, stir in the spinach leaves and sprinkle the nuts over the top. The spinach will wilt from the heat of the curry. Serve with chapatis, naan breads, or rice and your favorite relish or chutney.

Breaded Fish
& Tartar Sauce

Preparation time: 20 minutes
Cooking time: 12–15 minutes
Serves 4 (easily halved)

Home-breaded fish tastes so much fresher than frozen fish sticks (fingers) or fillets, and it doesn't have to be fried either. To smarten up the sauce for a more special occasion, swap half of the mayonnaise for crème fraîche or sour cream—or for kids, simply serve with ketchup.

4 thick slices white bread (day-old bread is best), about 7 oz (200 g)
1 handful fresh flat-leaf parsley
2 tablespoons mild olive oil
2 oz (50 g) Parmesan cheese (⅔ cup grated)
1 lemon
1¾ lb (800 g) sustainably sourced thick white fish fillet, such as cod, haddock, or pollack
3 tbsp all-purpose (plain) flour
1 large (UK medium) egg
2 tsp capers
1 large or 5 small pickles (gherkins)
½ cup (100 g) good-quality mayonnaise
salt and pepper
salad greens or peas, to serve

1

Preheat the oven to 425°F/220°C/
Gas Mark 7. Cut the crusts from the
bread and discard. Put the bread
into a food processor with half of
the parsley—stems (stalks) too—
and all of the oil.

2

Blend everything together to make
oily, herbed bread crumbs. Finely
grate the Parmesan and the lemon
zest, then mix into the crumbs with
salt and pepper. Transfer to a bowl.

**MAKE BREAD CRUMBS
FOR NEXT TIME**

If you've got more bread going
stale, why not make double
the bread crumb mix and freeze
half of it? Defrost overnight, then
use as above.

3

Cut the fish into chunky sticks
about 1¼ × 1¼ × 4 inches
(3 × 3 × 10 cm).

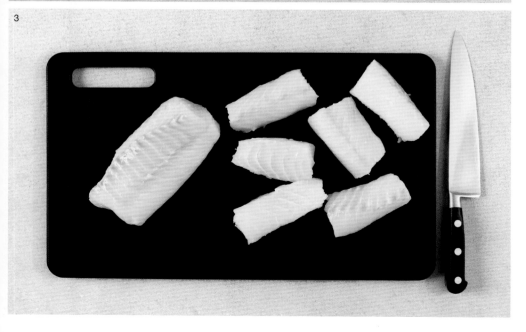

4

Put the flour onto a plate and season it generously with salt and pepper. Break the egg into a bowl, add salt and pepper to this, too, then beat it with a fork. Dust a piece of fish with the flour, then dip it into the egg. Let the excess egg drip off into the bowl below, then roll and pat the fish in the crumbs until covered in an even layer.

5

Place it onto a nonstick baking sheet and repeat with the rest of the fish. Rinse and dry your hands every now and again, because they can get sticky.

6

Bake the fish for 12–15 minutes, or until crisp and golden. Meanwhile, make the tartar sauce. Cut the lemon in half, squeeze one half, and cut the other into wedges. Finely chop the remaining parsley leaves, the capers, and pickles (gherkins), and put into a bowl. Add the mayonnaise and 1 tablespoon lemon juice. Season the sauce with salt and pepper.

7

Serve the fish with the tartar sauce, lemon wedges, and some salad leaves or just-cooked peas.

SHOPPING FOR FISH
It can be hard to tell if fillets of fish are fresh, especially if they're packaged. For that reason, it's best to buy from a fish supplier or fish counter. Fresh fish should look shiny and bright, not dull or dry. It should be firm when pressed (don't be afraid to ask), and smell like the sea. Anything that smells overly fishy is best avoided.

Lamb Chops with Tomato & Mint Salad

Preparation time: 20 minutes,
plus optional marinating time
Cooking time: 8–10 minutes
Serves 2 (easily doubled)

This mouthwatering lamb dish
makes a fabulous summer meal, and
it's smart enough for entertaining,
too. Bring out a hunk of crusty bread
to mop up the juices.

1 lemon

2 tbsp extra virgin olive oil

1 tsp sugar

1 tbsp capers

1 clove garlic

2 tsp mild olive, sunflower, or
    vegetable oil

4 lamb chops, cutlets, or leg steaks,
    at room temperature

1 (14-oz/400g) can lima (butter)
    beans, drained

½ red onion

1 bunch cherry tomatoes

1 handful fresh mint

salt and pepper

1

Squeeze the juice from half of the lemon into a small bowl, then add the extra virgin olive oil, and stir in the sugar and capers. Set aside.

2

Crush the garlic and put it into a small bowl. Finely grate the zest of the lemon, add to the garlic, then mix together with 1 teaspoon of the mild oil. Season with salt and pepper. Rub this mix all over the lamb. Marinate the lamb for anywhere from 5 minutes to several hours at this point, if you have time. Keep the meat chilled in the refrigerator if you do want to do this in advance. Remember to let the meat come up to room temperature before cooking.

Warm a plate in the oven on low heat.

3

Put a skillet or frying pan over medium heat. Add the second teaspoon of the mild oil, wait 30 seconds, then add the lamb. The first piece should sizzle immediately. If it doesn't, take it out and let the pan heat up a for little longer. Cook the lamb for 6 minutes, turning it halfway for meat that's medium-rare (pink and juicy in the middle). Cook for 2 minutes longer if you prefer lamb well done.

4

Lift the meat onto the warm plate, cover loosely with aluminum foil, and let stand for a few minutes while you make the salad. Set the pan aside for later. To make the salad, put the beans into a large bowl. Thinly slice the red onion and halve the cherry tomatoes. Pick the leaves from the mint, tear them into the bowl, then stir in the onion, tomatoes, and mint. Season with salt and pepper.

5

Return the pan to medium heat, then add the lemon and caper mixture prepared in step 1. Scrape up any tasty parts from the bottom of the pan, then add the resting juices that have collected under the lamb.

6

Spoon the salad onto plates, then nestle the lamb on top. Spoon the warm caper dressing over the lamb and salad and serve immediately.

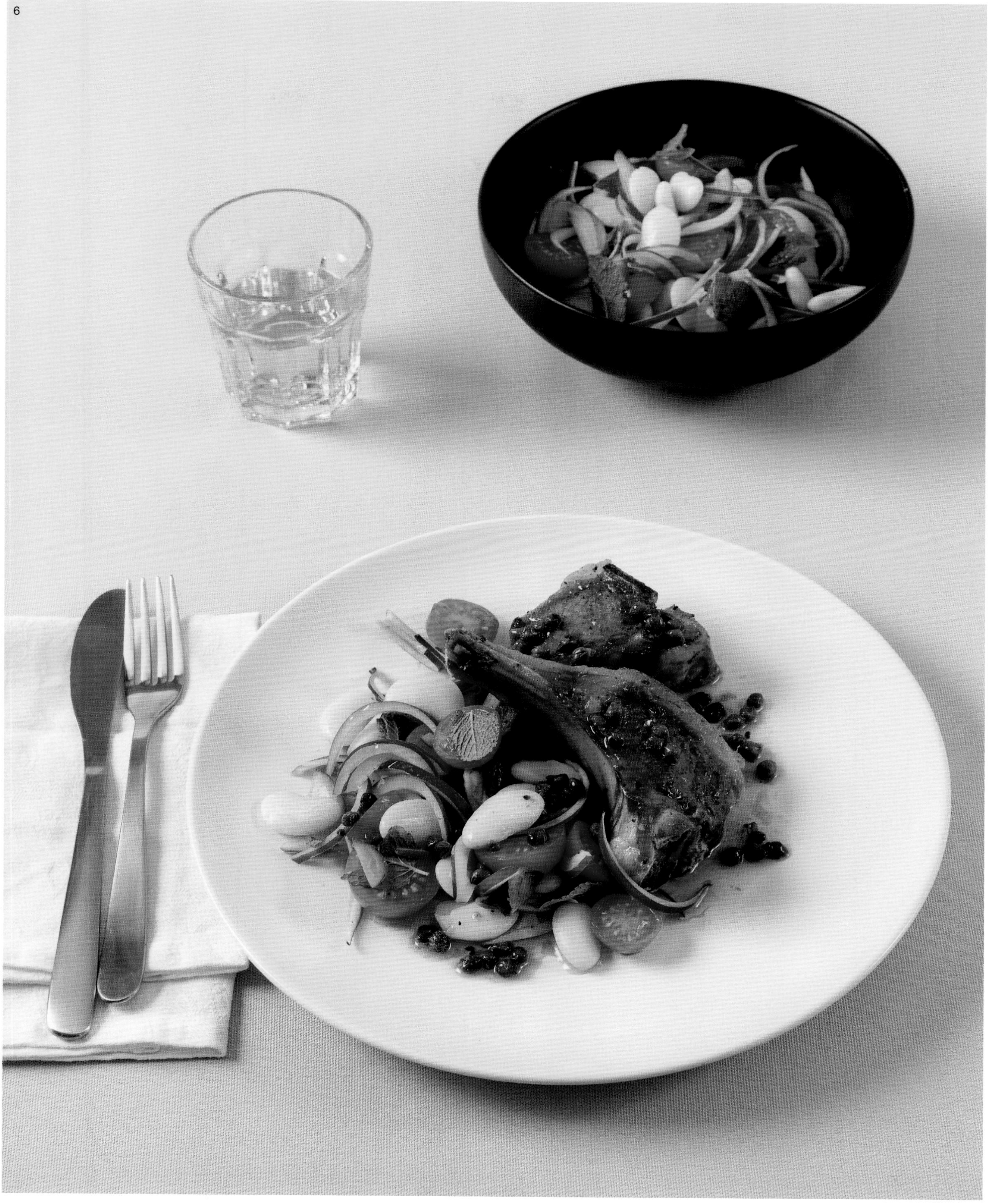

Spaghetti with Pesto

Preparation time: 10 minutes
Cooking time: 10 minutes
Serves 4

Fresh homemade pesto has so much more flavor than store-bought pesto in jars. Although best eaten as soon as it's made, any leftover pesto will keep in the refrigerator, covered with a layer of olive oil, for a week or so.

½ tsp salt

14 oz (400 g) spaghetti (although any pasta shape will work)

⅔ cup (80 g) pine nuts

1 clove garlic

1 large bunch fresh basil

⅔ cup (150 ml) extra virgin olive oil

2 oz (50 g) Parmesan cheese (⅔ cup grated), plus a little extra to serve

salt and pepper

1

Put a large saucepan of water over high heat and bring it to a boil. Add ½ teaspoon salt, then add in the pasta and bring to a boil. Stir once, turn the heat down a little, then boil for 10 minutes or until the pasta is just tender (firm but not chewy). Meanwhile, start the pesto. Heat a medium saucepan over low heat. Add the pine nuts and cook them for 3 minutes, stirring frequently, until they are golden and smell nutty. Tip onto a plate and let cool for a few minutes.

2

Coarsely chop the garlic and basil stems (stalks) and leaves, then put them into a food processor. Add the pine nuts and olive oil to the bowl and season with salt and pepper.

3

Blend the ingredients together until a bright green, slightly textured sauce comes together. Finely grate the cheese, then blend it into the sauce a couple of times.

4

Reserve a cupful of the pasta cooking water, then drain in a colander. Return the pasta to the pan. Spoon half the pesto, plus a couple of tablespoons of the reserved water, into the pasta. Toss well, using a pair of tongs, if you have them. If the pasta seems dry, add a little more of the reserved cooking water because it will help the sauce and pasta to marry.

5

Serve the pasta topped with a little more Parmesan, shaved thinly with a vegetable peeler, if you like.

Harissa Mackerel with Orange Salad

Preparation time: 20 minutes,
plus marinating
Cooking time: 15–20 minutes
Serves 6, easily doubled

Oily fish such as mackerel and sardines
are delicious with hot, spicy flavors,
such as harissa or curry paste, which
cut through the richness of the flesh.

6 smaller or 3 larger fresh mackerel,
    ask your fish supplier to clean (gut)
    them and to remove the heads
1 tbsp harissa paste
2 tbsp extra virgin olive oil, plus
    extra for greasing
3 large or 6 small oranges
11 oz (300 g) radishes (2½ cups
    sliced)
1 red onion
2 tbsp sherry vinegar
1 bunch fresh flat-leaf parsley
salt and pepper

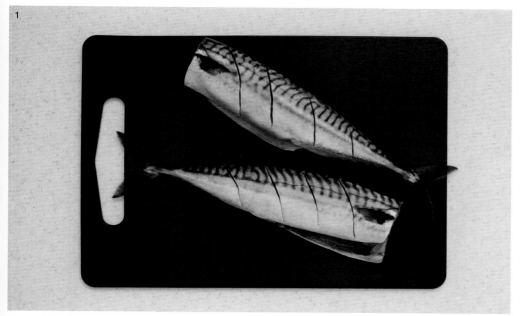

1

1
Rinse the fish under cold running water to remove any blood, then dry with paper towels. Slash the flesh 3–4 times on each side for small fish or 5 times for large fish.

2
Mix the harissa paste, 1 tablespoon of oil, and plenty of salt and pepper, then rub this all over the fish. Marinate in the refrigerator for a few minutes (or up to 3 hours), while you make the salad.

ABOUT HARISSA
This feisty paste of dried red chilies, garlic, and spices is originally from Tunisia, but it can be found in most large stores and delis. As an alternative, stir 1 tablespoon olive oil, 1 crushed garlic clove, and ½ teaspoon each ground cumin and ground coriander into 1 tablespoon chili paste or sauce.

2

3

Cut the top and bottom from each orange, then, using a serrated knife, cut away the skin and pith. Take care to follow the line of the orange flesh, so that you don't trim too much of it. Cut into thin slices.

4

Thinly slice the radishes and the red onion. Toss in a serving dish with the oranges, vinegar, and remaining olive oil. Season with salt and pepper.

5

Preheat the oven to 425°F/220°C/ Gas Mark 7. Grease a large baking pan, then put the fish on it. Roast for 15–20 minutes, depending on the size of the fish, until charred and cooked through. Test with a knife: The flesh at the backbone should flake easily. Toss the parsley leaves through the salad, then serve with the fish.

FEEL LIKE GRILLING?
Grill (barbecue) the fish over white hot coals or preheat your gas grill to 400°F/200°C. Brush the bars with a little oil. Cook small fish for 3 minutes on each side, 5 minutes for larger fish.

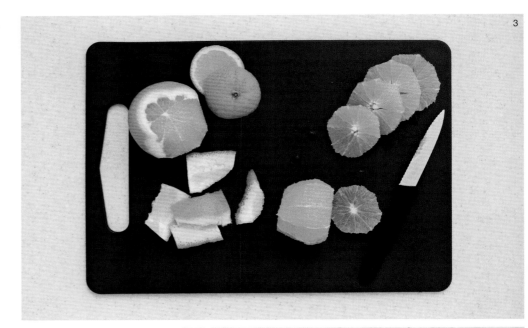

Asparagus & Poached Egg with Balsamic Butter

Preparation time: 10 minutes
Cooking time: 10 minutes
Serves 2, easily doubled or more

Most recipes for asparagus will involve steaming or boiling, but I love to cook it in a skillet or frying pan, or even roast it. Prepared this way, the asparagus retains all of its flavor, even intensifies it, and it's harder to overcook. For best results, buy the asparagus on the day of eating and look for the freshest firm, perky green spears.

---

9 oz (250 g) asparagus

chunk of Parmesan cheese,
   for shaving

1 tbsp white wine vinegar

2 extra-large (UK large) eggs,
   as fresh as possible

1 tbsp sunflower or vegetable oil

2 tbsp (25 g) unsalted butter

1 tsp balsamic vinegar

salt and pepper

1
Cut the bottom 2 inches (5 cm) from each asparagus spear, because the ends can often be tough.

2
Using a vegetable peeler, peel a handful of Parmesan shavings from the block.

3
Bring a deep saucepan of water to a boil, then add the wine vinegar and season generously with salt. Break 1 egg into a small dish or cup. When boiling, stir the water with a slotted spoon to make a whirlpool.

4
Gently slide the egg into the middle of the swirling water. Turn the heat to a simmer and cook the egg gently for 3 minutes, or until the white and yolk have set. Meanwhile, break the second egg into the dish or cup.

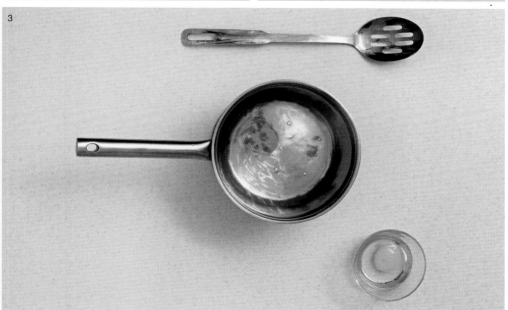

5
Lift the egg from the pan with the slotted spoon, then transfer it to a bowl of hot (not boiling) water. This will keep it warm while you poach the second egg.

6
While the second egg simmers, start cooking the asparagus. Put a large skillet or frying pan over high heat, then add the oil. Add the asparagus, season with salt and pepper, and fry for 3–5 minutes, depending on the thickness of the spears. Toss the spears frequently, until golden in places and just tender to the bite.

7
Take the pan from the heat and let cool for a few seconds. Add the butter and balsamic vinegar and let the butter melt.

8
Lift the asparagus onto warmed serving plates, then spoon over some balsamic butter from the skillet. Drain the eggs (pat dry underneath with paper towels or a clean dish towel/tea towel), then serve on top. Sprinkle with the Parmesan shavings. Sprinkle the eggs with salt and pepper and serve.

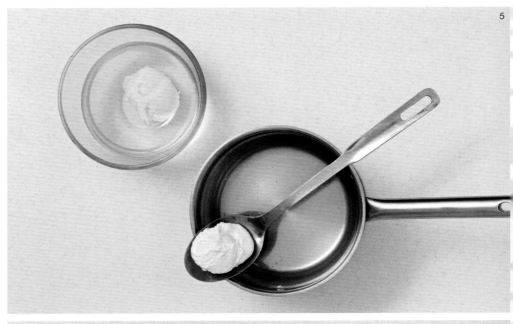

Carrot Falafel with Sesame Sauce

Preparation time: 15 minutes
Cooking time: under 15 minutes
Serves 4, easily doubled

The great thing about falafel (apart from they're good for you, easy, and filling) is that they reheat wonderfully or can be eaten cold, so you can make a batch and enjoy them whenever it suits. Why not try as a lunch-box filler with a small container of hummus and some veg sticks to make a change from the usual sandwiches.

2 cloves garlic

1 bunch fresh flat-leaf parsley

1 tbsp ground cumin

1 tbsp ground coriander

½ tsp dried crushed chilies
   or chili powder

1 (14-oz/400-g) can chickpeas,
   drained

1 extra-large (UK large) egg

2 carrots

1 lemon

1 tbsp olive oil

⅔ cup (150 g) plain (natural) yogurt

1 tbsp tahini

1 red onion

1 handful fresh mint

whole-grain (wholemeal) tortillas or
   pita bread

salt and pepper

pickled chilies, to serve (optional)

1

2

3

4

1
Coarsely chop the garlic and parsley, including the parsley stems (stalks). Put into a food processor with the spices, chickpeas, and egg.

2
Blend to make a finely chopped and fairly dry-looking mix. If you don't have a processor, mash the chickpeas with a potato masher and finely chop the garlic and herbs, then combine.

3
Coarsely grate the carrots and finely grate the zest of the lemon. Scoop the falafel mixture into a bowl, then add the carrots and lemon zest. Season to taste with salt and pepper.

4
Stir to combine, then shape the mixture into about 12 patties, pressing the mixture firmly together with cupped hands. The falafel can be kept in the refrigerator for up to 24 hours.

5

Heat a little oil in a nonstick skillet or frying pan, then fry the falafel in batches for about 3 minutes on each side, until golden. Don't be tempted to add more oil, because this will cause the patties to break.

6

Squeeze the juice from the lemon. Whisk together the yogurt, tahini, and 1 tablespoon lemon juice until smooth and spoonable. Add a little water if it's too thick. Season to taste with salt and pepper and more lemon juice, if you like.

7

Thinly slice the red onion and pick off the mint leaves. Toss with the remaining lemon juice and season with salt and pepper.

8

Warm the tortillas or pita breads in the microwave or in a hot skillet or frying pan according to the package instructions, then serve topped with the falafel, sesame yogurt, onion salad, and pickled chilies.

Spicy Shrimp, Fennel & Chile Linguine

Preparation time: 10 minutes
Cooking time: 15 minutes
Serves 2, easily doubled

This recipe is a regular in my home all year round. In the winter, I brown off good sausage meat instead of the shrimp (prawns), then simmer the sauce with canned tomatoes.

---

6 oz (175 g) linguine (or any other
    long pasta shape)
1 large or two smaller fennel bulbs
2 tbsp extra virgin olive oil,
    plus extra for drizzling
2 cloves garlic
1 large red chile
1 handful fresh flat-leaf parsley
1 lemon
¼ tsp fennel seeds (optional)
3½ oz (100 g) cherry tomatoes
7 oz (200 g) uncooked jumbo/tiger
    shrimp (large prawns), shelled and
    deveined, thawed if frozen
salt and pepper

1

Bring a large saucepan of salted water to a boil. Add the pasta, then once it has collapsed into the water, stir it and let boil for 8–10 minutes, until just tender.

IS MY PASTA COOKED?
Forget flinging a piece on the wall to see if it sticks. The easiest way to tell if pasta is cooked is to bite it. It should be tender, but with the slightest resistance in the middle— *al dente*—neither chewy nor soggy.

2

While the pasta cooks, cut the fennel bulb in half and remove any tough outer layers. You can also remove the core, if you like. Thinly slice the fennel. Reserve the feathery leaves, if there are any.

3

Heat the oil in a large skillet or frying pan, then add the fresh fennel. Fry for 10 minutes over medium heat, stirring often, until softened and sweet, and turning golden in places.

DEFROSTING FROZEN SHRIMP
To defrost frozen shrimp quickly, put them into a large bowl and cover with cold water. Let stand for a few minutes, then drain off the water and repeat. Pat dry and use immediately.

4

While you wait, thinly slice the garlic and chile. Seed the chile first, if you like. The easiest way to do this is by scraping out the middle with a teaspoon. Coarsely chop the parsley and cut the lemon into quarters.

5

Add the garlic, chile, fennel seeds, if using, and cherry tomatoes to the pan. Turn the heat up a little. Cook for 2 minutes or until fragrant and the tomato skins are starting to pop. Now add the shrimp and cook for about 3 minutes or until the shrimp have changed color all the way through.

6

Reserve a cup of the pasta cooking water, then drain the pasta in a colander.

7

Add the pasta, 5 tablespoons of the cooking water, the parsley, and any fennel leaves to the shrimp pan, then squeeze in the juice from 2 of the lemon wedges. Season generously with salt and pepper and toss everything together. Adjust to taste by adding more lemon juice, salt, and pepper, if needed. Serve drizzled with a little more oil and the remaining lemon wedges for squeezing.

Chipotle Chicken Fajitas

Preparation time: 10 minutes
Cooking time: 10 minutes
Serves 4, easily halved

Hot, tasty, and superfast, fajitas make great family food for busy weeknights. It's tempting to overfill the tortillas, but to avoid getting messy, think less is more—you can always roll another. To make my version of burritos see the tip on page 192.

---

2 bell peppers

1 onion

1 tbsp olive or vegetable oil

3–4 boneless, skinless chicken
   breasts

1 bunch fresh cilantro (coriander)

1 tbsp cumin seeds

1 tbsp chipotle paste

1 tbsp tomato paste (puree)

1 tsp sugar

3 oz (80 g) hard tasty cheese,
   such as mature Cheddar
   (¾ cup grated)

6–8 flour tortilla wraps

⅔ cup (150 g) sour cream, more
   if you like

salt and pepper

1
Seed then slice the bell peppers into chunky strips. Slice the onion.

2
Heat a large skillet or frying pan over medium–high heat. Add a splash of oil, wait a few seconds, then add the bell peppers and onions. Fry, stirring frequently, for 5 minutes, or until starting to soften and turn golden at the edges.

3
While you wait, cut the chicken into finger-width strips and put into a large bowl. Finely chop the cillantro (coriander) stems, then add to the chicken, along with the cumin seeds and some salt and pepper. Stir until the chicken is evenly coated.

4

Tip the cooked vegetables onto a plate or bowl, add another splash of oil to the pan, then fry the chicken for 5 minutes, stirring frequently, until golden and just cooked through.

5

While the chicken cooks, make the sauce. Stir together the chipotle paste, tomato paste (puree), and the sugar, and season with salt and pepper. Loosen with 2 tablespoons of water or until the sauce is the consistency of ketchup. Grate the cheese.

NO CHIPOTLE?
If you can't find this smoky, hot chili paste, then use 1 tablespoon ketchup mixed with 1 teaspoon chili sauce and a pinch of smoked paprika, if you have it. Add to the other ingredients and adjust the seasoning with more sugar, if needed.

6

Return the bell peppers and onions to the pan, then stir in the chipotle sauce. Keep cooking until coated and sticky, then remove from the heat.

7

Warm the tortillas according to the package instructions. Spoon some of the chicken mixture onto each tortilla, sprinkle with cheese, then finish with sour cream and a few cilantro leaves. Roll up and eat immediately.

BURRITOS
Roll the tortillas with only the chicken mix, then line them up in a large baking dish. Top with the cheese, then bake for 15 minutes at 400°F/200°C/ Gas Mark 6 until the cheese is melting, then top with the cilantro and sour cream.

Pan-Fried Fish with Salsa Verde

Preparation time: 15 minutes
Cooking time: 30 minutes
Serves 6

Crisp-skinned, tender fish with vibrant salsa verde makes one of the best simple suppers, and it's great for entertaining. The fish won't overcook if you follow these instructions—just ensure everything else is prepared before you start. Choose any sustainably caught, fresh white fish. Sea bass and bream work particularly well.

1 tsp salt

1 clove garlic

3 canned anchovy fillets, drained

1 lemon

1 small bunch fresh flat-leaf parsley

1 small bunch fresh basil

2 tbsp capers in liquid (brine), drained

3 tbsp extra virgin olive oil

2¼ lb (1 kg) baby (new) potatoes (see note on page 92)

6 fish fillets (see above), skin on and scales removed

2 tbsp all-purpose (plain) flour

2 tbsp sunflower or vegetable oil

1 tbsp butter, plus a little extra for the potatoes, if you like

salt and pepper

1
Preheat the oven to 275°F/140°C/
Gas Mark 1. Put a saucepan of
water on to boil and add the salt,
ready for the potatoes. While
it heats, make the salsa verde.
Coarsely chop the garlic and
anchovies and put them into the
bowl of a food processor. Finely
grate the zest from the lemon,
squeeze the juice, and add them to
the bowl along with the parsley and
basil leaves, capers, and extra virgin
olive oil.

2
Blend the ingredients to make a
slightly chunky, bright green sauce.
This sauce can be made up to
a day in advance and kept covered
in the refrigerator.

USING A MORTAR AND PESTLE
Traditionally, this sauce is made
in a mortar with a pestle, and the
anchovies, garlic, capers, and herbs
would be pounded together to
release their aromas. Feel free
to make it that way if you have
a mortar and pestle, but a food
processor makes it quicker.

3
Carefully put the potatoes into
the boiling water, then boil for
20 minutes. They're ready when a
table knife slips easily through one
of the potatoes. If you're not sure,
then lift one out and taste to check.

4

When the potatoes are ready, start the fish. Dry the fillets with paper towels, then slash the skin on each fillet 3 times using a sharp knife. Put the flour onto a plate, then season it generously with salt and pepper. Dust the fillets in a fine layer of flour, then set aside. The flour will give them a tasty crisp coating, and it will also protect the delicate fish from the heat of the pan.

CHOOSING FISH FILLETS
A good, fresh fish fillet should look and feel firm, and won't smell fishy. Buy fresh fish on the day you intend to cook it, or buy frozen and defrost in the refrigerator when you need it.

5

Have a plate ready, lined with some paper towels. Put a nonstick skillet or frying pan over medium-high heat, then add half the oil and half the butter. After about 30 seconds, slide in 3 fish fillets, skin side down. Cook for 3 minutes, without moving the fish, until the skin is golden and crisp and the flesh has turned white almost all the way to the top.

6

Carefully flip each piece of fish over with a spatula (fish slice), then cook for another 30 seconds. It shouldn't stick as you turn it. If the fish shows any sign of sticking, give it a little longer; it will come away from the pan when it's ready. Now lift the fish onto the plate and keep warm in the oven. Wipe out the pan with some paper towels, then heat the rest of the butter and oil and fry the second batch.

7

Drain the potatoes, toss them with a little more butter, and season. Serve the fish with spoonfuls of the salsa verde and potatoes to the side.

Weekend Cooking

Herb-Crusted Lamb with Pea Puree & Tomatoes

Preparation time: 20 minutes,
plus resting
Cooking time: 20 minutes
Serves 6

Depending on your guests' appetites,
serve two or three cutlets per person.
Fully trimmed lamb, right, is also
known as "French trimmed." All of
the skin, fat, and meat from around
the main eye of meat and the bones
around it are removed to create a neat
effect that looks special on the plate,
and it is easy to carve and eat.

1 handful fresh thyme

1¾ cups (80 g) fresh bread crumbs

2 tbsp extra virgin olive oil, plus
    extra for drizzling

2 racks of lamb, with 7–8 cutlets
    each, fully trimmed (ask your
    butcher to do this for you)

1 heaping tbsp Dijon mustard

1 large or 2 smaller onions

6 tbsp (80 g) unsalted butter

2¾ cups (400 g) shelled fresh or
    frozen baby peas (petits pois)

scant 1 cup (200 ml) vegetable
    broth (stock)

6 small bunches cherry tomatoes

1 handful fresh mint

salt and pepper

1

Pick the leaves from the thyme (you'll need about 2 tablespoons), finely chop, then mix with the bread crumbs, oil, and some salt and pepper. This can be made up to a day in advance, if you like.

2

Cut the racks of lamb into portions of 3 or 4 cutlets each. Season with salt and pepper, then smear the mustard over the top of each rack.

3

Press the bread-crumb mixture onto the racks using the palm of your hand. The racks can now be chilled for up to a day. Remember to remove them from the refrigerator 1 hour before cooking, so that your meat cooking times correspond with the recipe.

4

For the pea puree, finely chop the onion. Melt the butter in a medium saucepan, then add the onion with some salt and pepper. Fry gently for 10 minutes, until soft.

5

Add the peas and broth (stock) to the pan. Bring to a boil, then simmer for 2 minutes or until the peas are bright and tender.

6

Using an immersion (stick) blender, blend the peas until thick and smooth, then season to taste with salt and pepper. If you don't have a handheld blender, you can puree the peas in a blender or food processor instead.

7

Preheat the oven to 400°F/200°C/ Gas Mark 6. Roast the lamb for 20 minutes, adding the tomatoes to the pan halfway through cooking. When the lamb is ready, the crumbs will be golden and the tomatoes starting to split and turn juicy. These timings will cook the lamb medium rare—pink and juicy in the middle. If you like meat well done, add an extra 5 minutes (although this will make the meat tougher and drier and I wouldn't recommend it).

8

Let the lamb rest in the roasting pan for 5 minutes, then slice it into cutlets (you could serve the racks whole, if you like, but carving makes it easier for your guests to eat).

9

Spoon the pea puree onto plates, top with the lamb, then finish with a bunch of tomatoes, a drizzle of olive oil, and a sprinkling of torn mint leaves.

Roast Chicken with Tarragon Sauce

Preparation time: 10 minutes
Cooking time: 1 hour 20 minutes
Serves 4–6

Ideal for a spring Sunday, this chicken will have everyone asking for more (and it's all cooked in one pan, too). Tarragon, classic with chicken and creamy dishes, can also be replaced with flat-leaf parsley or chervil. Cook two chickens together if your family has a big appetite.

1 (3¼-lb/1.5-kg) chicken

1 onion

1 lemon

1 handful fresh tarragon

1 tbsp unsalted butter

1 lb 10 oz (750 g) baby (new) potatoes

1 tbsp olive oil

9 oz (250 g) asparagus spears or
    trimmed green (French) beans

scant ½ cup (100 ml) dry
    white wine

⅔ cup (150 ml) heavy (double) cream

1¼ cups (300 ml) chicken broth (stock)

1 cup (150 g) frozen young or baby
    peas (petit pois)

salt and pepper

1

Preheat the oven to 400°F/200°C/
Gas Mark 6. Put the chicken onto
a board, then cut away any string
that had been used to bind the bird.
Remove the giblets from the cavity
(between the legs). Cut the onion
and lemon in half, then put half the
onion, half the lemon, and several
sprigs of tarragon into the cavity.

2

Loosely retie the legs together
with kitchen twine (string). Spread
the butter over the breast and thigh
meat, then season with plenty
of salt and pepper. Roast for
20 minutes.

TRUSSING POULTRY
When chickens and turkeys are
bound too tightly, it makes it more
difficult for the heat to permeate
through the body. This means that
the breast meat, which doesn't need
so much cooking, can overcook
as you wait for the inner meat of
the thigh to cook completely. Tying
more loosely means that the hot air
can circulate all around the meat.

3

Cut any larger potatoes in half, then
add to the pan once the chicken
has roasted for 20 minutes. Drizzle
with 1 tablespoon oil and toss with
any juices in the bottom of the pan.
Return to the oven for another
40 minutes.

4

Cut the bottom 2 inches (5 cm) from
each asparagus spear, because the
ends can often be tough.

5

When the chicken is golden and cooked, and the potatoes are tender, transfer everything to a large platter. Put into the (turned-off) oven, leaving the door slightly open, to keep the chicken warm as it rests.

TESTING IF A WHOLE
CHICKEN IS COOKED
Your chicken is ready if the legs wobble freely at the hip joints—this indicates that the meat has cooked and contracted in the thickest part of the chicken, making the legs loose. Another way to test is to insert the point of a sharp knife or a skewer into the thickest part of the thigh. If the juices come out clear or with no trace of pink, it is cooked.

6

While the chicken rests, it's time to make the sauce and cook the green vegetables. Spoon the excess fat from the pan. Put the roasting pan over low heat, then add the wine and bubble for 1 minute. Add the cream and broth (stock).

7

Add the asparagus (or beans) to the pan, then simmer for 3 minutes. Add the peas, then return to a boil until the vegetables are just tender.

8

Coarsely chop the rest of the tarragon and stir it into the sauce. Season the sauce to taste—add a splash of the juice from the remaining lemon half, if you like. Serve the chicken with the potatoes, vegetables, and sauce.

Lemon Basil Gnudi with Fava Beans

Preparation time: 30 minutes,
plus at least 1 hour chilling
Cooking time: 15 minutes
Serves 4–6 (great as an appetizer too)

Cousins to potato gnocchi, these little ricotta dumplings are lighter, simpler to make, and a fantastic option for a vegetarian who's seen it all at dinner parties. If fresh broad (fava) beans are unavailable, boil 3 cups (500 g) frozen beans instead and then remove their pale green skins.

---

2 cups (500 g) ricotta cheese,
    drained of any liquid in
    the tubs
1 extra-large (UK large) egg
1 bunch fresh basil
1 lemon
4 oz (120 g) Parmesan cheese
    (1⅓ cups, grated)
1 tbsp all-purpose (plain) flour, plus
    plenty more for shaping
½ cup (25 g) fresh white bread
    crumbs
2¼ lb (1 kg) fresh fava (broad) beans
2 cloves garlic
6 tbsp (80 g) butter
1 tsp dried chili flakes
salt and pepper

1

Put the ricotta and egg into a large mixing bowl. Coarsely chop half of the basil leaves, add to the mixture, then finely grate in the zest of the lemon and 1 cup (90 g) of the Parmesan. Season with plenty of pepper and a little salt. Reserve the lemon.

2

Beat the ingredients together until smooth, then sift in the flour and add the bread crumbs.

3

Stir the flour and bread crumbs into the ricotta mix. Put plenty of flour into a baking pan or something similar, and have a floured plate ready. Spoon a couple of heaping teaspoons of the gnudi mixture separately into the flour in the pan, then roll them around in the flour until well coated. Shape the gnudi with dry hands to make a smooth ball or oval. Put onto the floured plate, then repeat with the rest of the mix. Chill the gnudi for at least 1 hour or up to 24 hours. This will firm up the mix ready for cooking.

4

Prepare the fava (broad) beans. Bring a saucepan of salted water to a boil. While it comes to a boil, break the pods and pop the beans out. Discard the pods.

5

Boil the beans for 3 minutes, by which point they should have floated to the top of the pan. Drain in a colander and cool under cold running water, then remove the bright green beans from their pale green skins. Cool under cold water and set aside for later.

6

When you're ready to cook the gnudi, bring a large, deep saucepan of well-salted water to a boil and put some serving plates in a low oven to warm. Add half of the gnudi to the pan (drop them in carefully one at a time and they won't stick). They will rise up to the surface. Once this has happened, cook for another 2–3 minutes. When ready, the gnudi will feel firm and bounce back when pressed lightly. Lift out and drain well using a slotted spoon onto the warmed plates. Repeat until all of the gnudi are cooked.

7

Just before serving, prepare the buttery sauce. Crush the garlic. Put a skillet or frying pan over medium-high heat, add the butter, and let it melt. Add the garlic and chili flakes, then sizzle for 1 minute.

8

Add the shelled (podded) beans and remaining basil leaves, and splash in a good squeeze of juice from the lemon—the butter will sizzle a little here and turn slightly golden. Season generously.

9

Spoon the garlic and bean butter over the gnudi, then serve with the rest of the grated Parmesan.

Fragrant Chicken with Quinoa Salad

Preparation time: 15 minutes, plus
marinating if you like
Cooking time: 40 minutes
Serves 6–8

Fresher than a North African tagine,
but with the same aromatic flavors, this
hearty salad is one of the easiest ways
to feed a crowd. Set the platter down,
perhaps with a bowl of thick yogurt on
the side, and let everyone tuck in.

---

10 pieces of chicken: 4 drumsticks,
   4 thighs, and 2 breasts is a
   good mix
2 cloves garlic
2 tbsp ras el hanout spice mix
1 tsp dried chili flakes
4 tbsp vegetable or sunflower oil
2 onions
1¾ cups (300 g) quinoa
2½ cups (600 ml) vegetable or
   chicken broth (stock)
11 oz (300 g) green (French) beans
   (3 cups prepared)
2 limes (you'll need 4 tbsp juice)
1 tbsp honey
2 tbsp walnut oil
3 heads red radicchio (chicory)
3 tbsp pomegranate molasses
1 large bunch fresh cilantro
   (coriander)
½ cup (50 g) pistachios,
   walnuts, or almonds
salt and pepper

1

Slash the chicken pieces through the skin a few times, then spread out in a large roasting pan.

2

Crush the garlic. Mix half of the garlic, all the ras el hanout, chili flakes, and 2 tablespoons of the oil with plenty of salt and pepper, then rub it all over the chicken pieces. If you have time, let the chicken marinate for 30 minutes, or even overnight in the refrigerator.

RAS EL HANOUT
This is a heady mix of spices, normally containing cinnamon, ginger, cumin, coriander, cardamom, allspice, and paprika among others, and often perfumed with rose petals. For a good homemade alternative, mix 1 teaspoon each ground cinnamon, cumin, sweet smoked paprika, ground coriander, and ground ginger, plus ½ teaspoon ground black pepper.

3

For the salad, thinly slice the onions. Heat 1 tablespoon oil in a large saucepan, then add the onions and cook over medium heat, stirring often, until softened and golden.

4

Tip in the quinoa and broth (stock), then bring to a boil.

QUINOA?
Quinoa is a nutritious whole grain and a great alternative to rice or couscous. In this recipe, I cook it with broth and softened onions in a sealed pan, so that it plumps up and absorbs all of the flavor—much like the way rice is cooked in Greece and the Middle East. You can also boil, then drain it. The grain is cooked when the little germ (this looks like a tail) pops out and the grains are tender but not mushy.

5

Cover the pan with a lid and simmer the quinoa for 10 minutes. While it simmers, trim, then chop the beans into short lengths.

6

After the quinoa has cooked for 10 minutes, add the beans to the pan, cover, and cook for another 5 minutes, until the beans are steamed and the quinoa cooked through. Spread the quinoa and beans over a platter or large baking sheet to help them cool as quickly as possible. Turn it over with a fork occasionally as they cool.

7

Make the dressing for the quinoa. Squeeze the lime juice, then mix with the honey, walnut oil, remaining garlic, and some salt and pepper. Separate as many radicchio (chicory) leaves as you can, then coarsely chop the inner leaves.

8

When you're ready to cook, preheat the oven to 400°F/200°C/Gas Mark 6. Put the chicken in to roast for 20 minutes, skin side up. After 20 minutes, take the breast portions out, then return the drumsticks and thighs to the oven, because they will need longer cooking. Cook for another 20 minutes, then return the breasts to the pan, drizzle the pomegranate molasses over all the pieces, then give everything a quick blast in the oven until the molasses is bubbling.

9

Just before serving, coarsely chop the cilantro (coriander). Toss the cilantro, radicchio, and dressing through the cooled quinoa. Top with the chicken (slice the breast meat), then pour the cooking juices over the meat. Sprinkle with the nuts and serve.

Eggplant Parmigiana

Preparation time: 45 minutes
Cooking time: 30 minutes
Serves 6

First softened in a pan, then layered with a rich herbed sauce, eggplants (aubergines) become a hero ingredient in this comforting recipe. The cheesy crust and the saucy layers below create a rich and satisfying dish, which makes a wonderful vegetarian alternative to lasagne.

4 large eggplants (aubergines),
    about 3¼ lb (1.5 kg)
scant ½ cup (100 ml) mild olive oil
2 cloves garlic
1 tbsp tomato paste (puree)
2 (14-oz/400-g) cans diced or
    chopped tomatoes
¼ tsp sugar
a few sprigs fresh oregano,
    or 1 tsp dried
1 small bunch fresh basil
2 slices good-quality white bread,
    about 3½ oz (100 g)
3 oz (80 g) Parmesan cheese
    (1 cup grated)
1 (4-oz/120-g) mozzarella cheese ball
salt and pepper

1
Cut the eggplants (aubergines) into slices about ¼ inch (5 mm) thick. Use a pastry brush to paint the top of each slice with some of the olive oil.

2
Heat a large skillet or frying pan over medium heat. Add several slices of eggplant, oiled side down. Fry for 5 minutes, or until golden and softened underneath. Brush the tops of the slices with oil, then turn and cook for another 5 minutes or until completely tender. Set aside and repeat with the rest of the slices.

3
While the eggplant is cooking, start the sauce. Thinly slice the garlic. Heat a saucepan over medium heat, then add 2 tablespoons of the oil. Add the garlic and cook for 1 minute, until softened. Add the tomato paste (puree), canned tomatoes, sugar, and half the oregano. Tear in the basil, then simmer the sauce for 10 minutes. Season with salt and pepper.

4
To make the crumb topping, tear the bread into the bowl of a food processor, discarding the crusts. Finely grate the Parmesan, then add half of it to the bread. Add the remaining oregano.

5

Blend until you have bread crumbs flecked with green.

IF YOU DON'T HAVE
A FOOD PROCESSOR
You can make the bread crumbs by grating the bread instead. Finely chop the herbs, then stir them together with the crumbs and Parmesan.

6

Preheat the oven to 350°F/180°C/ Gas Mark 4. Make layers of the eggplant and tomato sauce in an ovenproof dish, seasoning the eggplant with salt and pepper as you go.

7

Chop the mozzarella into small pieces. Sprinkle the mozzarella and remaining Parmesan over the top, then finish with the crumbs and a drizzle of oil.

8

Bake for 30 minutes or until golden and bubbling. Remove from the oven and let stand in the dish for 10 minutes before serving.

GETTING AHEAD
This dish can be prepared up to the end of step 7, then covered and chilled in the refrigerator for up to 2 days. If cooking from chilled, add an extra 10 minutes to the cooking time and cover it with aluminum foil if the topping browns before the time is up.

Creamy Fish Pie

Preparation time: 1 hour
Cooking time: 40 minutes
Serves 6

Perfect for informal get-togethers, a fish pie makes a luxurious but simple dish. Feel free to vary the fish, replace the dill with flat-leaf parsley, or add boiled eggs, if you like. Do use smoked haddock if you can find it; its gentle smokiness gives a backbone of flavor to the whole dish. If not, substitute more white fish and add a little smoked salmon at step 9.

3¼ lb (1.5 kg) floury potatoes, such as russets or Maris Piper

1 tsp salt

3½ cups (850 ml) whole milk

1¼ cups (300 ml) heavy (double) cream

1 bay leaf

4 cloves

1 onion

14 oz (400 g) smoked haddock fillet, skin on if possible

1 lb 5 oz (600 g) chunky white fish fillets, skin on

6 tbsp (80 g) butter

scant ½ cup (50 g) all-purpose (plain) flour

1 whole nutmeg, for grating

1 small bunch fresh dill

7 oz (200 g) large, shelled raw shrimp (prawns)

1 oz (25 g) Parmesan cheese (⅓ cup grated)

salt and pepper

1

Peel, then quarter the potatoes. Put into a large saucepan, just cover with cold water, add the salt, then bring to a boil. Once the water is boiling, turn the heat down and simmer the potatoes for 15 minutes or until tender.

2

Meanwhile, start the creamy sauce. Put 2½ cups (600 ml) of the milk and all the cream into a skillet or frying pan, then add the bay leaf and cloves. Cut the onion into quarters and add to the pan. Put over low heat, then bring to a simmer.

3

Once small bubbles start to appear, slide the fish fillets into the milk, skin side down. Cover, then cook the fish gently for 5 minutes, until the flesh has changed color and flakes easily. Carefully lift the fish from the pan and onto a plate. Turn off the heat under the pan, then let the milk and flavorings steep (infuse) for 10 minutes.

SKIN ON?
It's best for the fish to have skin on for this recipe, because it helps protect it from overcooking in the milk and also keeps it in one piece, ready for flaking into big pieces later.

4

Drain the potatoes in a colander. Put 2 tablespoons (25 g) of the butter and the remaining milk into the potato pan, then place over medium heat until the milk starts to boil and the butter is melting. Add the cooked potatoes, then take off the heat.

5

Mash the potatoes using a potato masher, or a potato ricer if you have one. Do this immediately, because the potatoes need to be hot in order to produce the best, fluffiest result. Season with salt and pepper.

6

Heat another saucepan over medium heat, then add the flour and remaining butter. Let the butter melt, then cook together, stirring, for 2 minutes, or until the flour starts to turn golden. Remove from the heat.

7

Strain the milk through a sieve into a pitcher (jug), then gradually whisk it into the flour and butter mixture. It will be thick at first, but keep whisking until a smooth sauce comes together. Return the pan to the heat and whisk until thickened.

8

Season generously with salt, pepper, and about ¼ teaspoon finely grated nutmeg. Chop the delicate dill leaves, then stir into the sauce.

9

Preheat the oven to 350°F/180°C/ Gas Mark 4. Flake the fish into a large ovenproof dish, discarding the skin and any bones. Keep the fish in chunky pieces. Pat the shrimp (prawns) dry with paper towels, then sprinkle them around the dish.

10

Spoon the sauce over the fish. Cover with spoonfuls of the mashed potatoes, then smooth and swirl them together. Finely grate the Parmesan, then sprinkle it over the top. The pie can be cooled, then chilled for up to 2 days.

11

Bake for 40 minutes (longer from chilled) or until the top is golden and the sauce bubbles around the edges. Stand for 10 minutes before serving.

HARD-BOILED EGGS?
If you want to add eggs, put 3 eggs into a saucepan of cold water and bring to a boil. After 8 minutes, cool, peel, and cut into quarters. Add them in step 9.

Lamb & Potato Curry with Fragrant Rice

Preparation time: 1 hour
Cooking time: 2½ hours
Serves 6

Like almost all stews, this rich lamb curry improves in flavor if made the day before and then reheated. Chill it overnight, then bring it slowly to a simmer the next day, ready to serve with a bowl of scented spiced rice.

3 onions
4 cloves garlic
2 tbsp vegetable oil
3½ tbsp (50 g) butter
1 tsp salt
1 large green chile
1 bunch fresh cilantro (coriander)
large chunk fresh ginger, or
    3 thumb-sized pieces
2 tsp ground turmeric
2 tsp ground cumin
2 tsp ground coriander
½ tsp ground black pepper
2¼ lb (1 kg) boneless lamb shoulder,
    trimmed of excess fat and cut into
    matchbox-size pieces (a butcher
    will be happy to do this)
2 tbsp tomato paste (puree)
1 (14-oz/400-g) can diced or
    chopped tomatoes
2 medium potatoes, about 9 oz
    (250 g)

For the rice
scant 2 cups (350 g) white basmati
    rice
6–7 cardamom pods
2 cinnamon sticks

1

Preheat the oven to 325°F/160°C/ Gas Mark 3. Thinly slice the onions and garlic. Place a wide, deep ovenproof casserole over low heat. After 30 seconds, add the oil and half of the butter. Once the butter foams, add two-thirds of the onions, all of the garlic, and ½ teaspoon of the salt. Fry gently for 10 minutes, stirring occasionally, until softened and starting to turn golden.

2

Meanwhile, seed and finely chop the chile, and finely chop the stems (stalks) from the fresh cilantro (coriander). Finely grate the ginger. Add these to the pan with the turmeric, cumin, ground coriander, and black pepper, then turn up the heat a little and cook for 3 minutes, stirring, until golden and fragrant. Take care not to let the spices burn.

3

Add the lamb and stir to coat it in the spices. Cook for 5 minutes, stirring occasionally, until the lamb has changed color all over. It doesn't need to be browned.

4

Stir in the tomato paste (puree), tomatoes, and ⅔ cup (150 ml) water.

5

Put the lid on the pan, leaving a little gap for steam to escape. Transfer the pan to the preheated oven and cook for 1¼ hours. Covering the pan this way lets the sauce cook down and reduce a little without becoming dry. While the curry cooks, peel the potatoes, then cut them into large chunks. Stir the potatoes into the curry and return to the oven for another 1¼ hours.

6

With about 45 minutes' cooking time left, start the rice. Heat a large saucepan over medium heat, then add the remaining butter. When it foams, add the remaining onion. Fry for 15 minutes, until the onion is golden and soft, stirring often.

7

While the onion cooks, rinse the rice. Put the rice into a sieve, then rinse it under the cold running water until the water runs clear. Let drain.

8

Stir the cardamom pods and cinnamon sticks into the onions, then add the drained rice. Stir until everything is well coated in the butter. Pour in 3 cups (700 ml) cold water (or just enough to cover the rice by a fingertip's depth), then add ½ teaspoon salt.

9

Bring to a boil, stir once, then cover and cook over medium heat for 10 minutes. Remove the pan from the heat, without removing the lid, and let stand for 15 minutes. The rice should be cooked through with no water remaining. If it seems slightly undercooked, add a splash of water, cover, and return to low heat for 5 minutes, then remove and let stand for 5 minutes.

10

Fluff up the rice with a fork to separate the grains, then cover the pan again until ready to serve.

11

To finish the curry, spoon off any excess fat that has risen to the top and season with salt and pepper. Coarsely chop the cilantro leaves and stir some of them through the curry. Sprinkle more cilantro leaves over and serve with the rice.

Tagliatelle with Bolognese Sauce

Preparation time: 40 minutes
Cooking time: 1½ hours
Serves 6 generously

A rich and meaty Bolognese sauce, or *ragù*, is a fabulous thing, but it can't be rushed. Ground meat (mince) is usually made from the tougher parts of the animal, so it needs long, slow cooking to become really tender. Browning the meat properly at the start is key to building an intense flavor, so take your time.

1 tbsp mild olive oil

1 lb 2 oz (500 g) lean ground (minced) beef

2 onions

2 stalks celery

1 carrot

2 cloves garlic

7 oz (200 g) dry-cured regular (streaky) bacon (about 8 slices/ rashers) or pancetta

1 handful fresh basil or 1 tsp dried mixed herbs

2 tbsp tomato paste (puree)

1 bay leaf

⅔ cup (150 ml) white wine

⅔ cup (150 ml) milk

2 (14-oz/400-g) cans diced or chopped tomatoes

1 lb 2 oz (500 g) tagliatelle

 salt and pepper

chunk of Parmesan cheese, to serve

1

Heat a large skillet, frying pan, or flameproof casserole over high heat, then add the oil. After 30 seconds, add the ground beef (mince). Make sure it sizzles in the pan rather than stews. Break up the meat with a wooden spoon as it browns.

2

After 10 minutes, the beef will have changed color from pink to gray to golden brown. It's possible that the meat will release water as it cooks at first, but keep the heat up and it will boil away, leaving the meat to fry. Transfer to a bowl.

3

While the meat browns, coarsely chop the onions, celery, carrot, and cloves garlic. Put into the bowl of a food processor.

4

Pulse the blades of the food processor in short bursts until the vegetables are finely chopped. A food processor will save lots of time here, but if you don't have one, chop the vegetables by hand. You may have to cook them for a little longer.

5

Chop the bacon or pancetta, add it to the pan, then fry gently for 8–10 minutes, until the fat has run out of the meat and it's crisp and golden. Pancetta will take slightly less time to crisp than bacon.

6

Add the vegetables to the bacon, then turn the heat down. Cook gently for another 10 minutes, until the vegetables have softened.

7

Return the meat to the pan and add torn basil leaves, if using, or the dried herbs. Stir in the tomato paste (puree), bay leaf, and wine, then let the mixture simmer for 2 minutes. Stir in the milk and tomatoes, plus a scant ½ cup (100 ml) water, then season with salt and pepper.

8

Partly cover the pan, then simmer for 1½ hours, until the beef is tender and surrounded with a rich, thick sauce. Taste to check the seasoning, adding salt and pepper, if necessary.

9

Just before serving, boil the pasta for 10 minutes (see page 173 for a full description if you need one). Reserve a cup of the cooking water, then drain. Finely grate some Parmesan cheese.

WHY TAGLIATELLE?
In Bologna, Italy, this sauce is served with tagliatelle instead of spaghetti. You can use spaghetti, if you like.

10

Put the pasta into the sauce, add a couple of tablespoons of the pasta cooking water, then toss well and serve, topped with grated or shaved Parmesan.

GETTING AHEAD
This meat sauce is a great recipe to double and keep in the refrigerator or freezer, ready to serve with pasta or make into Lasagne. If you double the quantity, you will need to brown the meat in batches.

Roast Lamb & Rosemary Potatoes

Preparation time: 30 minutes
Cooking time: 2 hours 10 minutes
Serve 6

Although some cuts of lamb, such as rack, are best served pink, the leg is a slightly tougher cut that benefits from a little more cooking. These timings give juicy and slightly pink meat. Choose a three-quarter (part-boned) leg if possible, because it makes carving so much simpler.

---

10 cloves garlic

1 handful fresh rosemary sprigs

1 (4½-lb/2-kg) part-boned leg
   of lamb

1 stalk celery

1 carrot

1 onion

3 tbsp mild olive oil

4½ lb (2 kg) potatoes, such as
   Yukon Gold or Maris Piper

scant ½ cup (100 ml) good red wine

2 cups (500 ml) good-quality lamb or
   beef broth (stock)

1 tbsp red currant or cranberry jelly

salt and pepper

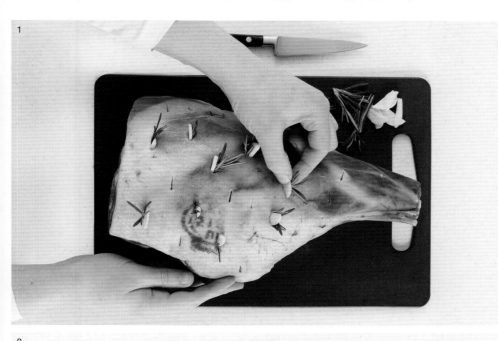

1

2

3

1

Preheat the oven to 425°F/ 220°C/ Gas Mark 7. Slice 5 of the garlic cloves into thin slivers. Pick small tufts of rosemary from the stems. Using a small, sharp knife, carefully poke about 25 holes into the lamb, cutting down about ¾ inch (1.5 cm) or so into the meat each time. Poke a piece of garlic and a tuft of rosemary into each hole. Season well with salt and pepper.

2

Chop the celery, carrot, and onion into big chunks. Put them into a heavy roasting pan. Sit the lamb among the vegetables, drizzle 1 tablespoon oil all over, then put into the middle of the oven and roast for 20 minutes. Turn the oven down to 375°F/190°C/Gas Mark 5, pour ½ cup (120 ml) water over the lamb, then set the timer for 1 hour. if at any point the garlic, rosemary, or lamb look as though they are coloring up too much, cover the pan with aluminum foil.

3

While the lamb cooks, peel the potatoes and cut into small chunks. Put these into a large roasting pan or onto a baking pan (tray), then add the remaining cloves garlic, still in their skins. Chop 1 tablespoon of rosemary, then sprinkle it over the potatoes, along with plenty of seasoning. Drizzle with the rest of the oil, then rub the oil around the potatoes with your hands.

4

When the lamb has had 1 hour's cooking, put the potatoes into the oven on the shelf above. Cook the lamb for another 30 minutes. The vegetables around the lamb will have softened and caramelized.

5

As soon as the lamb is cooked, take it out of the oven, turn up the heat to 425°F/220°C/Gas Mark 7, and let the potatoes crisp up for 20 minutes. Transfer the lamb from the pan to a board or platter and let it rest, uncovered.

6

Spoon the excess fat from the roasting pan, leaving a tablespoon or so behind, then put the pan over medium heat. Add the red wine and broth (stock), scraping up any bits from the bottom of the pan. Simmer until reduced by half, or until the sauce looks a little syrupy, then stir in the red currant or cranberry jelly to make a glossy sauce. Season to taste, and don't forget to add any resting juices.

7

Strain the sauce into a pitcher (jug). Serve the lamb with the potatoes, sauce, and your favorite vegetables.

PERFECT TIMING
If you want to cook a different-size piece of lamb, follow these timings. Always start with 20 minutes at 425°F/220°C/Gas Mark 7. For lamb that's golden brown on the outside and just pink nearer the bone, calculate 20 minutes cooking per 1 lb (450 g) of meat (the weight includes the bone). For rare lamb, calculate 15 minutes, and for well done, 25 minutes. As with all meat, cook the lamb from room temperature, or at least not straight from the refrigerator.

Paella

Preparation time: 30 minutes
Cooking time: 50 minutes
Serves 6

This classic Spanish rice dish is a great dish to cook for friends. The mix of seafood is up to you, but shrimp, mussels, and squid give great color and texture. Make sure you use the largest pan you can—the rice swells up a lot as it cooks.

3½ oz (100 g) chorizo (see note)

2 tsp mild olive oil

6 skinless, boneless chicken thighs, about 1 lb 2 oz (500 g)

2 onions

3 cloves garlic

2 red bell peppers

2 cups (350 g) paella rice (see page 238)

1 tsp smoked or regular paprika

generous pinch saffron strands (about ½ tsp)

scant ½ cup (100 ml) white wine

4¼ cups (1 litre) chicken or fish broth (stock)

6 small cleaned squid (optional)

11 oz (300 g) mussels

12 large shell-on raw shrimp (prawns), with heads on or off

1 handful frozen baby peas (petits pois)

1 handful fresh flat-leaf parsley

1 lemon

salt and pepper

1

Thinly slice the chorizo. Put a large skillet, frying pan, or flameproof casserole over medium heat, then add the oil. After 30 seconds, add the sausage. Fry for 5 minutes, until golden all over and the chorizo has released its red oil. Lift out of the pan and set aside. While the chorizo cooks, cut the chicken into bite-sized chunks.

CHORIZO
Chorizo is a spicy Spanish sausage flavored with paprika and garlic. There are two types: cooking chorizo, which is softer, and needs cooking like a regular sausage, and cured chorizo, which is firm and dry, and it is eaten raw, like salami. Either type will work in this recipe, but choose cooking chorizo if there's a choice.

2

Add the chicken to the pan, season with salt and pepper, and fry for 5 minutes, turning occasionally, until golden.

3

While the chicken fries, finely slice or chop the onion and garlic. Seed the bell peppers and cut them into chunky slices. Add the onions, garlic, and bell peppers to the chicken, stir, then cook gently for 10 minutes, until the onions and bell peppers are softened.

4

Add the rice and turn up the heat. Stir well to coat in the oil, then add the paprika, saffron, wine, and broth (stock) and season with salt and pepper. Simmer the rice for 20 minutes, or until it is nearly soft. Stir the pan several times as it cooks.

PAELLA RICE
Spanish cooks use a short, round-grain rice for paella, which is either labeled as "paella rice" or as one of the two most common varieties: Calasparra or Bomba.

5

Meanwhile, slice the squid tubes into thick rings, if using. Leave the tentacles whole. Scrub the mussels and pull any stringy threads away from them (these are known as beards). Tap any open mussels sharply on the work surface. Any that don't close after a few seconds must be discarded.

6

Add the shrimp (prawns) to the pan, tucking them into what sauce is left around the rice. Cover with a lid and cook for 5 minutes, then sprinkle the squid, mussels, peas, and chorizo over the top. Cover and cook for another 2 minutes, or until the mussels have opened and the squid has turned from translucent to white. The rice will have absorbed the broth.

7

Discard any mussels that haven't opened. Coarsely chop the parsley leaves, then sprinkle over the paella. Serve with lemon wedges to squeeze over.

Chicken, Bacon & Vegetable Pot Pies

Preparation time: 1¼ hours,
plus 30 minutes for cooling
Cooking time: 20 minutes
(or 30 for a large pie)
Makes 6 individual pies
or 1 large pie

Individual pot pies are easy to put
together, without any fiddly pastry
crimping. Serve with simply cooked
vegetables or potatoes for an ideal
family supper.

---

12 skinless, boneless chicken
    thighs, about 2¼ lb (1 kg)
8 slices (rashers) dry-cured smoked
    regular (streaky) bacon
1 tbsp mild olive oil
2 onions
2 stalks celery
3 medium leeks
several fresh thyme sprigs
1 tbsp butter
7 oz (200 g) button mushrooms
2 tbsp all-purpose (plain) flour, plus
    extra for rolling
1⅔ cups (400 ml) chicken broth
    (stock)
scant 1 cup (200 ml) crème fraîche
    or double (heavy) cream
1 tsp Dijon mustard
1 (17-oz/500-g) package frozen puff
    pastry or ready-to-roll pie crust,
    defrosted
1 large (UK medium) egg
salt and pepper

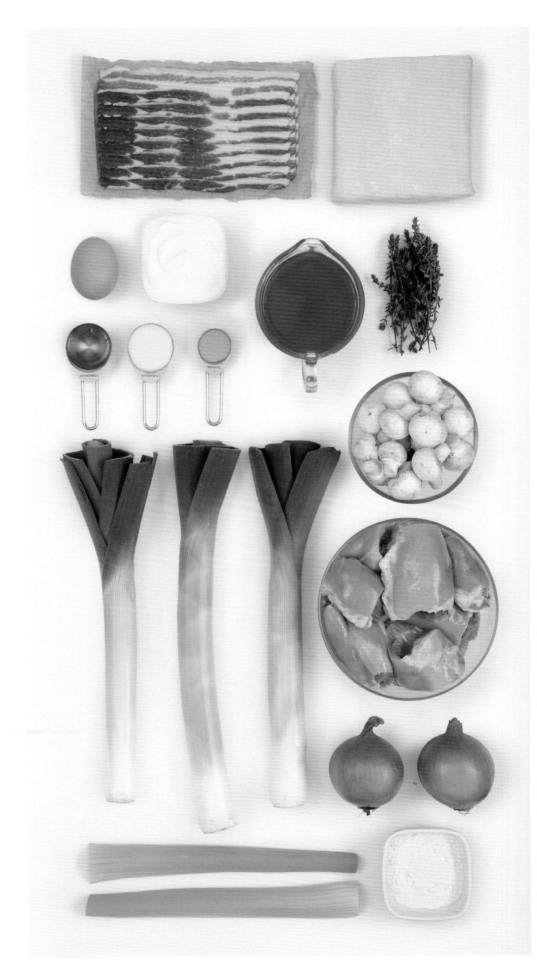

1
Cut the chicken thighs and bacon into bite-sized pieces.

2
Heat a large skillet, frying pan, or shallow, heatproof casserole over medium heat and add the oil. After 30 seconds, add half of the chicken and bacon and season with salt and pepper. Fry for 8–10 minutes, stirring often, until golden all over. Scoop onto a plate using a slotted spoon. Repeat with the second batch.

CAN'T FIND CHICKEN THIGHS? Most stores now sell boned chicken thighs. They're better than breasts for a recipe like this, because the meat stays moist, they have more flavor, and they are also better value. If you can't find chicken thighs, use breasts cut into chunks. Brown them, then return them to the pan during step 5, simmering for only 5 minutes, until the chicken is cooked through.

3
While the chicken cooks, finely slice the onions, celery, and leeks. Once both batches of chicken are cooked and set aside, add the vegetables to the pan, then cover and cook gently for about 10 minutes, until soft.

4
Pick the thyme leaves from their stems (stalks). Turn the heat back up a little, then add the butter, mushrooms. and thyme. Fry, stirring, for about 3 minutes, until the mushrooms and vegetables take on a golden tinge. Return the chicken to the pan.

5
Take the pan off the heat, then stir in the flour. Add the broth (stock) gradually to make a smooth sauce around the chicken and vegetables. Simmer for 20 minutes, until the chicken is tender.

6

Stir the crème fraîche or cream and mustard into the pie filling.

7

Taste the sauce for seasoning before you add any salt (the bacon will have added plenty). Season with pepper. Spoon the chicken pie filling into 6 individual pie dishes, leaving at least 1 inch (2.5 cm) at the top so that the filling can bubble without escaping. Let cool.

8

Flour the work surface a little, then roll the pastry to a square about 18 × 18 inches (45 × 45 cm). Cut 6 rectangles of pastry, each a little wider than the tops of the pie dishes. Use a fork to beat the egg with 1 tablespoon water to make a glaze. Dampen the rim of each dish with a little of the glaze. Press the pastry over the top.

9

Lightly brush the glaze over the pastry. Make a few small slashes in the top of each pie with a small sharp knife. The pies can be chilled for up to 2 days.

10

Preheat the oven to 400°F/200°C/ Gas Mark 6. Put the pies on a baking sheet and bake for 20 minutes, or until the pastry is golden and the filling is bubbling up in the middle. Pies cooked straight from the refrigerator will take a few minutes longer to cook.

GETTING AHEAD
Use fresh pastry instead of frozen, then freeze the pies, unbaked, for up to 1 month. Defrost overnight in the refrigerator before baking.

TO MAKE A LARGE PIE
Put the filling into a large pie dish, and cover with the pastry. Slash the top, then bake for 30 minutes, until risen and golden.

Crab Cakes with Herb Vinaigrette

Preparation time: 30 minutes,
plus 30 minutes for chilling
Cooking time: 12 minutes,
Serves 4–6 (makes 12 crab cakes)

Instead of serving your crab cakes
with a heavy mayonnaise, try spooning
over some citrus and herb dressing—it
brings every flavor to the fore. Serve
three crab cakes per person as a
main course for four, perhaps with
some boiled baby potatoes, or two
per person as an appetizer for six.

3-4 slices good-quality white bread,
    about 7 oz (200 g)
1 large green chile
1 lemon
1 small bunch fresh flat-leaf parsley
2 tbsp sour cream or crème fraîche
    (or good mayonnaise at a push)
2 tsp Worcestershire sauce
1 tsp cayenne pepper
1 large (UK medium) egg
1 lb 2 oz (500 g) white and brown
    crabmeat, picked over for shell
    (see note)
2 tsp capers
1 small bunch fresh tarragon
1 small bunch fresh dill
3 tbsp sunflower or vegetable oil
4 tbsp extra virgin olive oil
1 lime
1 tbsp butter
4–6 handfuls watercress
salt and pepper

1
Tear the bread into the bowl of a food processor, discarding the crusts, then process to fine crumbs.

2
Seed and finely chop the chile. Finely grate the zest from the lemon, then squeeze the juice. Coarsely chop the parsley leaves. Put the bread crumbs, sour cream, or crème fraîche, lemon zest, and 1 tablespoon of juice, the chile, parsley, Worcestershire sauce, cayenne, egg, and brown crabmeat into a large bowl.

WHITE OR BROWN CRABMEAT?
The ideal crab cake has a mixture of both white and brownmeat, which come from different parts of the crab. Around a 4:1 ratio of white to brown is about right. The white meat is flaky and delicately flavored, while the brown meat is intensely flavored and has more moisture. If you've bought mixed white and brown meat, just add it all in step 2.

3
Mix well until everything is evenly combined.

4
Now add the white crabmeat and mix in gently, so that small clumps of crab are left intact.

5

Shape the crab mix into 12 equal-sized patties. Put them onto a plate or tray in a single layer, then chill for 30 minutes in the refrigerator to let the mixture firm up.

GETTING AHEAD
The cakes can be covered with plastic wrap (clingfilm) and chilled for up to 24 hours, if you like.

6

While the cakes chill, make the vinaigrette. Coarsely chop the capers and leaves from the tarragon and dill. Put into a bowl, then add 2 tablespoons of the sunflower oil, all of the extra virgin olive oil, and the remaining lemon juice. Squeeze the juice from the lime and add it to the bowl. Season with salt and pepper.

7

Preheat the oven to 275°F/140°C/Gas Mark 1. Put a large skillet or frying pan over medium heat, then add ½ tablespoon each butter and sunflower oil. When the butter foams, add 6 of the crab cakes. Cook for 3 minutes or until crisp and golden underneath. Use a spatula (fish slice) to carefully turn the patties, then repeat. Lift onto paper towels, then keep warm in the oven. Wipe out the pan with paper towels, add the remaining butter and oil, then cook the second batch.

8

Serve the crab cakes with the dressing and a handful of watercress.

Roast Pork with Caramelized Apples

Preparation time: 30 minutes
Cooking time: 5 hours
Serves 6

Pork shoulder is a good-value cut that needs to be cooked slowly and for a long time, until the meat is meltingly tender. The skin and the fat below it crackle up to a wonderful crunch. Perfect cracklings starts with good quality free-range pork, with its skin well scored and rubbed with plenty of salt. Ask the butcher to score the skin for you, if possible.

---

1 tbsp mild olive oil

4½ lb (2 kg) pork shoulder, fat and
   skin well scored

1 tsp fennel seeds

1 tsp salt

1 onion

4 dessert apples, such as Jonagold,
   Braeburn, or Cox

½ lemon

several sprigs fresh thyme

3 bay leaves

2 tbsp (25 g) butter

scant 1 cup (200 ml) dry or medium
   hard cider

2½ cups (600 ml) chicken or pork
   broth (stock)

salt and pepper

1

Preheat the oven to 425°F/220°C/ Gas Mark 7. Rub most of the oil into the pork skin, then push the fennel seeds and salt into the slashes in the skin as evenly as you can. Put the pork into a roasting pan, then roast for 45 minutes.

2

Meanwhile, cut the onion into chunky slices. Quarter and remove the cores from the apples, but leave the skins on. Toss the apples with a squeeze of the lemon juice to prevent them from going brown.

3

When the pork has had 45 minutes, the skin will be starting to puff and crackle. Turn the oven down to 325°F/160°C/Gas Mark 3, then cook for another 4 hours, sprinkling the onions, most of the thyme, and the bay leaves around the pork when there's 1 hour of cooking time left.

4

When the pork is nearly ready, put the apples into a skillet or frying pan with the remaining oil and the butter. Place over medium heat and cook gently for about 15 minutes, turning regularly, until tender.

5

Lift the pork onto a board and let it rest, uncovered, while you make the gravy. Spoon any excess fat from the pan, then put the roasting pan over low heat. Pour in the cider, let it bubble, and reduce for 5 minutes, then add the broth (stock). Reduce the broth and cider mix for another 5 minutes, or until the liquid looks a little syrupy and has a good meaty flavor when seasoned with salt and pepper. Strain into a gravy boat or pitcher (jug).

6

Finish the apples. Turn up the heat under the apples, sprinkle in a few thyme leaves, then fry for another 2 minutes, or until glossy and golden.

7

When ready to serve, use a large sharp knife to carve the pork into thick slices. If the crackling is hard to cut through, cut it away from the meat in one piece, then snap it into shards before carving the meat. Serve the pork with the apples and gravy, along with vegetables such as Maple-Roast Winter Vegetables (page 284).

Vegetable Tagine with Chermoula & Couscous

Preparation time: 1 hour,
plus overnight soaking
Cooking time: 1¼ hours
Serves 6

A rich and tasty tagine is perfect for vegetarians or as a side dish to serve with roast lamb. Dried lima (butter) beans are worth the effort of presoaking, but you can use canned beans instead. Start from step 3, then add the beans to the pan with the rest of the vegetables in step 6.

1½ cups (12 oz/350 g) dried lima
    (butter) beans or 3 large cans
2 onions
4 large cloves garlic
½ cup (120 ml) olive oil
5 tsp ras el hanout spice mix
1 (14-oz/400-g) can diced or
    chopped tomatoes
2 tbsp tomato paste (puree)
2 cups (500 ml) vegetable or chicken
    broth (stock), plus 1¼ cups
    (300 ml)
1 lb 2 oz (500 g) squash, such as
    kabocha (pictured) or butternut
3 zucchini (courgettes)
¾ cup (150 g) dried plums (prunes)
    or apricots
2 tsp honey
1 large bunch fresh cilantro
    (coriander)
1 red chile
1 tbsp toasted sesame seeds
1 lemon
2⅓ cups (400 g) couscous
1 tbsp butter
salt and pepper

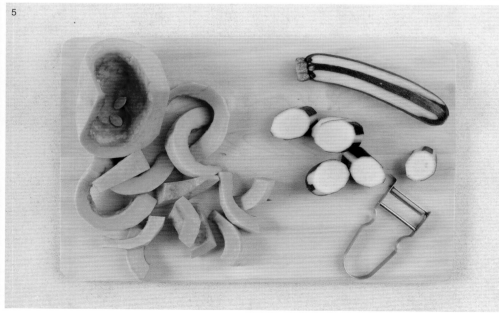

1

Put the lima (butter) beans into a large bowl of water and let them soak overnight. The beans will swell to about twice their original size.

2

Drain the soaked beans, put them into a large saucepan, cover with clean water, and bring to the boil. Cook for about 50 minutes, until tender but not soft. Drain well.

3

Meanwhile, coarsely chop the onions and 3½ garlic cloves. Heat 3 tablespoons of oil in a large flameproof casserole, then add the onions and garlic and fry over gentle heat for 10 minutes, until soft.

4

Stir the ras el hanout into the casserole, then cook for 2 minutes until the spices smell fragrant.

WHAT IS RAS EL HANOUT?
A classic Moroccan spice mixture, ras el hanout contains many aromatic spices including cinnamon, cumin, coriander, cloves, pepper, ginger, and even dried rose petals. If you can't find it, there is a recipe on page 213.

5

Add the tomatoes, the tomato paste (puree), 2 cups (500 ml) broth (stock), and drained lima beans. Cover, bring to a boil, then simmer for 30 minutes. The beans will be nearly cooked by now. Meanwhile, peel and seed the squash and chop into large chunks. Peel some of the skin from the zucchini (courgettes) to make stripes, if you like, then thickly slice them. It's not essential to peel the zucchini—the stripes are just for decoration.

6

Add the zucchini, squash, and dried fruit to the pan, then simmer again for 20 minutes, until the vegetables are tender and the tagine is thick and saucy. Stir in the honey.

7

While you wait, make the chermoula dressing and prepare the couscous. Coarsely chop the cilantro (coriander) leaves and put them into a bowl. Finely chop the chile and crush the remaining garlic, then add to the bowl with the rest of the olive oil, and most of the sesame seeds. Grate in the lemon zest and squeeze in half of the juice. Season with salt and pepper.

WHAT IS CHERMOULA?
Classically used as a marinade, chermoula consists of chopped fresh herbs, chile, garlic, oil, and lemon. Here, these flavors are used in a chermoula-inspired dressing to finish the dish.

8

For the couscous, mix the couscous and the rest of the lemon juice in a large bowl. Dot the butter over the top in small pieces. Bring the remaining broth to a boil, then pour it over the couscous. Cover tightly with plastic wrap (clingfilm), then set aside for 10 minutes.

9

When the 10 minutes is over, remove the plastic wrap and fluff up the couscous with a fork. Season generously with salt and pepper and serve with the tagine, with spoonfuls of the chermoula on top. Sprinkle with the remaining sesame seeds.

Goat Cheese
& Polenta Stacks

Preparation time: 30 minutes
Cooking time: 12–15 minutes
Serves 4–6, easily halved

This recipe is an ideal alternative to burgers when it's grilling (barbecue) season and will be enjoyed by vegetarians and meat eaters alike. Take the goat cheese out of the refrigerator at least an hour before you use it for the best creamy texture.

6¼ cups (1.5 litres) vegetable broth
  (stock)
2 oz (50 g) Parmesan cheese or
  other strong-tasting, hard cheese
  (⅔ cup grated)
2½ cups (375 g) quick-cooking
  Italian polenta
3½ tbsp (50 g) unsalted butter
¾ cup (175 ml) extra virgin
  olive oil
2 cloves garlic
1 bunch fresh basil or flat-leaf
  parsley
6 large Portobello (field) mushrooms
2–3 red bell peppers
3 (3½ oz/100 g) ripe, rinded
  goat cheeses
vegetable oil for brushing
2 tbsp olive paste (tapenade)
  or pesto
salt and pepper

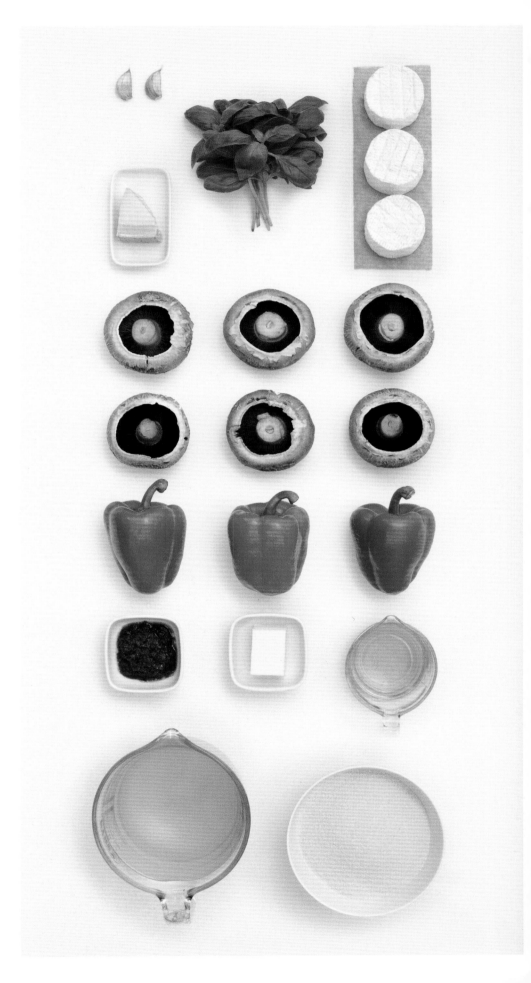

1

Pour the broth (stock) into a large saucepan, then bring to a boil. While you wait, finely grate the Parmesan. Carefully pour the polenta into the boiling broth in a steady stream, stirring all the while with a wooden spoon, until all of the polenta has been added.

The polenta will thicken up quickly. Cook for a couple of minutes until thick, stirring with a long-handled wooden spoon, because it will bubble and pop as it boils. Take the pan from the heat, then stir in the grated cheese, butter, and plenty of salt and pepper. Taste it—you may be surprised how much seasoning polenta can need.

2

Rub a little oil around the inside of a 8 x 12-inch (20 x 30-cm) baking pan, then pour in the polenta and smooth the top. Let cool for at least 10 minutes. It will set firm. You can do this a day in advance, if you like; just keep it covered and in the refrigerator.

3

Make the herbed oil and prepare the vegetables. Crush the garlic and finely chop the basil. Add to a bowl with the remaining oil and season with salt and pepper.

4

If the mushroom stems (stalks) are poking above the cap, then trim to cap level with a knife. Seed, then quarter the bell peppers. Brush the bell peppers and mushrooms with a little herbed oil.

5

Using a 4-inch (10-cm) cookie (biscuit) cutter (or you can use a saucer as a template to cut around), stamp 6 circles from the polenta. Cut the goat cheeses into 6 halves. Preheat the oven to 275°F/140°C/ Gas Mark 1.

6

Heat a large ridged grill (griddle) pan or skillet. Brush the polenta with a little oil and cook for 2–4 minutes on each side, or until golden. Keep warm in the oven.

7

Cook the mushrooms and bell peppers for about 5 minutes on each side, until golden and softened. Spoon some olive paste (tapenade) or pesto into the middle of each circle of polenta, then top with a piece of bell pepper, an upturned mushroom, then a circle of goat cheese. Drizzle with more of the garlic and basil oil, then serve.

TO GRILL (BARBECUE)
Before you begin cooking, check that the barbecue coals are glowing white hot, or your gas barbecue is preheated to 400°F/200°C. Lightly brush the polenta with a little oil. Cook the polenta for a couple of minutes on each side, either directly on the grill rack or on a griddle plate set over the barbecue, until golden and crisp. Set aside and keep warm at the side of the barbecue. Cook the mushrooms and bell peppers and follow as above.

Chargrilled Steak
with Garlic Butter

Preparation time: 15 minutes,
plus 10 minutes for chilling
Cooking time: 5–7 minutes
Serves 2

Cooking a steak well is surprisingly
easy. Buy good meat and follow a few
basic rules, and you'll be rewarded
with something special. The garlic
butter recipe will make more than you
need for two, but keep the leftovers
wrapped in the refrigerator for a week,
or in the freezer for a month.

---

1 clove garlic

1 handful fresh flat-leaf parsley

3½ tbsp (50 g) unsalted butter,
    softened

¼ tsp salt

2 New York strip (sirloin) steaks,
    about ¾ inch (2 cm) thick, at room
    temperature

1 tsp vegetable or sunflower oil

salt and pepper

1

Make the garlic butter first. Crush the garlic and finely chop the parsley. Put these into a small bowl. Add the butter, ¼ teaspoon salt, and season with pepper, then mix well with a fork.

2

Unroll a sheet of plastic wrap (clingfilm) onto the work surface. Spoon the butter onto the plastic wrap in a rough rectangle shape. Roll the wrap around the butter, then twist the ends to make a tight cylinder. Chill in the freezer for 10 minutes, until firm (or for longer in the refrigerator, depending on how much time you have).

3

Meanwhle, cut any excess fat off the steak (too much will just cause the kitchen to get smoky), leaving a layer about ¼ inch (5 mm) thick. Cut into this fat edge with a pair of kitchen scissors to prevent the steaks from curling up too much as they cook.

4

When you're ready to cook the steaks, rub them with the oil, then season generously with salt and pepper. Heat a skillet or ridged grill (griddle) pan over medium heat until hot but not smoking. Put the steaks into the pan, then cook, without moving them around, for 2 minutes. The steak should give a loud sizzle as the first edge hits the pan; if not, the pan isn't hot enough. Give it another minute to heat up, then try again. Press down a few times on the surface of the steaks with a spatula (palette knife) as they cook to encourage a deep, golden crust underneath.

5

Turn the steaks over and cook for another 2 minutes for medium rare— that is, pink and juicy in the middle. Press down on the meat as before to encourage good color and a crusty exterior. After 2 minutes on each side, press the steak. Instead of feeling soft or bouncy, a medium-rare steak will just yield to your finger. For medium steak, allow 3 minutes per side. To cook the fat along the edge of the steak, use tongs to hold the steak, fat edge down, against the pan. Hold the steak for about 30 seconds, until the fat turns golden.

6

Lift the steaks onto a warmed plate and remove the pan from the heat. Cover the steaks loosely with aluminum foil, then let rest for a couple of minutes. While you wait, preheat the broiler (grill) to high.

7

Return the steaks and their resting juices to the pan. Unwrap the butter and slice off 2 thick disks. Put them on top of the steaks.

8

Flash the steaks under the broiler for 30 seconds, or until the butter starts to melt over the steaks and into the juices below.

9

Serve the steak with the buttery juices and enjoy immediately.

GOLDEN RULES
Always take the steak out of the refrigerator at least 30 minutes before cooking. The thickness of steak is more important than its weight: a thinner steak will cook more quickly than a thicker steak. Remember you can't undo an overcooked steak, but you can always put an undercooked steak back in the pan.

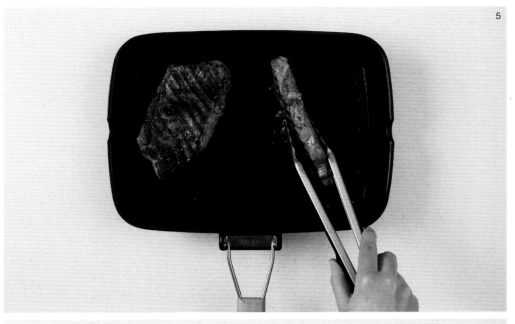

Chimichurri-Style Burgers

Preparation time: 30 minutes,
plus chilling
Cooking time: under 10 minutes
Makes 8 burgers, easily halved

Chimichurri is an Argentinian marinade or sauce, normally spooned over chargrilled steak. This recipe takes the essence of the original (lots of herbs, vinegar, and spice), and combines it with fresh tomatoes and onions to make a tasty, spoonable salsa.

2 red onions

1 large bunch fresh cilantro (coriander)

1 large bunch fresh flat-leaf parsley

2¼ lb (1 kg) good-quality ground (minced) beef

1½ tsp dried chili flakes

1 extra-large (UK large) egg

4 ripe tomatoes

2 cloves garlic

2 tbsp red wine vinegar

1 tsp sugar

1 tsp dried oregano

1 tbsp olive oil

a few shakes of Tabasco (optional)

mayonnaise, salad greens (leaves), and burger buns, to serve

salt and pepper

1

Finely chop 1 onion and half of the cilantro (coriander) and parsley leaves. Put into a large bowl with the ground (minced) beef, 1 teaspoon of the chili flakes, the egg, and plenty of salt and pepper.

CHOOSING MEAT FOR BURGERS
Ground chuck (steak mince) is made with the scraps (offcuts) from better quality beef, whereas ordinary ground beef (mince) is made with tougher cuts. Either will be fine for this recipe, although going to your butcher for ground chuck will mean that you can cook the burgers to juicy medium rare. The meat needs to contain some fat to keep the meat moist, but much of it will melt away as the burgers cook.

2

Work the ground meat and other ingredients together using your hands, until everything is well combined. Shape the meat into 8 patties, making sure they are nice and flat, then chill in the refrigerator for at least 30 minutes. The burgers can be made up to a day in advance.

TASTE FOR SEASONING
The beauty of making your own burgers is that you can fry a little off to check the flavor. Pinch off a little meat, heat a skillet or frying pan, and cook for a couple of minutes. Taste, then add more seasoning, if needed. I find that burgers normally need a surprisingly large amount.

3

Make the chimichurri salsa. Halve the tomatoes, scoop out the seeds with a spoon, then finely chop the flesh. Crush the garlic and finely chop the remaining onion and herbs, including their stems (stalks) if they are soft.

4

Mix the tomatoes with the garlic, onion, and herbs. Stir in the remaining chili flakes, vinegar, sugar, oregano, oil, and Tabasco. Season with salt and pepper. Although the relish contains lots of fresh herbs, it holds up well and can be made an hour or so ahead. Keep it chilled.

5

Heat a skillet, frying pan, ridged grill (griddle) pan, or the broiler (grill) until hot. Cook the patties for 2 minutes on each side for medium rare, or 3–4 minutes on each side for medium or well done. Split the buns and toast in the pan or under the broiler (grill), if you like. Top the bottom halves of the buns with a good spoon of mayonnaise and some salad greens (leaves). Add the burgers and spoonfuls of the chimichurri salsa to serve.

TO GRILL (BARBECUE)
Before you begin cooking, check that the barbecue coals are glowing white hot, or your gas barbecue is preheated to 400°F/200°C.

Coq au Vin
(Chicken with Red Wine)

Preparation time: 1 hour 10 minutes
Cooking time: 55 minutes
Serves 6

This is a very considerate recipe, because it can build in 24–48 hours for you to get ahead if you're entertaining. During this time, its flavors will improve and marry wonderfully under the lid. If you'd prefer to use skinless chicken, that's fine, just brown it for slightly less time and the sauce will be a little less rich.

---

18 shallots or small onions, about 1 lb 2 oz (500 g)

2 onions

2 stalks celery

3 carrots

6 slices (rashers) regular (streaky) bacon

4 tbsp mild olive oil

2 cloves garlic

scant ½ cup (50 g) all-purpose (plain) flour, plus 1 tbsp

6 chicken thighs and 6 drumsticks

5 tbsp (70 g) butter

1⅔ cups (400 ml) full-bodied red wine

2 cups (500 ml) chicken broth (stock)

11 oz (300 g) mixed mushrooms, such as button and cremini (chestnut)

salt and pepper

1

Put the shallots or small onions into a bowl, then pour over just-boiled water to cover. Let stand for 5 minutes, then drain and let cool. Trim the root ends and peel off the skins.

2

Finely chop or slice the onions and finely slice the celery. Cut the carrots into thick slices and the bacon into bite-sized pieces. Heat a large flameproof casserole over medium heat, then add 1 tablespoon of the oil. Add the vegetables and bacon to the pan.

3

Fry the vegetables and bacon together for 10 minutes, until softened.

4

Turn up the heat, then cook, stirring frequently, for 10 minutes, until everything is golden. Meanwhile, crush the garlic, then add it to the pan and cook for 1 minute. Turn everything out of the pan into a bowl.

5

Mix the scant ½ cup (50 g) flour with some salt and pepper in a sealable food bag. Put the chicken pieces into the bag, seal it, and shake to coat the meat.

6

Add 1 tablespoon butter and 1 tablespoon of the remaining oil to the pan. Cook one third of the chicken pieces for 10 minutes, turning halfway, until golden brown. Don't crowd the pan or the chicken will start to sweat rather than fry. After browning the first batch, spoon off excess fat, then add a splash of water. Scrape up any bits from the bottom of the pan and add to the vegetables in the bowl. These juices contain lots of flavor. Brown the remaining chicken in the same way.

7

After browning and removing all the chicken pieces, pour in the wine, then let it bubble for 5 minutes, or until it has reduced by a quarter.

8

Return all the chicken, vegetables, and juices to the pan, then pour in the broth (stock)—it's fine if the chicken pokes out of the liquid a little. Partly cover the pan with a lid and simmer the chicken for 50 minutes.

9

When the chicken is tender (check by cutting into one of the pieces— it should be easy to pull the meat away from the bone), scoop the chicken and vegetables out of the pan using a slotted spoon, and put them into a large bowl. Mix together 1 tablespoon flour and 1 tablespoon butter to make a smooth paste. Whisk into the sauce, then simmer for 5 minutes or until the sauce is glossy and has thickened slightly.

10

To finish the dish, fry the mushrooms. Cut any large ones in half. Heat the remaining 1 tablespoon butter in a skillet, and once it foams, add the mushrooms. Fry for 2–3 minutes on high heat, until the mushrooms are golden and just tender. Season with salt and pepper.

11

Gently stir the chicken and vegetables back into the pan, sprinkle the mushrooms over the top, then serve.

GETTING AHEAD

If you make the Coq au Vin in advance, let it cool, then chill for up to 2 days. Warm the pan gently and add a splash more broth or red wine to loosen the sauce if you need to, stirring gently. Fry the mushrooms and add them just before serving.

Sides

Roast Potatoes

Preparation time: 30 minutes
Cooking time: 40–50 minutes
Serves 6 generously

No roast dinner is complete without a pile of crunchy-on-the-outside, fluffy-in-the-middle roast potatoes. Good roast potatoes start with a floury variety of potato, such as russets or King Edward. Goose fat is great because it adds its own rich, luxurious flavor. Of course, you can use oil instead—a light, flavorless oil such as vegetable, sunflower, or peanut (groundnut) is best.

4½ lb (2 kg) medium floury potatoes
½ cup (100 g) goose or
  duck fat or scant ½ cup
  (100 ml) vegetable, sunflower,
  or peanut (groundnut) oil
1½ tsp salt

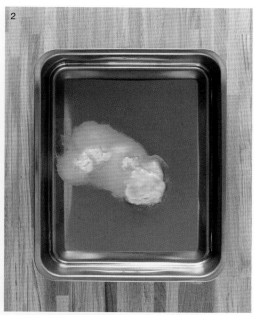

1

Preheat the oven to 425°F/220°C/ Gas Mark 7. Peel the potatoes, then cut them into quarters, or pieces about the size of a small egg. Put the potatoes into a large saucepan and cover with cold water. Put over high heat, bring to a boil (which will take about 10 minutes from cold), add ½ teaspoon salt, then, when the pan is bubbling fiercely, turn the heat down a little and boil the potatoes for 2 minutes.

2

Spoon the goose fat or pour the oil into a large roasting pan. Put it into the oven to heat up when the potatoes are almost ready.

3

Tip the potatoes into a colander and let them drain thoroughly. Let them sit for 5 minutes. As the steam rises, they will dry out a little. Return the potatoes to the pan, cover with a lid, then shake the pan briefly, holding the lid firmly, letting the potatoes roll about inside. This will fluff them up for a crispier finish.

4

Carefully, remove the roasting pan from the oven, then carefully spoon the potatoes into the fat. Turn them in the hot fat a little to coat, then season with the remaining salt.

5

Roast the potatoes for 40 minutes, or until crisp and golden, turning once during cooking. The exact timing of the potatoes will depend on the size of the chunks and the variety of potato, so give them 10 minutes more if you think they need it. Serve immediately.

Dauphinoise Potatoes

Preparation time: 25 minutes
Cooking time: 1–1¼ hours
Serves 6

Simplicity itself, yet so delicious,
a dish of dauphinoise potatoes makes
a wonderful accompaniment to roast
meat or steaks, and can be prepared
well in advance if you're entertaining.
This recipe is rich without being over
the top, but you could add more
cream and less milk, if you like.

1⅔ cups (400 ml) heavy (double)
   cream
1¼ cups (300 ml) whole milk
1 clove garlic
1 whole nutmeg, for grating
3¼ lb (1.5 kg) medium floury
   potatoes, such as russets or
   King Edward
1 tbsp butter
3 oz (80 g) Gruyère or Cheddar
   cheese (¾ cup grated)
salt and pepper

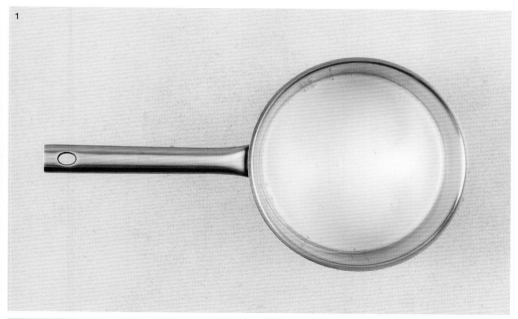

1

Put the cream and milk into a medium saucepan. Crush the garlic clove, add to the pan, then bring to a boil. As soon as small bubbles start to pop around the edge of the pan, remove it from the heat. Finely grate ¼ teaspoon nutmeg, stir it into the pan, then let steep (infuse) for at least 10 minutes.

2

Meanwhile, peel the potatoes, then slice them to a thickness of about about 3-mm (⅛-inch). If the potatoes slip too much on the board, cut them in half. Rest the potatoes on their flat edge, then slice them.

3

Preheat the oven to 350°F/180°C/ Gas Mark 4. Spread the butter over the inside of a large baking dish. Sprinkle a layer of potatoes in the bottom of the dish, then season with salt and pepper. Repeat until all of the potatoes have been used up.

4

Pour the flavored cream over the potatoes. Only the top of the potatoes should stick out of the liquid, but this can depend on the depth and width of your baking dish. Add a splash more cream, if needed. Grate the cheese, then sprinkle it over the top of the potatoes.

5

Bake the potatoes for 1 hour, or until the top is golden and bubbling and the potatoes are tender. Check this by inserting a knife into the middle of the dish. The knife should slide easily through to the bottom. If the potatoes need longer but the top is already golden, cover the dish with aluminum foil and bake for another 15 minutes. Let the potatoes settle for a few minutes before serving.

Dressed Green Beans

Preparation time: 10 minutes
Cooking time: 10 minutes
Serves 4–6

If boiled or steamed greens seem boring, try this easy way to transform the humble green (French) bean into a special side dish, perfect with roast chicken. Serve just warm or at room temperature.

---

4 slices (rashers) dry-cured regular
   (streaky) bacon

1 tsp mild olive oil

1 lb (500 g) fine green beans

½ tsp salt

2 shallots or ½ small red onion

2 tsp whole-grain mustard

2 tbsp red or white wine vinegar,
   or apple cider vinegar

salt and pepper

1
Cut the bacon into small pieces with a knife or kitchen scissors. Put a skillet or frying pan over medium heat, then add the oil. After 30 seconds, add the bacon.

2
Fry the bacon gently for 10 minutes until crisp, golden, and surrounded with the melted bacon fat.

3

While the bacon cooks, bring a medium saucepan of water to a boil. Trim the stem (stalk) ends from the beans, leaving the slender tops. Put the beans and salt into the boiling water. Bring the pan back to a boil, then cook the beans for 5 minutes, or until they are just tender.

4

Meanwhile, peel, then finely chop or slice the shallots or onion.

5

Taste one of the beans to check they're cooked to your liking. Drain them in a colander. Stir the shallots or onion, mustard, and vinegar into the bacon pan, then season with pepper and a little salt. Add the beans to the pan.

6

Turn the beans over in the dressing until well coated, then serve.

Maple-Roast Winter Vegetables

Preparation time: 15 minutes
Cooking time: 50 minutes
Serves 4–6

Boiling winter root vegetables leaches out their flavor and goodness into the cooking water. Roasting, however, intensifies their flavor, and the skins crisp up, too. Celeriac (celery root), sweet potatoes, butternut squash, and Jerusalem artichokes could all easily be substituted, if you like. This is a great side dish with any of the roasts in this book.

---

1 medium rutabaga (swede), about
  1 lb 5 oz (600 g) in total
4 medium parsnips, about 1 lb 5 oz
  (600 g) in total
5 medium carrots, about 1 lb 5 oz
  (600 g) in total
4 tbsp mild olive oil
2 sprigs fresh rosemary
6 cloves garlic
1 tbsp maple syrup or honey or
  more, if you like
salt and pepper

1

2

1

Preheat the oven to 425°F/220°C/ Gas Mark 7. Peel the rutabaga (swede), but simply scrub the parsnips and carrots, leaving the skins on. Cut all of the root vegetables into large pieces, all about 1¼ inches (3 cm) across. Put into a large (ideally nonstick) roasting pan. It looks like a lot of vegetables, but they will shrink considerably in the oven as they roast. Spoon over the olive oil, then rub it all over the vegetables with your hands. Season with plenty of salt and pepper. Roast the vegetables for 30 minutes, until starting to soften.

2

Meanwhile, pick the needles from the rosemary sprigs, then chop them finely. Stir the garlic cloves (still in their skins) and rosemary into the vegetables. Return the pan to the oven, then roast again for another 20 minutes, or until the vegetables are tender and golden around the edges. The garlic cloves will be tender within their papery skins.

3

While the vegetables are still sizzling hot, drizzle over the maple syrup or honey. Serve the vegetables immediately, making sure everyone gets a garlic clove on their plate, ready to squeeze out the soft pulp.

Tomato & Mozzarella Salad with Gremolata

Preparation time: 10 minutes
Serves 4–6

Traditionally Italian, gremolata is chopped parsley and garlic mixed with lemon zest and can be sprinkled over a salad or cooked fish, meat, or pasta. If you'd prefer a straight-up mozzarella, tomato, and basil salad, then simply tuck the leaves from a bunch of basil in among the cheese and tomato, then season with salt, pepper, and oil.

---

1 lemon

1 small clove garlic

1 small bunch fresh flat-leaf parsley

about 1 lb 5 oz (600 g) assorted ripe
   tomatoes, at room temperature

2 large or 3 smaller balls buffalo
   mozzarella cheese

3 tbsp extra virgin olive oil

salt and black pepper

1
Finely grate the zest of the lemon. Finely chop the garlic and parsley leaves, then mix with the lemon zest and some salt and pepper in a bowl.

2
Slice the tomatoes and mozzarella.

HEIRLOOM TOMATOES
These colorful tomatoes, sometimes called "heritage," are old varieties that have come back into vogue for their flavor and look. Find them in some grocers and larger stores at the peak of the tomato season.

3
Arrange the slices of tomato and cheese on a large plate, seasoning with salt and pepper as you go. Sprinkle the gremolata over the salad, then drizzle with the olive oil to serve.

Green Salad with Seeds & Croutons

Preparation time: 10 minutes
Cooking time: 2 minutes
Serves 4–6, easily doubled

A versatile, goes-with-everything kind of salad that is anything but boring. I've used store-bought croutons to keep things simple. If you want to make your own, toss seasoned cubes of bread with a little oil, then bake at 400°F/200°C/Gas Mark 6 until crisp and golden.

2 tbsp sunflower seeds
1 small clove garlic
3 tbsp olive oil
1 tbsp red or white wine vinegar
1 tsp Dijon mustard
1 tsp honey
1–2 ripe avocados
5 cups (150 g) mixed arugula
    (rocket), watercress, and spinach
    salad (or a similar mix of
    flavorful leaves)
a good handful store-bought
    croutons
salt and pepper

1

Put the sunflower seeds into a skillet or frying pan, then cook over medium heat for a few minutes until they are toasty and sizzling. Tip onto a plate and let cool.

2

Crush the garlic, then put into either a small bowl or a jar. Add the oil, vinegar, mustard, honey, and a pinch of salt and pepper. Whisk or shake the ingredients together to make a thickened vinaigrette.

MAKE A BATCH OF DRESSING
If you like to eat salad most days, then why not save yourself time and make a batch of dressing? Multiply the recipe and keep in a jar in the refrigerator for up to a week. Give it a shake before using.

3

Cut the avocado in half, remove the pit (stone), then peel off the skin. Slice thinly. If you want to do this in advance, toss the sliced avocado in a little lemon juice (to prevent discoloration), then cover with plastic wrap (clingfilm) and chill.

4

Put the leaves into a large bowl, add the avocado, croutons, and the cooled seeds, then pour in the dressing. Toss well to make sure everything is coated, then serve immediately.

Potato, Bacon & Watercress Salad

Preparation time: 10 minutes,
plus cooling
Cooking time: 15–20 minutes
Serves 4–6

I'm a big fan of the way German cooks make potato salad. It often includes pickles (gherkins), bacon, and mustard, and it's dressed while warm so that the potatoes absorb all of the flavors in the dressing. My version is a great side for the barbecue, picnic, or dinner table.

1½ lb (700 g) baby (new) potatoes

6 slices (rashers) regular (streaky)
    bacon (dry-cured is best)

1 tbsp whole-grain mustard

1 tbsp red or white wine vinegar

2 tbsp mild olive oil

2 tbsp mayonnaise

4 pickles (gherkins)

1 bunch scallions (spring onions)

3½ oz (100 g) watercress (3 cups
    chopped)

salt and pepper

1

If some of the potatoes are on the larger side, cut them in half first. Put the potatoes into a large saucepan of salted water, then bring to a boil. Boil for 15–20 minutes, or until tender.

SKINS ON
I like small, waxy potatoes for my potato salad, because they don't need to be scraped or peeled before cooking. The skin acts as a helpful barrier as they are boiled, preventing them from overcooking, and also provides lots of flavor and nutrients, too.

2

Meanwhile, cut the bacon into bite-sized pieces. Put into a skillet or frying pan over medium heat. Fry the bacon for 10 minutes, or until golden and crisp.

3

In a large bowl, mix together the mustard, vinegar, oil, and mayonnaise. Finely chop the pickles (gherkins) and thinly slice the scallions (spring onions).

4

Drain the potatoes well, then cool for 15 minutes or so until warm. Toss with the dressing, cornichons, and scallions, then let cool completely. If making in advance, cover with plastic wrap (clingfilm) once cold.

5

When ready to serve, check the seasoning of the potatoes. If they seem a little dry, add a splash of water, and stir well. Coarsely chop the watercress, stir through the salad, sprinkle with the bacon, then serve.

Hasselback Sweet Potatoes

Preparation time: 10 minutes
Cooking time: 1 hour
Serves 6, easily doubled

Strictly speaking, a Hasselback potato would be a normal white potato, skin left on, flesh slashed and stuffed with bay leaves, then roasted in the oven. The idea works wonderfully with sweet potatoes, which open out as they roast, ready to soak up lots of maple syrup, chili, lime, and sour cream.

6 large sweet potatoes

2 sprigs fresh rosemary

3 tbsp olive oil

3 tbsp maple syrup, or more,
    if you like

1 tsp dried chili flakes, or
    more, if you like

1 lime

6 tbsp plain (natural) Greek yogurt,
    sour cream, or crème fraîche

salt and pepper

1

Preheat the oven to 400°F/200°C/ Gas Mark 6. Cut slits in the sweet potatoes at ½ inch (1 cm) intervals, going almost all the way through the potato.

2

Finely chop the rosemary leaves. Put the potatoes into a roasting pan. Rub the oil over them, then sprinkle with the rosemary, and plenty of salt and pepper. Try and get as much of the rosemary into the potatoes as you can.

3

Bake for 1 hour or until tender in the middle, crisp outside, and the potatoes have fanned out.

4

Just before serving, drizzle the hot potatoes with the maple syrup and sprinkle with the chili flakes. Squeeze over the juice of the lime, then add spoonfuls of yogurt, sour cream, or crème fraîche.

Spiced Carrot & Herb Salad

Preparation time: 20 minutes, plus cooling
Cooking time: 5 minutes

Carrots rarely take center stage, so this is a special salad to show off all that's good about the humble orange root. Cooked carrot salads a little like this are commonplace in Moroccan and Portuguese cooking, but the flavors go with a multitude of dishes from across the world.

2¼ lb (1 kg) young or small
   carrots
2 cloves garlic
1 tsp fennel seeds
1 tsp coriander seeds
2 tsp cumin seeds
4 tbsp red wine vinegar
2 tbsp sugar
4 tbsp extra virgin olive oil, plus
   extra for drizzling (optional)
2 tbsp sesame seeds
1 bunch fresh mint
1 handful fresh dill
salt and pepper

1
Trim the tops from the carrots, then thinly slice lengthwise. There's no need to peel them first. Thinly slice the garlic.

2
Put both the carrots and garlic into a large saucepan, cover with cold water, and season with salt. Bring to a boil over high heat, then simmer for 5 minutes, or until the carrots are just tender.

3

Meanwhile, heat a skillet or frying pan, then add the fennel, coriander, and cumin seeds. Cook for a couple of minutes until the spices smell aromatic. Coarsely crush the seeds in a mortar with a pestle.

4

Drain the carrots, then toss in a bowl with the toasted spices, vinegar, sugar, oil, and seasoning. As the carrots cool, they will absorb all of the flavors.

5

Wipe out the pan that you used for the spices, then add the sesame seeds. Cook the seeds for a few minutes, stirring often, until lightly golden.

6

When the salad has cooled, coarsely chop the mint and dill leaves. Toss with the carrots and sesame seeds, then transfer to a serving dish. Drizzle with a little more oil, if you like.

Fresh & Fluffy Flatbreads

Preparation time: 15 minutes, plus rising
Cooking time: 6 minutes
Serves 8, easily doubled

Yes, OK, you can buy perfectly good pita bread in the stores, but this is about having fun in the kitchen. It's easier than you might think. The breads go perfectly with the the lamb kofte on page 134, or any time you need some tasty bread for dipping and sharing. The milk and water mix makes the dough extra soft in the middle.

3⅔ cups (450 g) white bread (strong) flour, plus extra for rolling out

2 tsp (7 g) instant dry (fast-action) yeast

2 tsp fine salt

⅔ cups (150 ml) milk, plus a little more for brushing

3 tbsp extra virgin olive oil, plus extra for greasing

1 tbsp sesame seeds

1 tbsp poppy seeds

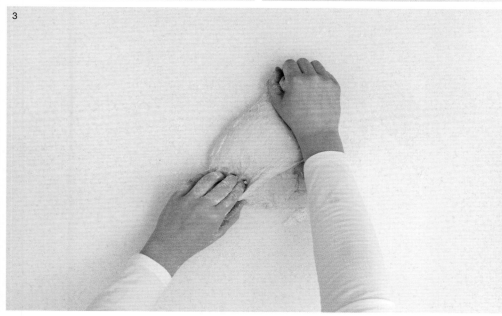

1

Put the flour into a large bowl, add the yeast and salt, and mix well. Make a well in the middle with a wooden spoon. Mix the milk, oil, and ⅔ cup (150 ml) just-warm water in a pitcher (jug).

2

Pour the liquid ingredients into the dry, then quickly mix together to make a rough dough. Try to avoid getting any overly wet or dry patches. Set aside for 10 minutes.

3

After 10 minutes, flour the work surface and your hands, then tip the dough out from the bowl. Knead the dough until smooth and springy, about 5 minutes. If you have a food processor or mixer with a dough hook, you can use that instead. Add a little more flour, if needed, but avoid adding too much, because it will dry the dough. As you work the dough it will become less and less sticky.

HOW TO KNEAD
As long as the dough is stretched and folded enough, it doesn't matter how you do it. I hold the dough down with my left hand, then grab the dough at the farthest edge with my right and push it away to make the dough stretch. I then fold the stretched dough over itself, squash it down with my knuckles, and turn it 90 degrees. Repeat until the dough is springy and bounces back when prodded.

4

When the dough is silky smooth and springy to the touch, stop kneading. Pour a little more oil into a large bowl, add the dough, and turn it over a few times until coated.

5

Cover with plastic wrap (clingfilm) then let it rest somewhere warm, but not hot, for about 1 hour, or until doubled in size.

GETTING AHEAD
If you want to make the dough the day before, let it rise in the refrigerator. It will rise to the same size, only more slowly, and will have a richer flavor.

6
When the dough is ready, preheat the oven to 450°F/230°C/Gas Mark 8 and sprinkle 2 baking sheets with flour. Using a large knife dipped in flour, cut the dough into 8 pieces. Don't knead the dough before you roll it because you want to retain the bubbles of air in it. It will also be easier to roll out. With extra flour on the rolling pin, roll the dough into a round or a slipper shape, until about 3 mm (⅛ inch) thick.

7
Lift the dough onto the prepared baking sheets. Using a pastry brush, brush the dough with a little milk, then sprinkle with the sesame or poppy seeds. The dough doesn't need to rise again.

8
Bake the flatbreads for about 6 minutes, until light, and puffed, and smelling delicious. To keep the breads soft, wrap in a clean dish towel (tea towel) while they are still hot, then let cool.

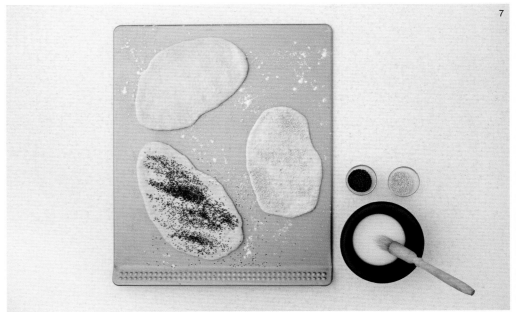

Roasted Vegetable & Feta Couscous

Preparation time: 10 minutes,
plus cooling
Cooking time: 40 minutes
Serves 4–6 as a side, easily doubled

Instead of making this an overtly
Moroccan-flavored couscous salad,
I've kept things simple with a little
lemon, crunchy pecans, and a touch
of sweetness from dried cranberries
so that it will go with just about
anything. A great barbecue or
picnic side and lunch-box filler.

½ butternut squash

1 red onion

2 zucchini (courgettes)

2 bell peppers, ideally 1 red and
   1 yellow for color

2 tbsp extra virgin olive oil, plus
   more to dress, if you like

scant 1 cup (80 g) pecan halves

1¾ cups (300 g) couscous

scant ½ cup (50 g) dried
   cranberries

1 lemon

2 cups (450 ml) chicken or vegetable
   broth (stock)

1 bunch fresh flat-leaf parsley

3½ oz (100 g) feta cheese
   (⅔ cup crumbled)

salt and pepper

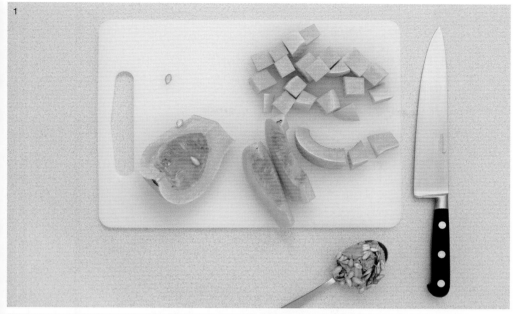

1

Preheat the oven to 400°F/200°C/Gas Mark 6. Scoop the seeds from the squash using a spoon and discard. Cut the squash into bite-sized cubes using a large, sharp knife. There's no need to peel the skin from the squash unless you really want to, because it will soften as it roasts.

2

Peel the onion and cut it into chunky wedges. Slice the zucchini (courgettes) into thick rounds. Halve and seed the bell peppers, then cut into chunky pieces. Put all of the vegetables into a large roasting pan, drizzle with the olive oil, and season well with salt and pepper.

3

Roast the vegetables for 20 minutes, turn them over a few times in the oil, then add the pecans. Return to the oven for another 20 minutes.

4

While the vegetables cook, prepare the couscous. Put the grains into a large bowl and stir in the cranberries. Finely grate in the lemon zest.

5

Put the broth (stock) into a pan and bring to a boil. Pour it over the couscous. Cover the bowl with plastic wrap (clingfilm) or a large plate to keep in the steam. Let the couscous stand for 15 minutes, or longer if you have time.

6

When ready, the roasted vegetables should be tender and golden and the nuts will be toasty. Squeeze the juice of the lemon over the vegetables and let cool.

7

The couscous is ready when all of the broth has been absorbed. Fluff up the grains with a fork and let it cool a little. Toss with the vegetables and season to taste with salt and pepper. Coarsely chop the parsley leaves and crumble the cheese.

8

Toss the parsley and feta through the salad just before serving, adding a drizzle more oil, if it seems dry. This is best served just warm or at room temperature.

Desserts

Flourless Chocolate Cake

Preparation time: 20 minutes
Baking time: 35 minutes
Serves 12

A flourless chocolate cake is
a real dessert hero, especially
when feeding friends who are
avoiding wheat. Nuts and plenty of
chocolate give the cake its structure
and a decadently gooey texture
within. The espresso bolsters the
chocolate flavor rather than adding
a coffee taste of its own.

1¾ sticks (200 g) butter, plus extra
   for greasing
1 cup (125 g) skinned (blanched)
   hazelnuts or 1¼ cups (125 g)
   almond meal (ground almonds),
   see note
1 cup packed (200 g) light brown
   sugar
8 oz (200 g) bittersweet (dark) chocolate, 70% cocoa solids
2 tbsp fresh espresso or 1 tbsp
   instant coffee granules mixed
   with 2 tbsp just-boiled water
1 tsp vanilla extract
5 large (UK medium) eggs, room
   temperature
¼ tsp salt
1 tbsp unsweetened cocoa powder,
   for dusting

1
Generously grease a 9-inch (23-cm) round springform cake pan with butter, then line the bottom with parchment (baking) paper. Preheat the oven to 350°F/180°C/Gas Mark 4. Put the nuts into a food processor with 1 tablespoon of the sugar, then process until finely ground. If using almond meal (ground almonds), skip this step and add the sugar later on.

2
Break the chocolate into a medium heatproof bowl and add the butter, coffee, and vanilla. Melt together gently, either set over a saucepan of barely simmering water or in the microwave (see note). Stir until smooth, then set aside.

MELTING CHOCOLATE
Place the bowl over a saucepan of barely simmering water (the bowl should be just larger than the rim of the pan, so that it sits easily on top), making sure the bottom doesn't touch the water. Let the chocolate melt for about 5 minutes, stirring once or twice, until smooth throughout. Alternatively, microwave on high in 20-second bursts, stirring after each one, until smooth. It's important to use a heatproof bowl, such as Pyrex, otherwise it can become too hot and scorch the chocolate.

3
Crack the eggs into a large bowl, add the rest of the sugar, then whisk for 5 minutes with an electric mixer until thick, mousselike, and doubled in volume.

4

Pour the melted chocolate around the edge of the bowl (this prevents it from knocking too much air out of the foam). Using a large metal spoon, fold the chocolate in. It might take longer than you expect to get the batter to an almost even brown and before little ribbons of chocolate stop appearing.

5

Sprinkle the ground nuts and salt into the bowl, then fold them in until evenly blended. Carefully pour the batter into the prepared pan. Preserving the air is the name of the game.

6

Bake on the middle shelf of the oven for about 35 minutes, or until the cake has risen and is set on top, with a just-perceptible wobble underneath the papery crust when you jiggle the pan. Put the pan on a cooling rack as it cools. The cake will sink and crack a little, which is fine. Let cool completely.

7

Unclip the sides of the pan and use a spatula (palette knife) to loosen the cake and its lining paper away from the bottom and put onto a serving plate. Put the cocoa in a fine-mesh sieve and give the cake a good dusting. Serve with cream or ice cream, and perhaps some berries, if you like. The cake can be made up to 2 days in advance (I actually prefer it the next day) and kept in a cool place. Let it come to room temperature before serving.

Key Lime Pie

Preparation time: 30 minutes,
plus at least 4 hours for chilling
Cooking time: 20 minutes
Serves 8–10

With its delicious citrus bite, sweet
cream topping, and an irresistibly
crumbly ginger crust (base), one
slice of this pie just isn't going to be
enough. It's a perfect dessert for a
retro-style dinner party—it seems
impressive but it's actually simple.

7 tablespoons (100 g) unsalted
  butter, plus extra for greasing
1 (11-oz/300-g) package gingersnap
  (ginger nut) cookies (biscuits)
8 limes, or 14–18 key limes
2 large (UK medium) eggs
1 (14-oz/400-g) can sweetened
  condensed milk
2½ cups (600 ml) heavy (double)
  or whipping cream
1 tbsp confectioners' (icing) sugar

1

Use a little butter to grease the bottom and sides of a fluted 9-inch (23-cm) loose-bottomed tart pan, then line it with a circle of parchment (baking) paper. Preheat the oven to 350°F/180°C/Gas Mark 4. Put a small saucepan over medium heat. Add the butter and let it melt. Break the cookies (biscuits) into the bowl of a food processor, then process them to fine crumbs. Alternatively, put the cookies into a large food bag, squeeze out the air, then seal the top. Crush with a rolling pin until the cookies are reduced to fine crumbs.

2

Turn the food processor on, then drizzle the butter onto the cookie crumbs. If you crushed the cookies in a bag, transfer them to a bowl and stir in the melted butter. When ready, the crumbs will look like wet sand.

3

Tip the buttery crumbs into the tart pan and smooth them out over the bottom and up the sides using the back of a spoon, pressing them down firmly in an even layer.

4

Put the pan onto a baking sheet, then bake for 10–15 minutes, or until the crust has turned a dark, golden brown.

5

Meanwhile, make the filling. Finely grate the zest from the limes, saving a little for decoration later, if you like, then squeeze their juice; you'll need about ⅔ cup (150 ml) for a really tangy pie. Beat the juice, zest, eggs, condensed milk, and 1¼ cups (300 ml) of the cream together.

6

Pour the filling into the cooked pie crust. Bake the pie for 20 minutes, or until the filling is set around the outside but still quivery in the middle. Cool completely, then chill for at least 4 hours or ideally overnight. If wrapped well, the pie will keep chilled for up to 2 days at this point.

7

Using a balloon whisk or electric mixer, whip the rest of the cream with the confectioners' (icing) sugar until it just holds its shape in loose folds.

8

Remove the pie from the pan, if you like. Transfer the pie onto a serving plate, then spread the cream over the filling, swirling it a little as you go.

9

Sprinkle with the rest of the lime zest, then serve.

KEY LIMES

Key limes are a small, strongly flavored variety of lime grown in southern states of the United States. Ordinary limes are fine, but if you use key limes, you'll need to squeeze around 16 in order to obtain ⅔ cup (150 ml) juice.

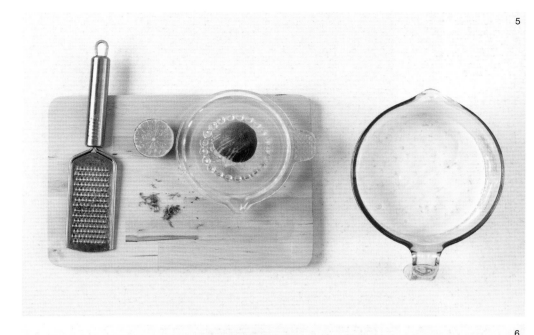

Panna Cotta with Raspberries

Preparation time: 30 minutes,
plus 30 minutes for cooling and
6 hours for chilling
Serves 6

Italian for "cooked cream," a
panna cotta with fresh vanilla and
raspberries makes for an impressive
but simple dinner party dessert.

---

5 sheets leaf gelatin (gelatine)
1 vanilla bean
1¾ cups (450 ml) heavy (double)
   cream
1¾ cups (450 ml) whole milk
generous ⅓ cup (80 g) superfine
   (caster) sugar
1⅔ cups (200 g) raspberries

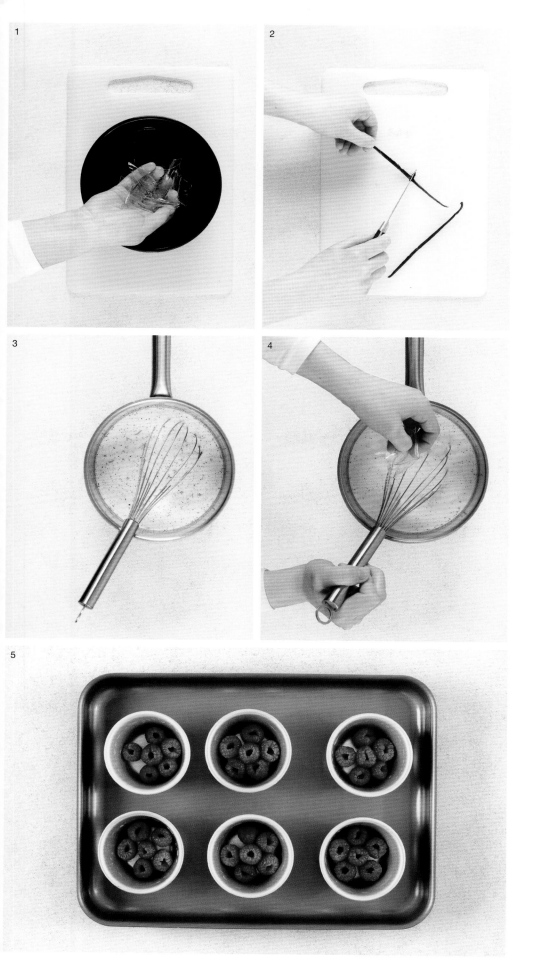

1
Fill a small bowl with cold water, then add the gelatin (gelatine) sheets. After a couple of minutes' soaking, they will have softened.

GELATIN POWDER
If you can't find sheets of leaf gelatin, use 1 tablespoon gelatin powder instead. Follow the instructions on the package, or sprinkle it evenly over 2 tablespoons cold water in a heatproof bowl. Let stand until it has swollen and absorbed the liquid. Heat a shallow saucepan of water, then set the bowl with the gelatin in it, keeping the heat low. The gelatin will melt. It's important not to overheat it, because this can impair the flavor of the dish. Once melted, stir into the warm cream, as in step 4.

2
Scrape the seeds from the vanilla bean. To do this, slit the bean along its length with a small sharp knife to make 2 halves. Run the knife along the cut edge of each half to remove the seeds.

3
Put the vanilla seeds, cream, and milk into a saucepan, then whisk to separate any clumps of vanilla. Put the pan over medium heat and bring to a boil. Take the pan off the heat.

4
Stir the sugar into the cream, then let it dissolve for 2 minutes. Remove the gelatin from the water and squeeze it out. Stir the gelatin into the still-warm cream until it has completely dissolved.

5
Put ⅔ cup (150-ml) small ramekins or dessert molds on a baking sheet or roasting pan. Put 6 raspberries into the bottom of each.

6

Transfer the cream mixture to a pitcher (jug), then pour it carefully into the ramekins or molds. Let cool for 30 minutes.

7

Cover the surface of each panna cotta with a piece of plastic wrap (clingfilm) to prevent a skin from forming on the top, then chill them in the refrigerator for at least 6 hours or ideally overnight.

8

When ready to eat, remove the plastic wrap. If you have used dessert molds, dip each mold into a bowl of hot water for a few seconds before turning the panna cotta onto a plate. If you have used ramekins, serve as they are. Sprinkle a few raspberries around to decorate.

6

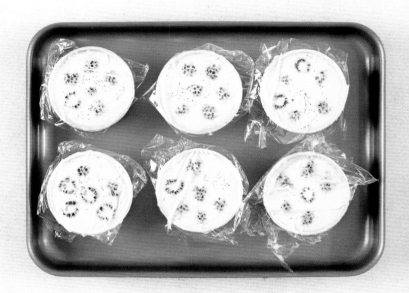

7

Peach & Raspberry Cobbler

Preparation time: 25 minutes
Cooking time: 40–50 minutes
Serves 6

Adding almond meal (ground almonds) and a handful of raspberries to a classic cobbler lifts the flavor of the peaches and lightens the topping. Choose yellow-fleshed peaches if you can, for the best color. The peaches can be replaced by nectarines, then by plums a little later in the year.

6 just-ripe peaches
1½ cups (175 g) fresh or defrosted frozen raspberries
2 tbsp cornstarch (cornflour)
generous ⅓ cup (80 g) sugar, plus 3 tbsp
6 tbsp (80 g) cold unsalted butter, plus 1 tbsp
1 cup (125 g) self-rising (raising) flour
½ cup (50 g) almond meal (ground almonds)
½ tsp baking powder
¼ tsp salt, if needed (see page 12)
⅔ cup (150 ml) buttermilk or milk
1 tsp vanilla extract
1 handful slivered (flaked) almonds (optional)
cream or ice cream, to serve (optional)

1

Preheat the oven to 375°F/190°C/ Gas Mark 5. Cut the peaches in half, and remove the pit (stone) with the tip of the knife. Cut each half into 3 or 4 slices. If it clings to the pit, just cut the flesh into chunks around it. Put the peaches and half of the raspberries into a large baking dish or shallow casserole. Sprinkle the cornstarch (cornflour) and the 3 tablespoons sugar over the top, then splash on 6 tablespoons water. Stir well. Cut the 1 tablespoon butter into small pieces, then dot it over the fruit.

2

Make the cobbler topping. Put the flour into a large bowl, then stir in the almond meal (ground almonds), and baking powder (and salt if using UK self-raising flour). Sometimes the almonds can clump, so break them up with your fingers, if necessary. Cut the remaining butter into cubes and add to the dry ingredients.

3

Rub the ingredients together. To do this, use both hands to lift the butter and flour from the bowl, then gently pass them between your fingers and thumbs as they drop back into the bowl. As you repeat the action, the butter will gradually work its way into the flour. Lift the mixture as you go to keep it cool and aerated.

4

The mixture should resemble fine bread crumbs.

5

Stir in the generous ⅓ cup (80 g) sugar, then the buttermilk or milk and vanilla. Stop stirring as soon as a lumpy batter comes together. Gently mix in the remaining raspberries, taking care not to squash them.

6

Spoon the cobbler topping over the peaches, then sprinkle with the slivered (flaked) almonds, if using. The topping will spread out as it cooks, so don't worry about smoothing the surface.

7

Place the cobbler on a baking sheet and bake for 40–50 minutes, or until the topping is golden brown and well risen, and the fruit is saucy and bubbling beneath.

8

Serve hot, warm, or cold with cream or ice cream.

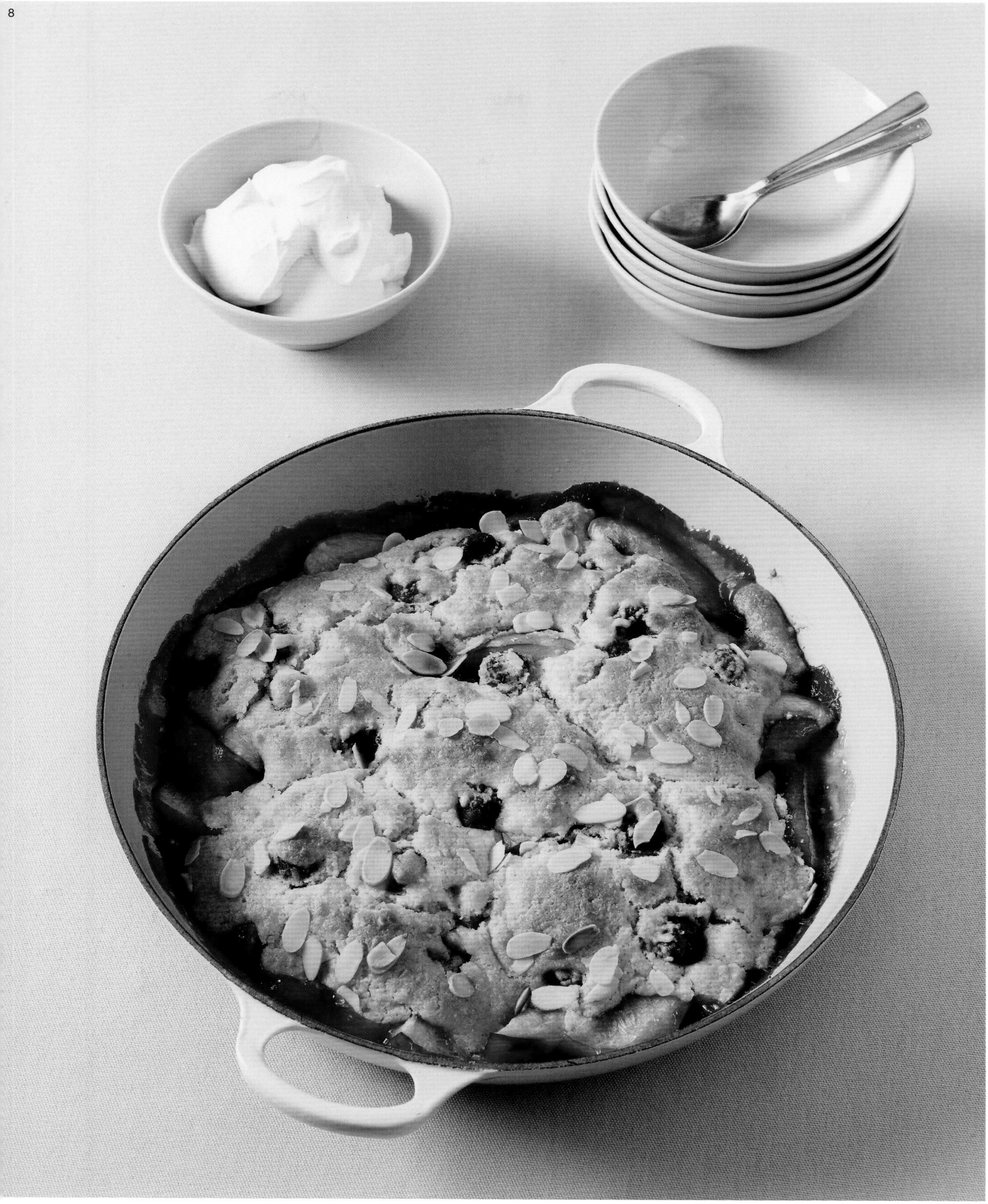

Summer Pudding Trifle

Preparation time: 20 minutes,
plus cooling and chilling
Cooking time: 10 minutes
Serves 8

This recipe takes all of my favorite parts from summer pudding (a British dessert made with bread and lots of intense fruit) and a traditional trifle (rich vanilla custard, liquor, and cream) to create the taste of the season. The berries can be varied: as long as you have about 6 cups (900 g) of small berries, plus about 2½ cups (350 g) ripe strawberries, it will turn out fine.

3¼ cups (400 g) raspberries

2 cups (300 g) blackberries

scant 1 cup (100 g) red currants or
   blueberries, if not available

scant 1 cup (100 g) black currants
   or blueberries, if not available

scant ⅔ cup (120 g) sugar,
   plus a little extra

12 oz (350 g) strawberries (2¼ cups
   prepared)

4 extra-large (UK large) eggs

2 tbsp cornstarch (cornflour)

1¼ cups (300 ml) whole milk

2½ cups (600 ml) heavy (double)
   cream

1 vanilla bean

7 oz (200 g) good-quality
   brioche or pound (Madeira) cake

5 tbsp orange liqueur
   (or orange juice for a
   nonalcoholic version)

1

Put three-quarters of the raspberries, blackberries, and currants or blueberries into a medium saucepan, then add two-thirds of the sugar and 2 tablespoons water.

DESTEMMING CURRANTS
To remove currants from their stems (stalks), hold over a bowl, then run a fork along the stem from top to bottom. The currants will come off easily.

2

Simmer for 2 minutes, until the berries are surrounded with juice but mainly still intact. Hull the strawberries by slicing off their tops, then cut each one in half or quarters, if large. Stir most of the strawberries into the hot fruit, then let cool.

3

To make the custard, separate the eggs (see page 343), putting the yolks into a large bowl. (Use the egg whites in another recipe.) Add the remaining sugar and the cornstarch (cornflour).

4

Whisk everything together until smooth.

5

Put the milk, 1¼ cups (300 ml) cream, and half of the vanilla seeds (see note) into a medium saucepan, then bring just to a boil.

DESEEDING VANILLA BEANS
To scrape the vanilla seeds from the bean, slit the bean along the length, then run a small knife along each side.

6

Pour the hot liquid onto the egg yolk mixture, whisking constantly as you pour, until smooth and even.

7

Return the custard to a clean saucepan, then bring to a boil over medium heat until thick and smooth, stirring all the time. Strain into a bowl, sprinkle the surface with a little sugar (this will stop a skin from forming), and cool until warm. Cover and transfer to the refrigerator to cool completely.

8

When the fruit and custard have cooled, it's time to layer up the trifle. Tear the brioche or cake into pieces and put some into the bottom of a large serving bowl or trifle dish at least 3½ inches (9 cm) deep and 6-cup (1.5-litre) capacity. Sprinkle with some of the liqueur and let soak in for a few seconds.

9

Spoon over some of the fruit and its juice, then layer the rest of the brioche and fruit until it has all been used and the brioche is totally covered in juice. Keep adding a little liqueur as you go, saving 1 tablespoon for later.

10

Give the custard a quick whisk to make sure it's smooth, then spoon it on top of the fruit and spread to the edges. Chill the trifle for a few hours or overnight.

11

Whip the remaining cream with the rest of the vanilla and liqueur, until thickened but not stiff.

12

Spoon the cream over the trifle, then decorate with the reserved fruit.

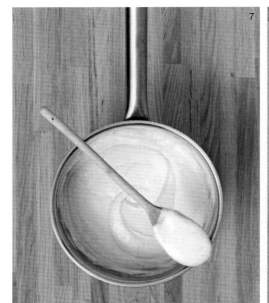

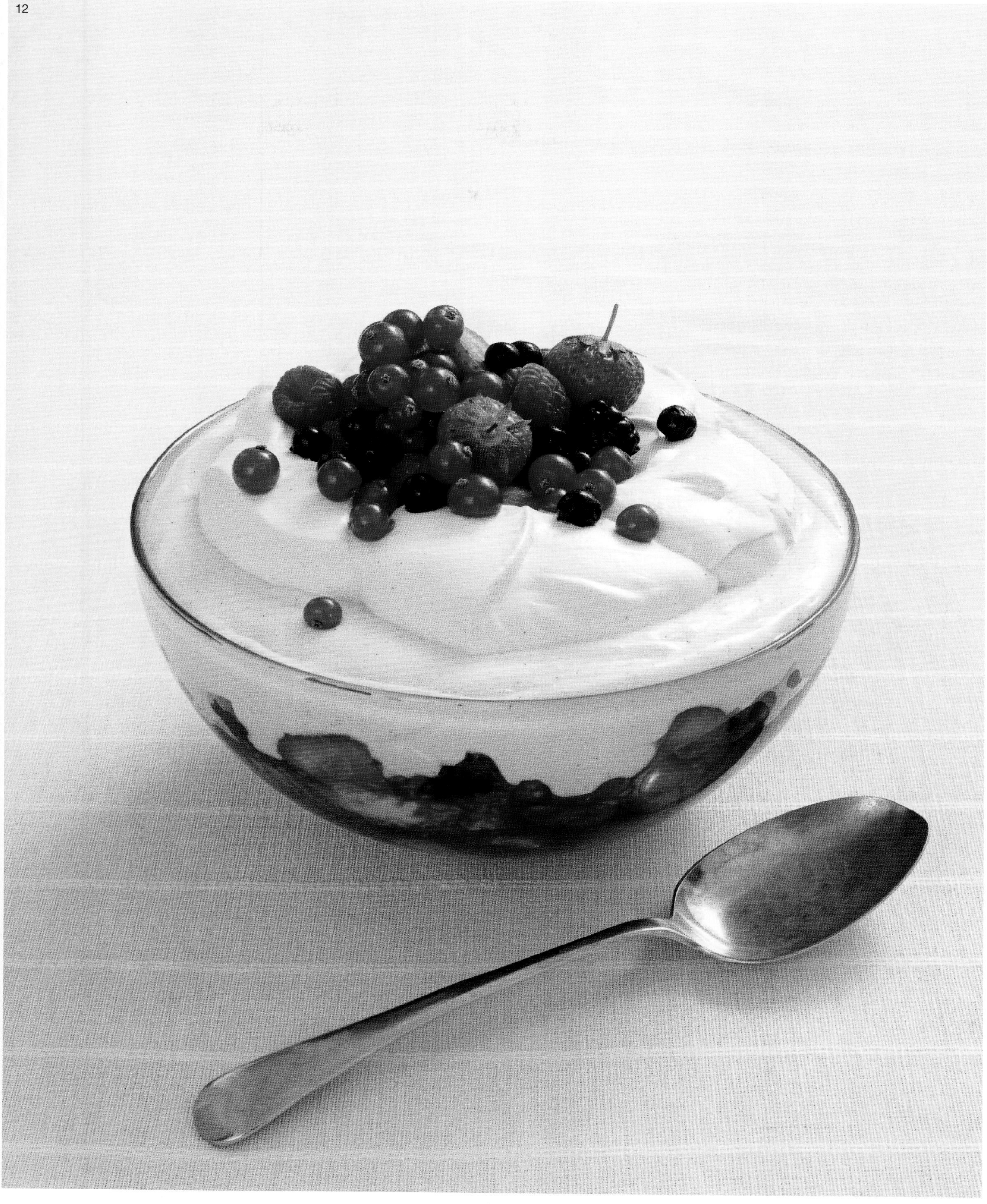

Berry Ice Cream with a Crumble Topping

Preparation time: 30 minutes, plus freezing time
Cooking time: 25 minutes
Serves 8–10

Condensed milk is the secret ingredient here, creating a silky smooth ice cream that doesn't need churning the "proper" way but tastes really convincing. The basic vanilla mix would also be great with choc chips, honeycomb, rum-soaked raisins... whatever you like. Add them at step 10 and freeze.

2½ cups (600 ml) heavy (double) cream
1 tsp vanilla extract
scant 1 cup (200 ml) sweetened condensed milk
¾ cup (100 g) all-purpose (plain) flour
1 pinch fine salt
3½ tbsp (50 g) unsalted butter, cold
4 tbsp superfine (caster) sugar
about 3 cups (350 g) mixed berries (fresh or frozen)

1

Pour the cream into a large mixing bowl, then add the vanilla. Using an electric mixer, whip the cream until thickened but not stiff.

2

Add the condensed milk to the cream, then use a spatula or large metal spoon to fold it in until evenly mixed. Try to conserve as much of the air in the cream as you can.

3

Put the mixture into a large freezer-proof container (I used a small 7 x 10-inch/18 x 25-cm roasting pan, or a baking dish would be fine, too), cover with plastic wrap (clingfilm), then freeze for 3 hours, or until set but still spoonable.

4

Prepare the crumb topping and fruit while you wait. Preheat the oven to 350°F/180°C/Gas Mark 4. Mix the flour and salt in a large bowl, then add the butter, cut into cubes.

5

Rub the butter into the flour, passing it through fingers and thumbs until the cubes of butter start to incorporate into the flour. If the mixture starts to feel warm or the butter sticky, chill it for 5 minutes, then continue. Keep rubbing together until the mixture looks like clumpy bread crumbs, then stir in 2 tablespoons of the sugar.

6

Spread out the crumb mixture over a large baking sheet. Bake for about 25 minutes, until golden and crisp, taking a look halfway through. If the crumbs are browning unevenly, break up with a spoon and stir them about a little, then return to the oven. Let cool.

7
Put the fruit into a saucepan with the remaining 2 tablespoons sugar.

8
Heat the pan gently until the fruit turns soft and saucy, then cool completely.

9
When the ice cream base is almost frozen but still spoonable, swirl in the fruit and its juice.

10
Sprinkle with the crumb topping, cover with plastic wrap, then freeze for at least 4 hours, ideally overnight or for up to 1 month. Take the ice cream out of the freezer 15 minutes before you want to serve it to let it soften ready for scooping.

Melba Sundaes

Preparation time: 10 minutes
Serves 4, easily doubled or halved

The combination of raspberry sauce, peaches, and vanilla ice cream makes a delicious sundae that everyone will love. I've suggested using nectarines, because fuzzy peach skin spoils the texture for me, but choose whatever you like, looks best, and smells most fragrant in the store. Adults might like a little splash of amaretto liqueur over the top of the ice cream.

1-quart (1-litre) container vanilla ice cream
1⅔ cups (200 g) raspberries
2 tbsp confectioners' (icing) sugar, or to taste
4 ripe nectarines or peaches
12 crisp amaretti cookies (biscuits)

1

Take the ice cream from the freezer 10 minutes before you need to scoop it. Using either an immersion (stick) blender or a food processor, blend the raspberries and confectioners' (icing) sugar together to make a coulis. Taste and add more sugar, if you like, although remember that the ice cream will be fairly sweet. There's no need to worry about straining (sieving) out the seeds.

2

Halve the nectarines, then remove the pits (stones). Slice each half into 4 wedges.

3

Crush the cookies coarsely. To serve the sundaes, have ready 4 large sundae glasses or regular glasses. Start with a scoop of ice cream, a few pieces of nectarine, a drizzle of raspberry sauce, and sprinkling of amaretti. Repeat the layers until the glasses are full to overflowing, then serve immediately.

Mango & Black Currant Sorbet

Preparation time: 30 minutes,
plus freezing
Cooking time: 10 minutes
Serves 6–8

This gorgeous sorbet will brighten
the end of any meal. When choosing
mangoes, pick those that are ripe but
not too ripe, with just a slight yield
when pressed. You could turn the
mix into sorbet ice pops (lollies), if
you have a set of molds—fill them
at step 8, then freeze.

1½ cups (300 g) sugar

3–4 large, just-ripe mangoes,
about 3¼ lb (1.5 kg) in total

3 large, or 4–5 smaller limes

scant 1 cup (100 g) black currants or
blackberries if not available, fresh,
or frozen and defrosted

1 large (UK medium) egg (optional)

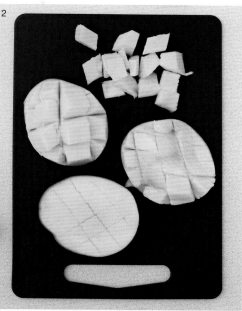

1

Put 1 cup plus 2 tablespoons (225 g) of the sugar into a medium saucepan, then pour in 1 cup (250 ml) cold water. Put the pan over gentle heat and stir every now and again until the sugar has dissolved. When it has dissolved, and not before, boil the mixture for 1 minute, then let cool while you cut up the mango.

2

Cut the cheeks of the mango away from the pit (stone) in the middle, then cut away any flesh from around the middle, too. Cut deep crisscrossed cuts into the cheeks, stopping when you get to the skin, then push the flesh inside out so the flesh sticks out. Cut away the flesh.

3

Squeeze the juice from the limes—you will need scant ½ cup (100 ml). Put the lime juice and mango chunks into a food processor, then blend until smooth. Add the cooled syrup and process again.

4

Line a 2-quart (2-litre) freezer-proof container with a large sheet of plastic wrap (clingfilm)—a little oil will help it to stick to the sides of the container, if it's being difficult—then pour in the sorbet mixture. Put into the freezer until it has set solid or is almost there. This will take about 6 hours or overnight is best.

5

Make the black currant or blackberry ripple. Put the berries into a saucepan, then add the remaining 6 tablespoons (75 g) sugar and 1 tablespoon water. Put the pan over gentle heat and let the whole lot bubble together until the fruit is soft. Pass the sauce through a fine-mesh sieve and let cool. Discard what's left in the sieve.

6

When the mango mixture is firm, turn it out of the container and cut it into pieces.

7

Put the pieces into the bowl of the processor and blend until smooth and thick. You might need to wait a few minutes for the mixture to soften a little, if it's frozen really hard. If you want to use the egg white, separate the egg and add it now.

WHY AN EGG WHITE?
Adding an egg white to the final mixing gives the sorbet a smoother, more silky texture, and most sorbets are made this way. If you are concerned about serving a dish containing raw whites, then omit the egg. Alternatively, you can buy pasteurized whites from some stores.

8

Give the berry sauce a quick stir, because it tends to set a little like a jelly or jam as it cools. Spoon half of the mango mixture back into the freezer container, then swirl over half of the berry sauce. Repeat, then cover, and freeze the sorbet for another 6 hours or until firm again. The sorbet will keep for up to 1 month.

9

Take the sorbet from the freezer 10 minutes before you want to eat it, then scoop and serve in small bowls or ice cream cones.

Muscat & Honey Poached Peaches

Preparation time: 15 minutes,
plus cooling
Cooking time: 15 minutes
Serves 6

Glowing gold and scented with
vanilla and wine, these peaches are
heavenly by themselves and low in
fat, too. Should your halo slip, add
a spoonful of cream or mascarpone
to the side of your plate for one of
the best summer desserts there is.

---

1 lemon

1 vanilla bean

1 cinnamon stick

1½ cups (375 ml) sweet Muscat
    dessert wine (see note)

3 tbsp honey or orange flower honey

½ cup (100 g) sugar

6 just-ripe peaches

thick heavy (double) cream or
    mascarpone cheese, to serve
    (optional)

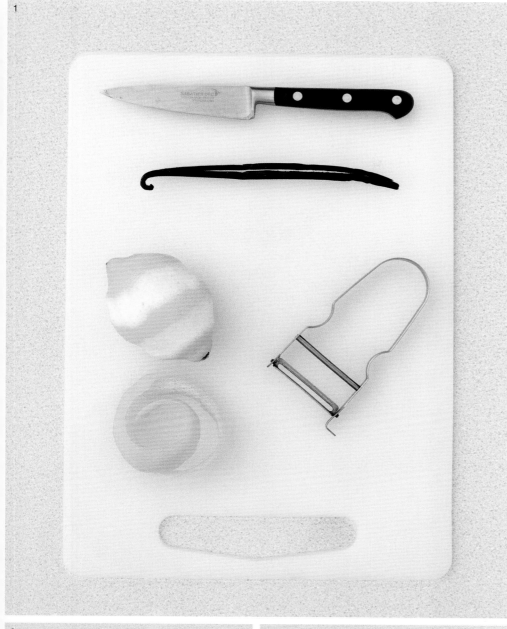

1
Pare the zest from the lemon using a vegetable peeler and split the vanilla bean down the middle.

2
Choose a saucepan that's big enough to hold the peaches in a single layer. Put the zest, vanilla, cinnamon stick, wine, honey, and sugar into the pan, then add 1¼ cups (300 ml) water. Heat gently until the honey and sugar have dissolved. Bring the liquid to a simmer, then add the peaches to the pan (the liquid might not completely cover them, but that's OK).

3
Cover the peaches with a large scrunched up round of parchment (baking) paper. This will help to keep them submerged in the syrup.

NO DESSERT WINE?
Muscat wine is rich and sweet, with plenty of body (a sauternes would also work). If you can't find it, then go for a fruity white wine, such as Viognier, and add ¼ cup (50 g) more sugar, or to taste.

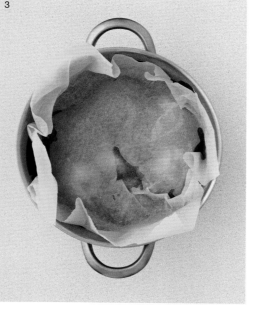

4

Cook the peaches, lifting the paper and turning them over gently 4 times, for about 15 minutes in total, or until softened but not squashy.

5

Lift the peaches out of the syrup, then let stand until cool enough to handle. Remove the vanilla bean, cinnamon stick, and lemon zest, too. Boil the syrup for 5 minutes to concentrate the flavors. Let it cool.

6

Slip the skins from the cooled peaches. I find this easiest if I make a little cut in the skin at the bottom of the peach, then ease the skin away carefully with my finger and thumb. Discard the skins.

7

Pour the cooled syrup over the peaches, then serve. If making ahead, chill, then remove them from the refrigerator an hour or so before eating.

Raspberry & Passion Fruit Mallow Meringue

Preparation time: 30 minutes
plus cooling time
Cooking time: 1 hour
Serves 8 generously

Crisp on the outside, light, fluffy,
and soft within, this crowd-pleaser
is easier to make than you may think.
I like to use a mixture of cream and
yogurt to top the meringue, and
crown it with juicy fruit.

5 extra-large (UK large) eggs

¾ cup (150 g) superfine (caster)
   sugar

1¼ cups (150 g) confectioners'
   (icing) sugar, plus 1–2 tbsp for
   the topping

1 tsp cornstarch (cornflour)

1¼ cups (300 ml) heavy (double)
   cream

1¼ cups (300 g) Greek yogurt

1 tsp vanilla extract

4 large, ripe, wrinkly passion fruit

2 cups (250 g) raspberries

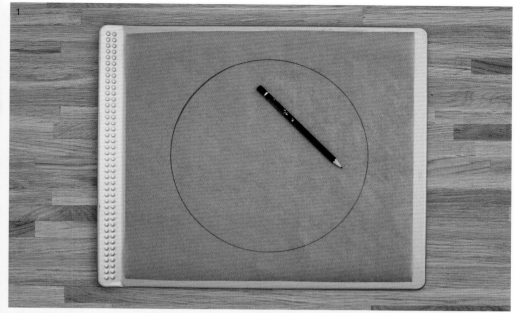

1
Use a pencil to mark a circle about 10 inches (25 cm) in diameter on a piece of parchment (baking) paper. A large dinner plate is about the right size to use as a template. Use this to line a large baking sheet, remembering to turn the paper over or you'll end up with a pencil mark on your meringue. Preheat the oven to 300°F/150°C/Gas Mark 2 and set a shelf in the middle of the oven.

2
Separate the eggs and put the whites into a large and spotlessly clean glass or metal bowl.

SEPARATING AN EGG
Gently crack the shell against the side of a small bowl. Slowly pull the shell apart as cleanly as possible along the crack, tipping the yolk into 1 half of the shell. Let the white drain away into a bowl below. Drop the yolk into another small bowl. Separate the next egg over a third bowl—that way if you accidentally break the yolk, it won't contaminate the clean whites.

FAT FREE
Grease is the enemy of egg whites and, if any does end up in the bowl, the whites will not foam. I like to wipe the bowl with a piece of paper towel dampened with vinegar or lemon juice before adding the whites. Never use a plastic bowl, because grease can hide in scratches in the surface, even if the bowl looks clean.

3

Using an electric mixer, whisk the egg whites until the beaters leave a stiff peak when you pull them away from the bowl. Take care not to overwhisk the whites at this stage.

4

This photograph shows overwhisked egg whites, which look dry and cotton wool-like at the edges, and slightly separated and watery at the bottom of the bowl. Overwhisking the whites at this stage makes it hard to get a good result later on.

5

Add 1 tablespoon of the superfine (caster) sugar, then whisk the mixture back to stiff peaks. Keep adding and whisking the sugar, one spoon at a time. The meringue will start turning from fluffy to thicker and have a pearly sheen.

When all of the superfine sugar has been added, the meringue will look thick and pearlescent like shaving foam.

6
Sift in 1¼ cups (150 g) confectioners' (icing) sugar and the cornstarch, then fold them into the mixture using a large metal spoon.

FOLDING
Don't undo all your hard work with the whisk at this point. Cut the confectioners' sugar into the whites, then fold in a figure 8, keeping a light touch to conserve the air bubbles. Stirring the meringue will cause it to lose volume.

7
Use a few dots of the meringue to act as glue between the paper and the baking sheet. Spoon the meringue onto the paper, then spread it out to fit within the circle. Create a rough nest shape, with a shallow indentation in the middle.

8

Bake the meringue for 30 minutes, then turn the temperature down to 275°F/140°C/Gas Mark 1 and bake for another 30 minutes, until the meringue is crisp on the outside and has taken on the palest hint of gold. Let stand in the oven until cold. In an ideal world, make the meringue the evening before you need it and leave it in the oven overnight. A few small cracks are to be expected, but cooling it slowly will prevent any major crevasses from appearing.

9

To make the topping, whip together the cream, yogurt, vanilla extract, and remaining confectioners' sugar together until thick but not stiff. Cut the passion fruit in half and scoop out the pulp.

CHOOSING PASSION FRUIT
As they ripen, passion fruit become more wrinkly, and the pulp inside the hard shell becomes sweeter and more perfumed. Avoid any that look too shriveled, and pick those heavy for their size and with a purple-yellow hue.

10

Swirl the creamy mixture over the top of the meringue, then sprinkle with the raspberries and drizzle with the passion fruit seeds.

Classic Baked Cheesecake

Preparation time: 20 minutes,
plus cooling and chilling
Baking time: 55 minutes
Cuts into 12 generous slices,
more if you need it to

Creamy and cool, with a crisp crust
(base) with just a hint of ginger, this
cheesecake is baked but not cloying.
The cooling time in the oven is all
important, so make this the last thing
you do in the kitchen on the day you
make it. Serve with seasonal fruit,
or pale and interesting, all by itself.

For the base

1 stick (110 g) soft butter
9 oz (250 g) graham crackers
    (digestive biscuits)
2 tbsp superfine (caster) sugar
½ tsp ground ginger (optional)

For the filling

2 lb (900 g) regular (full-fat) cream
    cheese, at room temperature
1 cup (200 g) superfine (caster)
    sugar
1 tbsp cornstarch (cornflour)
1 vanilla bean or 1 tsp vanilla paste
1 lemon
5 large (UK medium) eggs, room
    temperature
1 cup (250 g) regular (full-fat) crème
    fraîche or sour cream

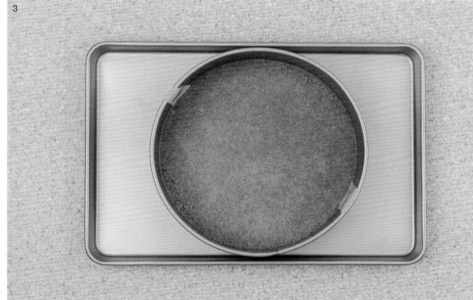

1

Preheat the oven to 400°F/200°C/ Gas Mark 6. Melt the butter in a medium saucepan, then use a little to grease a 9-inch (23-cm) round springform cake pan. Line the bottom with a circle of parchment (baking) paper (see note). Crush the crackers (biscuits) until fine and sandy. You can do this by putting them in a strong plastic food storage bag, squashing out the air, then banging them with a rolling pin. Or use a food processor, as I have here.

2

Mix the melted butter, 2 tablespoons sugar, and the ginger, if using, into the crumbs, until evenly blended and like wet sand. Press into the bottom of the cake pan, spreading firmly with the back of a spoon, until evenly spread.

3

Put the cake pan on a baking sheet, then bake for 10 minutes or until golden. Let cool.

4

To make the filling, put the cream cheese and sugar into a large bowl, then sift the cornstarch (cornflour) over it. If using a vanilla bean, split it in half lengthwise and scrape out the seeds. Finely grate the zest from the lemon, and add the vanilla and lemon zest to the bowl. Using a spatula, beat until smooth. A spatula is better than a whisk here, because you don't want to beat in too much air, which can cause cracks.

LINING THE CAKE PAN
Look closely at the photo for step 3 and you'll see I put a strip of parchment paper beneath the lining parchment in the pan. This helps me to get a hold on the cheesecake once it's ready, and makes it easier to get it off the bottom.

5

Separate 2 eggs (see page 343), saving the whites for another time. Beat the 3 whole eggs and 2 yolks into the cheese mixture one by one, until smooth.

6

Finish by beating in ½ cup (125 g) crème fraîche or sour cream. Pour the mixture onto the crumb crust (base), then level the top.

WHAT IS CRÈME FRAÎCHE?
Easily found in Europe and now more popular in the United States, this cultured cream is thick, rich, and fantastic for baking. It has a sour flavor but is creamier than regular sour cream. Its slightly higher fat content makes for a good cheesecake.

7

Bake for 10 minutes, then turn the oven down to 300°F/150°C/Gas Mark 2 and bake for another 45 minutes, or until the middle wobbles slightly as you jiggle the pan, and the top has turned pale gold at the edges. Check the cake after two-thirds of the baking time and give it a turn, if needed. When it's ready, loosen the edge of the cake from the pan using a spatula (palette knife), then return to the turned-off oven and let it cool in the oven with the door slightly open for 1 hour. Remove and let cool to room temperature for a couple of hours, then chill overnight.

8

For optimal creaminess, take the cheesecake from the refrigerator half an hour before you want to eat it. Smooth the rest of the crème fraîche or sour cream over the top, then serve.

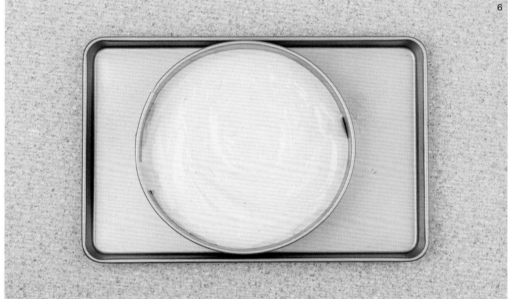

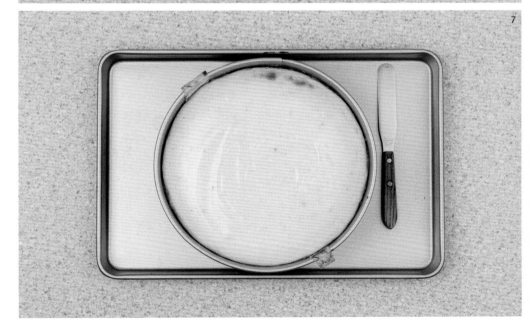

Pumpkin Pie

Preparation time: 1 hour, including
blind baking, plus chilling
Baking time: 45 minutes
Serves 12

Essential baking for fall (autumn),
this pie is delicately set and spiced,
with a good crisp crust (case). A big
dollop of boozy maple cream on the
side really complements the flavor of
the pumpkin.

For the dough

all-purpose (plain) flour, for rolling
1 quantity sweet shortcrust dough
    (see page 370), or use 12 oz
    (350 g) store-bought pie dough

For the filling

3 large (UK medium) eggs
½ cup packed (100 g) light brown
    sugar
¼ cup (50 g) superfine (caster) sugar
1 tsp vanilla extract
1½ tsp each ground cinnamon
    and ginger, mixed with ½ tsp
    ground nutmeg
½ cup (120 ml) heavy (double) cream
½ cup (120 ml) milk
2 tbsp maple syrup, or 2 tbsp
    more sugar
1 (15-oz/425-g) can solid-pack
    pumpkin puree (or see note
    page 350)
a pinch of salt

For the cream

⅔ cup (150 ml) heavy (double) cream
1 tbsp maple syrup
1 tbsp bourbon or whiskey

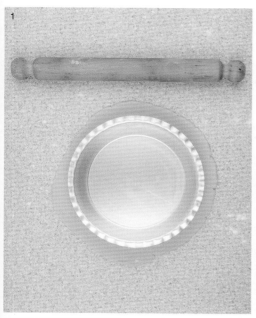

1

Lightly flour the work surface, then roll out the dough until large enough to line a 9-inch (23-cm) pie pan (one with a lip is best). Use the pan as a guide for size, and try to keep the dough as round as you can. See page 362 for full rolling instructions, if needed.

2

You can either use the rolling pin to lift the dough into the pan, or try this method: Dust the top of the dough with a little flour, then fold it first in half, then into a triangle. Lift it into the pan, then unfold.

ANY HOLES?

Don't worry if your dough tears before cooking, just press it back together. If cracks or holes appear after cooking, dampen a small piece of leftover dough and smooth it over carefully.

3

Press the dough against the edges of the pan, then trim off the overhanging dough with a sharp knife. Prick the bottom all over with a fork, right down to the metal. Crimp the edges, if you like, pushing the dough between your thumb and index finger to make deep, V-shaped indents. Repeat all the way around, then chill the dough for 15 minutes, or longer if you have time.

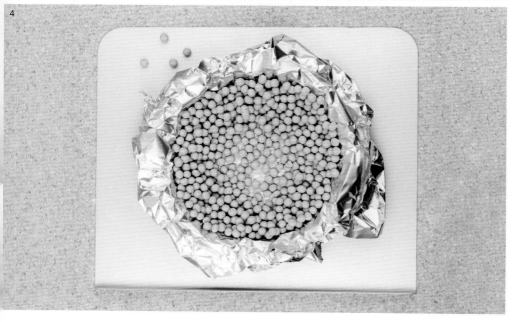

4

Preheat the oven to 375°F/190°C/ Gas Mark 5. Put the pan on a baking sheet. Tear a sheet of aluminum foil large enough to completely cover the dough, edges and all. Pour in pie weights (baking beans) to cover the bottom, mounding them up a little toward the edges. Bake for 20 minutes.

5

Check under the foil; if the pastry looks dry and set, remove the foil. If not, bake for another 5 minutes. When ready, carefully spoon out the hot baking weights, then remove the foil. Bake for another 15–20 minutes, or until it is golden and feels sandy. If the edges color before the bottom is ready, cover them with foil.

6

Make the filling while you wait. Beat the eggs, saving 1 tablespoon to glaze the pastry later. Beat the rest of the filling ingredients into the eggs to make a thin custard.

HOMEMADE PUMPKIN PUREE
To make your own puree, roast large chunks of butternut squash or pumpkin with a little oil for 30 minutes at 400°F/200°C/ Gas Mark 6, or until softened, or microwave them. Puree or mash well, then pass through a sieve until smooth. Add 1¾ cups (425 g) to the rest of the filling ingredients once cooled.

7

To seal the pastry (the filling has a lot of liquid), brush the pastry all over with 1 tablespoon reserved beaten egg, then bake for 2 minutes, until shiny.

8

Pull the oven rack out a little. Pour the filling into the crust, but don't overfill it. Slide the oven rack back.

9

Bake for 45 minutes or until the edges rise slightly and the center wobbles gently. Let cool in the pan. To make a cream, whip all the ingredients until just thickened.

10

Serve the pie at room temperature or chilled, with the cream.

Strawberry Meringue Cake

Preparation time: 30 minutes
Baking time: about 1 hour
Serves 12

This playful recipe is inspired by the British classic Eton mess and makes a great alternative to a meringue for an unusual summer dessert. Just like Eton mess, the cream is absolutely key to the finished recipe. Pour it lavishly over each portion so it soaks into the cake and mingles with the berries and meringue.

For the cake

1 stick (110 g) butter, plus extra for greasing
4 tbsp heavy (double) or whipping cream, plus extra to serve
1 tsp vanilla paste, or use extract
9 oz (250 g) ripe strawberries (1¾ cups/200 g prepared)
1⅓ cups (175 g) all-purpose (plain) flour
1 cup (100 g) almond meal (ground almonds)
½ tsp baking powder
¼ tsp salt
3 large (UK medium) eggs, plus 2 egg yolks
¾ cup (150 g) superfine (caster) sugar

For the topping

2 large (UK medium) egg whites
½ cup (100 g) superfine (caster) sugar
more ripe strawberries, or other berries
1 tbsp confectioners' (icing) sugar

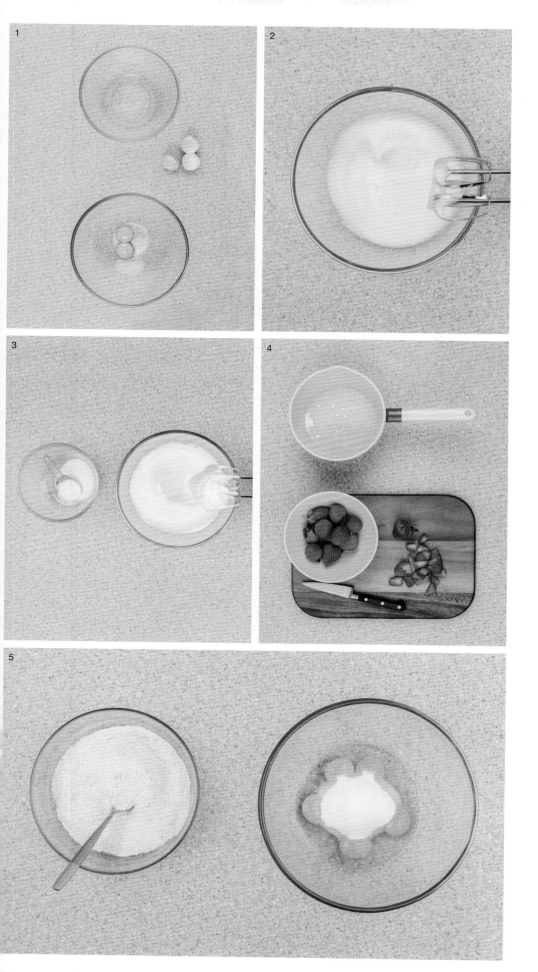

1

Preheat the oven to 350°F/180°C/
Gas Mark 4. Use a little butter to
grease a 9-inch (23-cm) round
springform cake pan, then line the
bottom with parchment (baking)
paper. Get the meringue topping
ready first. Separate 2 eggs (see
page 343), putting the yolks into a
large bowl to use in the cake batter
later, and the whites into a separate
large bowl.

2

Using an electric mixer, whisk the
egg whites until the beaters leave a
stiff peak when you pull them away
from the bowl. Be careful not to
overwhisk them.

3

Add 1 tablespoon of the sugar,
then beat until the mixture becomes
thick, shiny, and holds stiff peaks.
Keep adding and whisking back
to stiff peaks until all the sugar
has been used and the meringue
has taken on a pearly sheen.

NICE IDEA, NO TIME?
Just press a handful of crushed
store-bought meringue shells into
the cake batter before baking.

4

Now for the cake. Melt the butter
in a small saucepan, then remove
from the heat and stir in the cream
and vanilla. Remove the stems
(stalks) from the strawberries, then
cut into fingertip-sized chunks.

5

Mix the flour, almond meal (ground
almonds), baking powder, and
salt and set aside for later. Crack
the 3 whole eggs into the bowl
containing the 2 yolks from earlier,
then add the superfine (caster) sugar.

6

Using the electric mixer, beat the eggs and sugar together until doubled in volume, thick, and mousselike, which will take about 5 minutes.

7

Pour the butter mixture into the eggs, whisk briefly, then sift the flour and almond mixture over the top. Whisk briefly again, until evenly blended. Fold in the chopped strawberries, using a large spoon or spatula.

8

Pour the batter into the prepared cake pan and level the top. Spoon the meringue over the cake to make a crown, with pointy peaks if you can. Leave some of the center of the cake uncovered, or it will take too long to bake. If the meringue has set a little in the bowl, just fold it a few times with the spoon until smooth.

9

Bake for 10 minutes, then turn the oven down to 325°F/160°C/ Gas Mark 3) and bake for another 45–50 minutes, or until the cake is golden, has risen in the center, and the meringue is crisp and feels dry and hard. Insert a toothpick or skewer into the center of the cake to see if it is ready. It will come out clean or just a little sticky when done. Let cool for a while in the pan, then carefully unclip it. Let cool on a rack, then remove the bottom and transfer to a serving plate once cooled.

10

Serve the cake with a few more strawberries on top and at the side, a dusting of confectioners' (icing) sugar, and a generous helping of cream.

Tarte au Citron (Lemon Tart)

Preparation time: about 1 hour
10 minutes (including blind baking),
plus chilling and cooling
Baking time: 5 minutes
Serves 12

I turn to classic lemon tart again and
again for a dessert that works for
just about any meal. The lemon curd
filling is sharp, fresh, and citrussy,
and the pastry is a crisp, sweet shell
(case) that's simple to make, with no
need to worry about overmixing.
There's enough dough for two tarts,
so put half in the freezer.

For the pastry

1 large (UK medium) egg
2 sticks (225 g) soft butter
1 tsp vanilla extract
scant ½ cup (50 g) confectioners'
    (icing) sugar, plus extra to serve
    (optional)
½ tsp fine salt
2¾ cups (350 g) all-purpose (plain)
    flour, plus extra for rolling

For the lemon curd filling

8 large (UK medium) eggs
1½ sticks (175 g) butter
1 cup (200 g) superfine (caster)
    sugar
5 large lemons

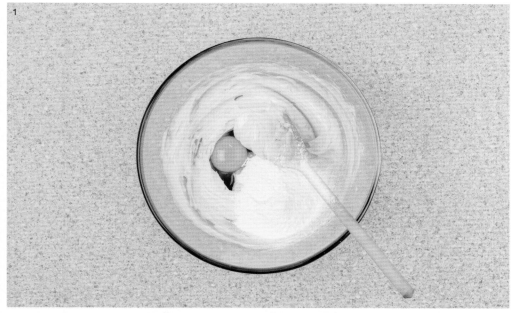

1

To make the dough, first separate the egg (see page 343). You will only need the yolk. In a large bowl, beat the butter until it is soft and smooth. Next, add the egg yolk, vanilla, sugar, and salt.

2

Beat together until evenly combined and creamy. Sift in the flour, then work it into the creamed mixture until you have a clumpy but evenly mixed dough with hardly any dry flour left at the bottom of the bowl.

MAKE IT IN A PROCESSOR
It's easy to make the dough by hand, but if you have a food processor, then simply process the butter by itself until creamy. Blend in the yolk, vanilla, sugar, and salt, then finish with the flour.

3

Turn out the dough onto the work surface and make a smooth ball. It will seem soft, even a little sticky. Shape into 2 equal-sized disks, then wrap in plastic wrap (clingfilm). Chill one piece for at least 30 minutes (you need it to be firm but not hard, or it will crack as it rolls), and reserve the other for another time. It can be frozen for up to 1 month.

4

Preheat the oven to 400°F/200°C/ Gas Mark 6 and use the dough to line a 9-inch (23-cm) loose-bottomed tart pan. Before rolling, flour the work surface and rolling pin. Press shallow ridges across the dough, then rotate it by a quarter turn. Repeat this until the dough is about ½ inch (2 cm) thick. If any cracks do appear, pinch them together.

5

Now roll out the dough to a circle. Roll the pin evenly over the dough, going forward and backward in only one direction. If you roll it in several directions, the dough may roll unevenly and stretch, which causes shrinking. Turn it by a quarter turn every few rolls, until it is just large enough to line the tart pan, allowing about a 1-inch (2.5-cm) overhang.

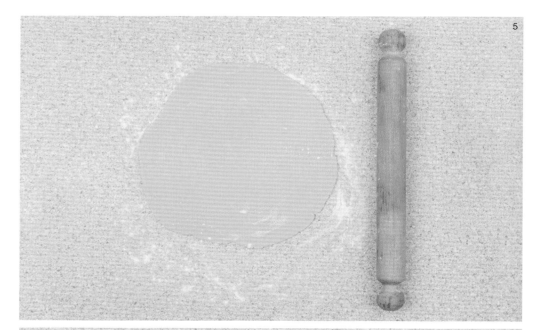

6

Flip the farthest edge of the dough over the rolling pin, then lift it and carefully drape it over the pan. Taking it a section at a time, gently push the dough down and into the corner of the pan so it sits at a clean right angle. Pinch off a small ball of excess dough and use it to press the dough into the ridges of the pan.

7

Trim the excess dough away with a roll of the rolling pin across the top of the pan. Pinch the dough between your finger and thumb so that its edge meets the top of the pan, or better still, comes slightly higher (if your dough does shrink, it will still be the same size as the pan). Prick the bottom all over with a fork, right down to the metal. Lift onto a baking sheet and chill for 10 minutes in the freezer until hard, or longer in the refrigerator if you have time.

ANY HOLES?

If any holes or tears appear, dampen a little piece of the leftover dough and press it into the hole or tear. If cracks appear during baking, smooth a blob of dough over the hot pastry, bake for a few minutes to set, and it will melt and form a delicate seal. Be careful when doing this, though, because too much pressure on the edge of a baked pastry shell (case) can cause crumbling—this is only for emergency measures!

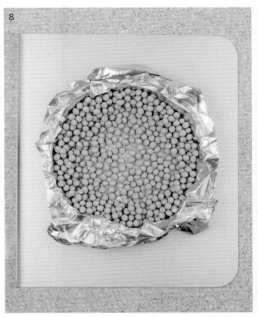

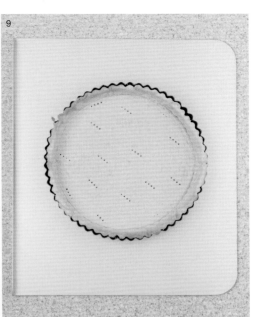

8
When ready to bake, line the dough with a sheet of aluminum foil, making sure all the edges are covered. I tend not to use parchment (baking) paper for this, because it can make the pastry sweaty underneath. Fill with pie weights (baking beans), mounding them up a little at the sides, to support the dough as it bakes.

9
Bake for 15–20 minutes, or until the pastry looks set and is fairly dry underneath the foil. It should not have taken on much color at this point. Removing the weights too soon can cause the pastry to sag, so if you're not sure, give it another 5 minutes. Remove the foil and weights from the pan.

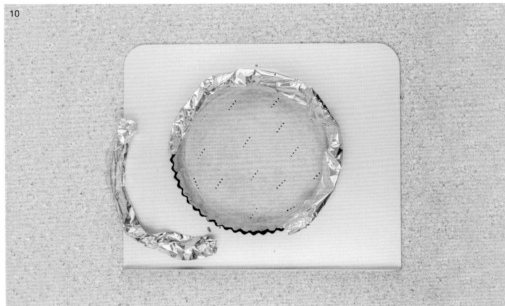

10
Turn the oven down to 325°F/160°C/ Gas Mark 3. Bake for another 10–15 minutes, or until the bottom of the pastry is pale gold and feels sandy. If the outside edges are looking brown before the middle of the pastry is ready, carefully wrap in foil and return to the oven.

11
While the pastry is baking, make the filling. Separate 4 eggs. You will only need the yolks for this recipe. Beat them with the 4 whole eggs in a large bowl. Cut the butter into small pieces, and put into a heavy-bottomed pan with the sugar. Juice the lemons and add 1 cup (250 ml) lemon juice to the pan.

12

Gently melt the butter and sugar into the lemon juice. Once melted, begin to whisk the eggs with one hand, and simultaneously pour the hot lemon mixture onto them with the other. Pour slowly at first so that the eggs don't get too hot too quickly and scramble.

13

Return the mixture to the pan and cook it over medium heat for 3–5 minutes, or until thickened and smooth. Try to avoid letting it boil, and keep stirring all the time, concentrating on the edges of the pan where it is hottest.

14

Pour the lemon curd into the cooked pastry shell (case), then bake again for 5 minutes, which just helps the curd to set.

15

Transfer the tart to a cooling rack, let cool completely, then chill until ready to serve. Sprinkle with confectioners' (icing sugar), if you like.

LEMON MERINGUE PIE
To transform the tart into a lemon meringue pie, follow the meringue technique on page 357, beating 4 of the leftover egg whites with 1 cup (200 g) superfine (caster) sugar. Whisk 1 teaspoon cornstarch (cornflour) into the thick finished meringue. Dollop evenly over the warm lemon filling, then spread it up to and slightly over the pastry edges, peaking the meringue in dramatic curls as you go. Bake at 400°F/200°C/Gas Mark 6 for 20 minutes or until golden, let cool for at least 1 hour, then serve warm or cold on the day of making.

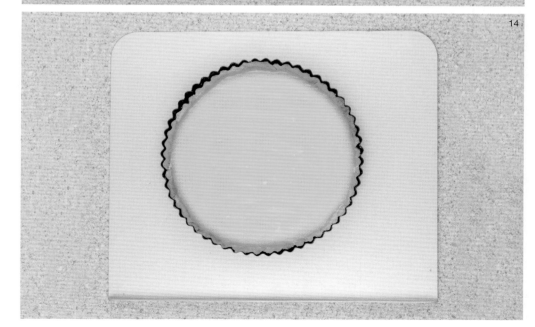

Chocolate Profiteroles

Preparation time: 20 minutes
Baking time: 30 minutes per batch
Serves 6 (makes 18)

Once you've discovered the trick to making choux pastry at home, you'll be making profiteroles again and again. Cooled, unfilled choux puffs (buns) will keep in an airtight container for 3 days or freeze for 1 month. Refresh in a hot oven to crisp them up, then continue from step 8.

For the paste

1 cup (125 g) all-purpose (plain) flour
1 tsp sugar
a pinch of salt
6 tbsp (80 g) butter, plus extra for greasing
1 cup plus 1 tbsp (250 ml) water
3 large (UK medium) eggs

For the chocolate sauce

7 oz (200 g) bittersweet (dark) chocolate, 60–70% cocoa solids, broken into pieces
⅔ cup (150 ml) heavy (double) cream
scant ½ cup (100 ml) milk
1 tsp vanilla paste or extract
a pinch of salt

For the filling

2 cups (450 ml) heavy (double) cream
2 tbsp confectioners' (icing) sugar
½ tsp vanilla paste or extract

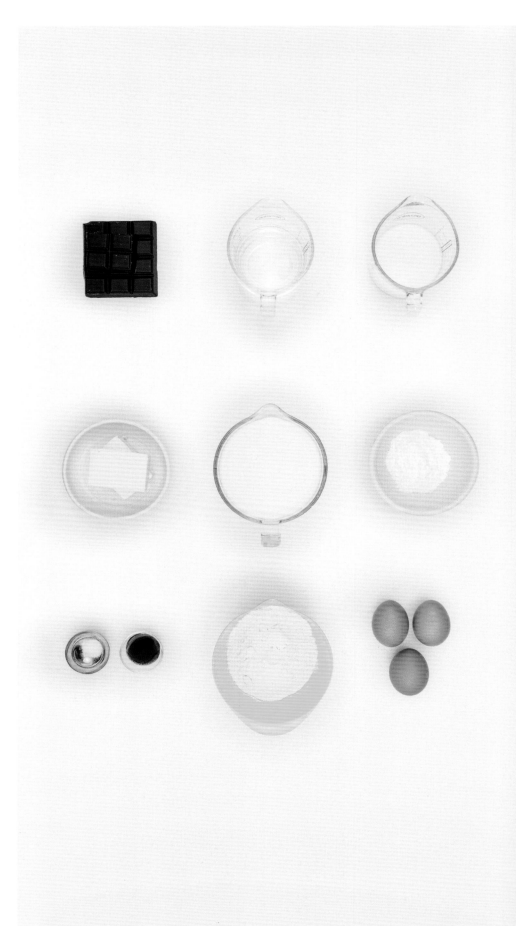

1

For the paste, first sift the flour, sugar, and salt together onto a piece of parchment (baking) paper.

2

Put the butter and water into a medium saucepan. Heat over fairly low heat until the butter has completely melted. Once melted, increase the heat and bring the water to a rolling boil. Keep a wooden spoon on hand. With the pan still on the stove, and using the parchment like a chute, quickly pour the flour mixture into the pan, then grab the wooden spoon and start mixing it vigorously. Turn off the heat. It will seem weirdly lumpy at first, but keep beating. You need to add the flour quickly after the water comes to a boil to avoid letting too much of it evaporate.

3

After a short period of beating, the lumpy mixture will transform into a shiny, thick smooth paste that comes away cleanly from the edge of the pan. Stop beating.

4

Spoon the paste onto a cold plate and spread it out with the wooden spoon. This helps to cool it quickly. When it's barely warm to the touch, move on to step 5.

5

Beat the eggs together in a measuring pitcher (jug). Put the paste into a large bowl, then add the eggs in small additions, beating until fully incorporated each time. The paste will get stiffer, then looser. You can do this with an electric mixer, if you prefer. Stop adding egg when the mixture is smooth and silky, and falls in a smooth dollop from the spoon when shaken sharply. The paste can be chilled for up to a day at this point.

6

When ready to bake, preheat the oven to 425°F/220°C/Gas Mark 7. Grease and line 2 large baking sheets (trays) with parchment paper. Spoon 18 heaping teaspoons paste onto the sheets, aiming for walnut-sized balls. If you want to be neat, pipe the paste onto the sheets using a ½-inch (1-cm) tip (nozzle) and a large pastry (piping) bag. Smooth any points with a wet finger.

7

Bake for 10 minutes, then turn down the oven to 400°C/200°C fan/Gas Mark 6 and cook for 20 minutes, or until crisp and golden brown. The pastry should hardly give at all when gently squeezed. Don't open the oven door to turn the sheets until the pastry has risen well and is changing color, or they will deflate.

Once cooked, cut each puff (choux bun) partway open, then bake for another 5 minutes. This lets the steam out from the centers and will help keep the pastry crisper for longer. Remove and let cool.

8

To make the sauce, chop the chocolate. Bring the cream and milk to a simmer, add the chocolate, vanilla, and salt, then remove from the heat and stir until smooth and silky. It can be made in advance and warmed gently when ready to serve.

9

These puffs are best filled shortly before serving, but you can do it 2 hours ahead and store them in the refrigerator. Put the cream, sugar, and vanilla into a large bowl and whip until thickened but not stiff. Spoon it generously into the cold puffs.

10

Pour the warm chocolate sauce over them to serve.

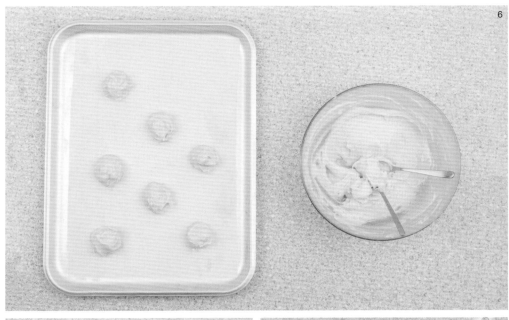

One-Crust Apple & Blackberry Pie

Preparation time: 25 minutes,
plus chilling (if making own dough)
Baking time: 35–50 minutes
Serves 8

This is an easy pie to make and
needs no special equipment.
A simple, sturdy but tender pastry
crust holds the juicy contents
inside (or you can use 12 oz/350 g
store-bought pie dough). Try using
rhubarb and strawberries or perhaps
peaches and blueberries once
you've got the hang of it.

___

For the sweet shortcrust dough

1⅔ cups (200 g) all-purpose (plain)
  flour, plus extra for rolling
¼ tsp salt
¼ cup (50 g) cold vegetable
  shortening (fat) or lard
5 tbsp (70 g) cold butter
1 large (UK medium) egg
2 tbsp sugar

For the filling

1 lb 7 oz (650 g) tangy dessert
  apples (3–4), such as Jonagold,
  Braeburn, or Cox
1 lemon, or 1 tbsp lemon juice
  from a bottle
2 tbsp cornstarch (cornflour)
½ tsp ground cinnamon or nutmeg
⅔ cup (100 g) blackberries, fresh or
  frozen, and defrosted
½ cup (100 g) granulated sugar
2 tbsp semolina or fine corn flour
  (cornmeal)
1 tbsp butter
1 tbsp turbinado (demerara) sugar

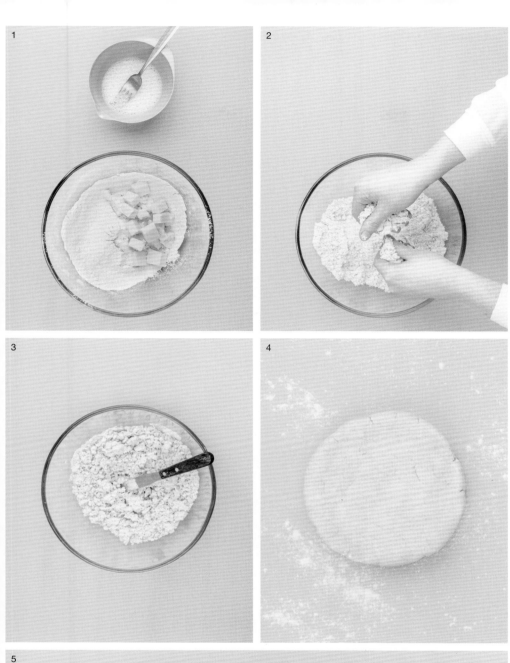

1

Make the dough first. Sift the flour into a large bowl and add the salt. Cut the shortening (fat) and butter into cubes, then add to the bowl. Separate the egg and beat the yolk with 2 tablespoons water. Reserve the egg white for later on.

2

Rub the fat into the flour with your hands until the mixture resembles fine crumbs, then stir in the sugar. A food processor makes light work of this job, if you have one.

3

Splash the egg yolk and water over the rubbed-in mixture, then quickly work it in using a blunt table knife until it comes together. If using a processor, process until the dough forms a smooth ball. Try to avoid adding more liquid, or mixing it too much once the dough starts to take shape. If the dough won't come together, add 1 teaspoon water. Some flours are drier than others, so the amount of liquid you need can vary.

4

If making by hand, knead the dough briefly to make a smooth ball. Shape into a disk, wrap in plastic wrap (clingfilm), and chill for 30 minutes, or until firm but not rock hard, while you prepare the filling. Preheat the oven to 375°F/190°C/Gas Mark 5. Put a baking sheet in the oven to heat up. This will provide a boost of heat to the bottom of the pastry and help it crisp up.

5

Peel the apples, chop the flesh away from the cores in big chunks, then slice them thinly. Toss in a large bowl with 1 tablespoon lemon juice, the cornstarch (cornflour), spice, and berries. Don't add the sugar yet, or it can make the fruit a little wet by the time the pastry is ready.

6

Cut a large square of parchment (baking) paper and sprinkle it lightly with flour. Using a floured rolling pin, press ridges evenly across the dough. Rotate the dough and paper by a quarter turn and repeat. Do this until the dough is about ½-inch (1-cm) thick. If any cracks appear at the edges, pinch them back together.

7

Roll the dough out into a 12-inch (30-cm) round. Roll forward and back, not side to side, and turn the dough and paper a quarter turn every few rolls. This helps the dough stretch without becoming tough.

8

Slide the dough, still on its paper, onto a baking sheet. Sprinkle the semolina or corn flour (cornmeal) over the middle. Toss the granulated sugar into the fruit and mound it in the middle of the dough, leaving a border of about 3 inches (7 cm). Lightly beat the egg white with a fork, then brush it around the edges with a pastry brush.

9

Push the dough up and around the fruit, pinching it to make a kind of basket shape. If any cracks appear, just pinch the dough together to reseal. Dot the butter over the fruit. Brush the outside of the dough with the egg white and sprinkle with turbinado (demerara) sugar.

10

Slide the baking sheet on top of the preheated baking sheet. Bake for 35–40 minutes, or until golden and crisp and the apples are just tender. If they are not cooked but the pastry is, reduce the temperature to 350°F/180°C/Gas Mark 4 and give it another 10 minutes. Cool for at least 10 minutes to let the juices settle, then serve hot or warm with ice cream, cream, or custard.

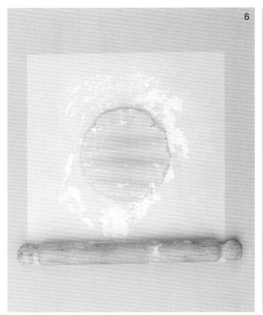
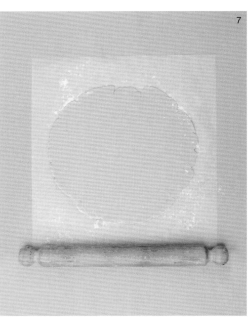

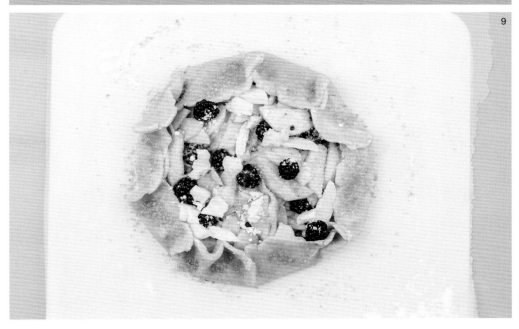

Upside-Down Fruitcake

Preparation time: 20 minutes
Baking time: 55 minutes–1 hour
Makes 12 slices

I love the way that despite its glossy
looks, this is a down-to-earth cake,
ready to change with the seasons as
they roll around. Cherries, apricots,
peaches, apples, pears, even the
classic pineapple will easily meld
into the bottom of the rich almond
sponge cake. Serve slightly warm
with whipped cream or crème
fraiche, or custard if it's cold outside.

For the cake

2¼ sticks (250 g) soft butter, plus
    extra for greasing

1¼ cups packed (250 g) light brown
    sugar

1 cup plus 2 tbsp (140 g) all-purpose
    (plain) flour

2 tsp baking powder

¼ tsp salt

1 cup (100 g) almond meal (ground
    almonds)

½ cup (125 g) sour cream or crème
    fraîche

4 large (UK medium) eggs, room
    temperature

½ tsp almond extract

For the fruit

8–10 ripe plums, not too soft

4 tbsp packed light brown sugar

374

1
Preheat the oven to 350°F/180°C/
Gas Mark 4. Use a little butter to
grease a 9-inch (23-cm) round
springform pan, then line the bottom
with parchment (baking) paper. For
the fruit, halve and pit (stone) the
plums, then cut each half into
3 wedges. Toss them with the light
brown sugar.

2
Arrange the fruit in the bottom
of the pan in neat rings, if you have
time, or be more rustic. They must
be in a single layer. Make sure you
add all the sugar.

3
For the cake, put the butter into
a large mixing bowl with the dry
ingredients, sour cream or crème
fraîche, eggs, and almond extract.

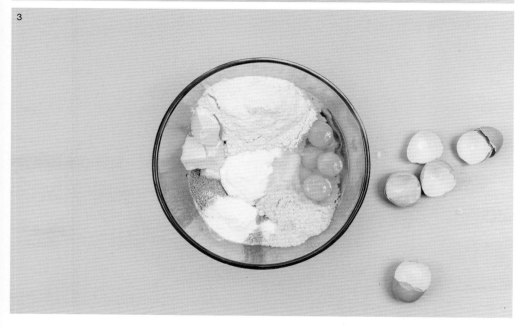

4

Use an electric mixer to beat everything to a smooth, fairly thick cake batter.

5

Spoon the batter on top of the fruit, then smooth the top.

6

Bake for 55 minutes–1 hour, or until the cake is golden and has risen; a toothpick or skewer should come out clean when inserted into the middle. Run a spatula (palette knife) around the edge of the pan to loosen the cake, then let cool on a cooling rack.

7

Serve the cake warm. If you need to reheat it, cover it loosely with aluminum foil and let it warm through in a low oven for 15 minutes.

PEAR & CHOCOLATE CAKE
Toss 1 lb (450 g) sliced just-ripe pears (about 3 medium) with the sugar. Add a generous ½ cup (100 g) bittersweet (dark) chocolate chips to the cake batter.

PINEAPPLE CAKE
Toss 2⅔ cups (450 g) pineapple chunks (drained, if canned) with the sugar. For a really retro touch, poke candied (glacé) cherries here and there between the fruit.

SPICED APPLE CARAMEL CAKE
Toss 1 lb (450 g) sliced, peeled apples (about 3 medium) with the sugar. Mix 2 teaspoons pumpkin pie spice (ground mixed spice) in with the flour. Drizzle with store-bought caramel sauce or dulce de leche to serve.

Chocolate Mousse
with Cherries

Preparation time: 20 minutes,
plus chilling
Makes 6 large or 8 smaller portions

What better excuse to eat
chocolate mousse than the arrival
of the cherry season. The slightly
retro flavor combination is well
worth revisiting—good chocolate
and a splash of kirsch (clear brandy
made with cherries) will really make
the fruit flavor pop.

---

5 oz (150 g) bittersweet (dark)
  chocolate, 70% cocoa solids

1½ cups (350 ml) heavy (double)
  cream

2 extra-large (UK large) eggs,
  at room temperature

1 tbsp kirsch, brandy, or water

4 tbsp superfine (caster) sugar

12 oz (350 g) ripe cherries
  (2 cups pitted)

1 lemon

1

Chop the chocolate into small pieces, then put into a large heatproof bowl. Pour ⅔ cup (150 ml) of the cream into a small saucepan, then bring just to a boil.

2

When the cream has bubbles appearing at the sides and the surface is shimmering, it's ready. Pour the hot cream onto the chocolate and let melt for about 3 minutes.

3

While you wait, separate the eggs (see page 343) and put the whites into a clean, grease-free bowl. Beat the yolks with the kirsch, brandy, or water. Stir the chocolate and cream together until even, then add 2 tablespoons of the sugar and all of the yolk mixture. Stir until smooth and even.

4

Pour another ⅔ cup (150 ml) cream into a bowl. Using an electric mixer, first whisk the egg whites until thick and foamy, but not stiff. Then whisk the cream until thick but not stiff. Do it this way around and you won't need to wash the beaters in between—(cream on the beaters would prevent the whites from whipping).

5

Fold the cream into the chocolate mix using a large metal spoon or a rubber spatula.

6

Now add a quarter of the whites and stir them in. This will loosen the mixture ready for the rest of the whites. Spoon in the remainder, then fold in gently until the mixture is thoroughly blended, with no traces of white.

FOLDING
Using a figure 8 motion, cut instead of stir the egg whites into the creamy chocolate mix. Try to conserve as much air as you can.

7

Spoon the mousse into 6 larger or 8 smaller serving glasses or cups and chill for at least 2 hours or until firm.

8

To prepare the cherries, first cut them in half and remove the pits (stones).

9

Put the cherries into a skillet or frying pan with the remaining sugar and 2 teaspoons lemon juice. Cook the cherries over high heat for 1 minute or so, until the sugar melts and bubbles around the cherries. Let cool.

10

Softly whip the remaining cream, then spoon it on top of the set mousses. Serve with the cherries.

TRY THIS
For cute little Black Forest cake cups, why not layer the cherries, mousse, and some store-bought chocolate cake in glasses, then top with whipped cream and more cherries.

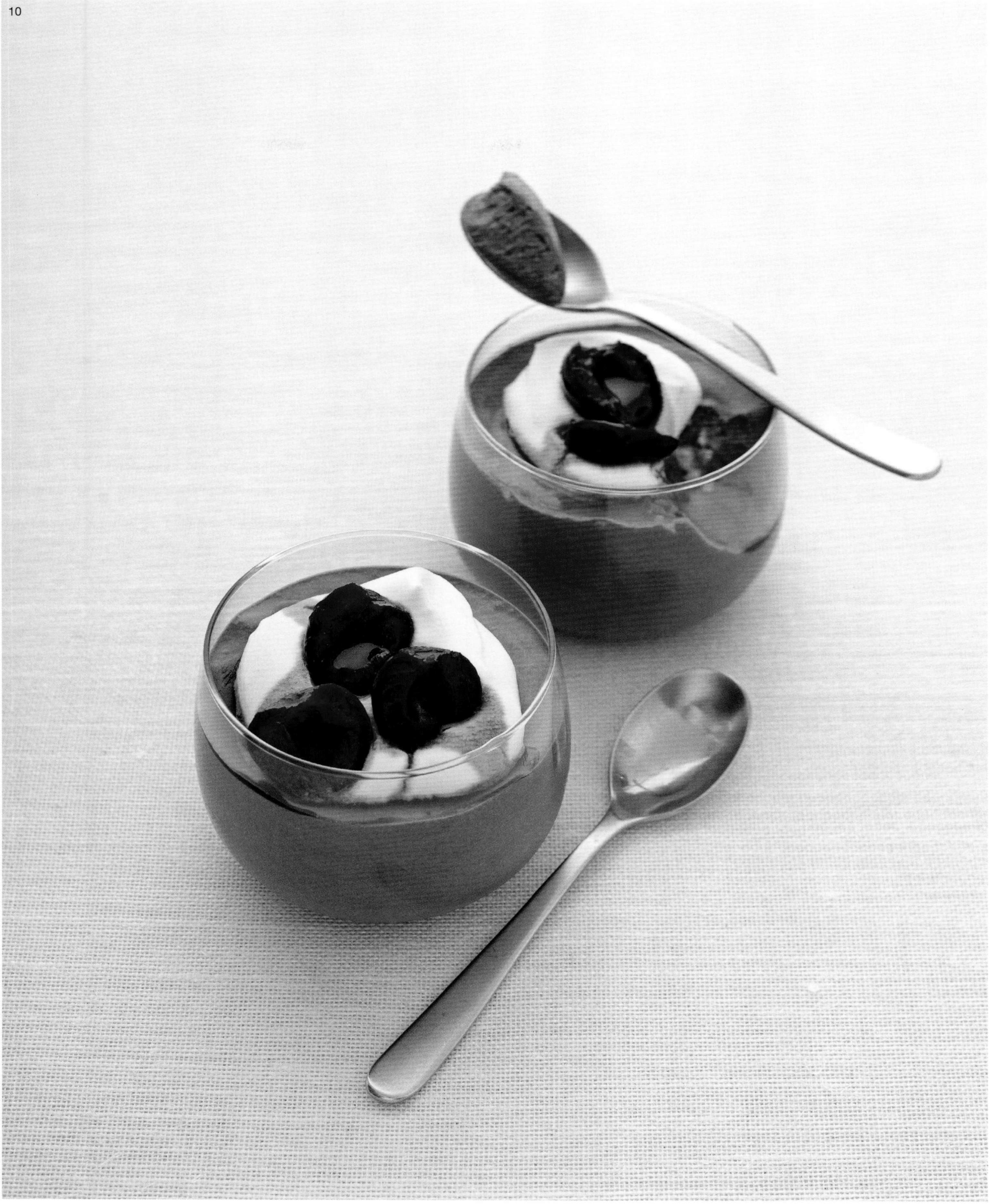

Baking

Butterscotch Banana Bread

Preparation time: 20 minutes,
plus cooling time
Cooking time: 1 hour 10 minutes
Makes 8 slices

This moist, filling quick bread is the
perfect use for bananas going spotty
in the fruit bowl. The frosting isn't
essential, because the bread is also
delicious sliced and buttered, but its
smooth toffee taste is worth trying
at least once.

3 medium, very ripe bananas, total
　peeled weight about 11 oz (300 g)
1½ sticks (175 g) softened unsalted
　butter, plus extra for greasing
¾ cup plus 2 tbsp packed (175 g)
　light brown sugar
½ tsp salt
3 large (UK medium) eggs
1 tsp vanilla extract
¾ cup plus 1 tbsp (100 g) all-
　purpose (plain) flour
1 cup (120 g) whole wheat (whole-
　meal) flour
2 tsp baking powder
½ cup (50 g) chopped walnuts,
　plus extra to decorate if you like
scant ½ cup (100 g) regular (full-fat)
　cream (soft) cheese

1
Rub a little butter over the inside of a 2-lb (900-g) loaf pan measuring 9 x 5 x 3 inches (23 x 13 x 7 cm), then line it with a strip of parchment (baking) paper, leaving some overhang at either end. Preheat oven to 325°F/ 160°C/Gas Mark 3.

2
Peel the bananas and put them into a bowl. Use a fork to mash the fruit to a lumpy pulp.

3
Put the bananas, 1 stick plus ½ tbsp (120 g) of the butter, ½ cup plus 2 tbsp (120 g) of the sugar, the salt, eggs, vanilla, flours, and baking powder into a large bowl, then use an electric mixer to beat the ingredients until smooth.

WHOLE WHEAT FLOUR
This will add a little extra nuttiness and texture to your loaf. If you'd rather use all white flour, that's fine.

4
Stir in the walnuts, then turn the batter into the prepared pan.

5

Bake the loaf for 1 hour 10 minutes, or until risen, golden, and springy to the touch. Test if the cake is done by inserting a toothpick or skewer into the middle of the thickest part. If it comes out clean, the cake is ready. If there are traces of batter, bake for another 10 minutes, then check again. Cool in the pan for 10 minutes, then transfer the loaf to a cooling rack and let cool.

6

While it cools, make the frosting. Put the remaining butter and sugar into a saucepan with 1 tablespoon water. Put it over gentle heat, then wait until the sugar has dissolved. Let the mixture simmer for 3 minutes, until it looks like a silky caramel. Remove from the heat and let cool.

7

Put the cream cheese into a bowl, then add the caramel. Beat or whisk the two together to make a smooth, coffee-colored frosting.

8

Spread the frosting over the cake, then sprinkle with a few more nuts to decorate, if you like.

Pecan Cranberry Pie

Preparation time: 50 minutes, plus
chilling and cooling time
Cooking time: 35 minutes
Cuts into 10 slices

Studded with jewel-like cranberries,
this is a pecan pie fit for any
celebration. The cranberries offer
a welcome tanginess among the
sticky maple and dark sugar filling.

2 cups (200 g) pecan nuts
all-purpose (plain) flour, for dusting
1 quantity sweet shortcrust dough,
    made with all butter (see page
    370), or buy store-bought pie
    dough
3½ tbsp (50 g) unsalted butter
½ cup (120 ml) maple syrup
1 cup packed (200 g) dark brown
    sugar
1 tbsp brandy (optional)
¾ cup (100 g) dried cranberries
salt
1 tsp vanilla extract
2 large (UK medium) eggs
crème fraîche or whipped cream,
    to serve (optional)

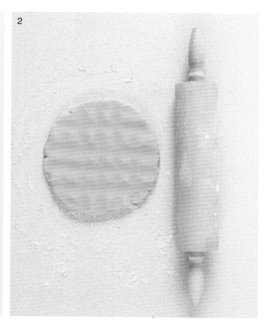

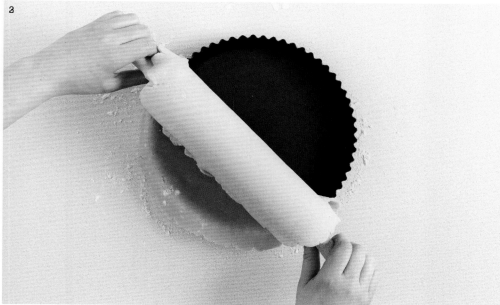

1

Preheat the oven to 400°F/200°C/
Gas Mark 6. Put the pecan nuts into
a baking pan and roast them for
5 minutes, until golden and smelling
toasty. Let cool.

2

Dust the work surface and a rolling
pin with flour. Have ready a 9-inch
(23-cm) loose-bottomed tart pan.
Using the rolling pin, press shallow
ridges evenly across the dough, then
rotate it by a quarter turn. Repeat
this until the dough is about ½ inch
(1 cm) thick. This will help the dough
to stretch without becoming tough.

3

Now roll out the dough. Push the
rolling pin in only one direction,
turning the dough by a quarter
turn every few rolls, until it's about
⅛ inch (3 mm) thick. Using the
rolling pin to help, lift the dough
over the pan.

4

Ease the dough gently into the pan,
then press it gently into the edge
of the pan, using your knuckles or
pinch off a small ball of dough and
use that instead.

5

Trim the top of the dough with a
pair of kitchen scissors so that it
just overhangs the pan or use the
rolling pin method (see page 362).
Lift onto a baking sheet, then chill in
the freezer for 10 minutes (or longer
in the refrigerator if you have time),
until the dough feels firm. Make sure
there's a shelf set in the middle of
the oven.

6

Tear a sheet of parchment (baking) paper large enough to completely cover the tart pan and overhanging dough. Scrunch up the paper, then cover the dough. Cover the paper with a layer of pie weights (baking beans; see page 132), mounding them up a little at the edges.

7

Bake the pastry shell (case), still on its baking sheet, for 15 minutes. Remove the paper and the weights. The pastry should be pale but feel dry and be turning gold at the edges. Turn the oven down to 325°F/160°C/Gas Mark 3. Return to the oven and cook for a further 5–10 minutes until the base is starting to brown. Remove from the oven.

8

While the pastry cooks, make the filling. Reserve 12 of the pecans, then chop the rest fairly finely.

9

Melt the butter in a saucepan, then stir in the maple syrup, dark brown sugar, brandy, cranberries, a pinch of salt, the vanilla extract, and eggs. Beat with a fork until evenly combined. Stir in the chopped pecans.

10

Pour the mixture into the baked pastry shell, then sprinkle the remaining whole pecans over the top. Carefully transfer the pie, still on its sheet, to the oven.

11

Bake for 35 minutes, or until the filling is set around the outside and has just the slightest wobble in the center. If the pastry is going too brown, cover with aluminum foil. Cool the pie completely before taking it out of the pan. Serve in thin slices, with crème fraîche or whipped cream, if you like.

11

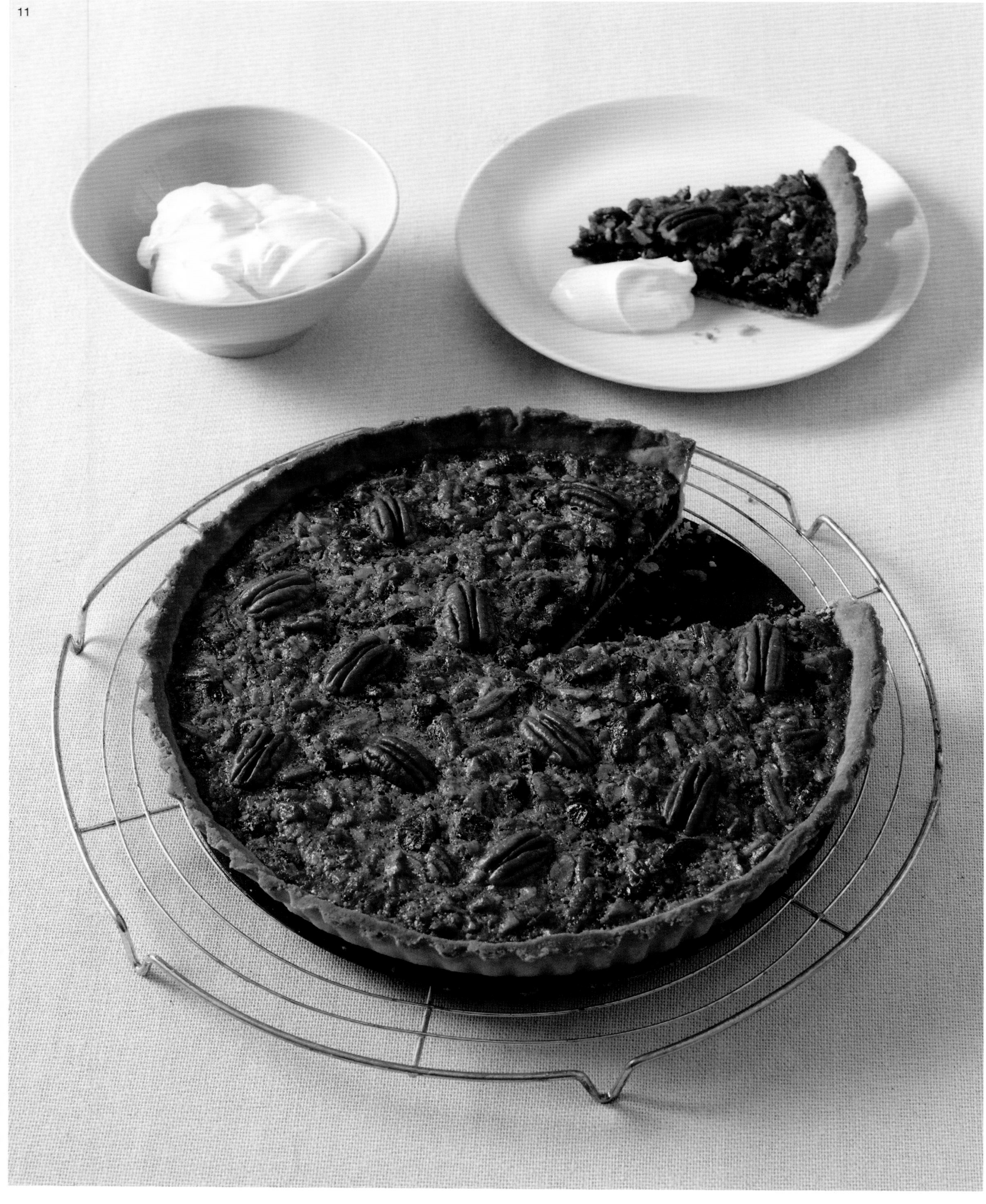

Chocolate Truffle Cake

Preparation time: 30 minutes,
plus cooling time
Cooking time: 35–40 minutes
Cuts into 12 slices

Squishy, dark, and rich, this cake
makes a showstopping birthday
cake. It's perfect for dessert, too.
The sponge cakes can be made
up to 2 days ahead and kept in an
airtight container, if needed.

2 sticks (225 g) softened unsalted
   butter, plus extra for greasing
11 oz (300 g) bittersweet (dark)
   chocolate, 70% cocoa solids
1½ cups (300 g) superfine (caster)
   sugar
4 large (UK medium) eggs
⅔ cup (170 g) buttermilk or plain
   (natural) yogurt
1 tsp vanilla extract
1¼ cups (150 g) self-rising
   (raising) flour
½ tsp baking powder
½ tsp salt, if needed (see page 12)
¼ cup (25 g) unsweetened cocoa
   powder
scant ½ cup (50 g) confectioners'
   (icing) sugar
⅔ cup (150 g) sour cream
   or heavy (double) cream

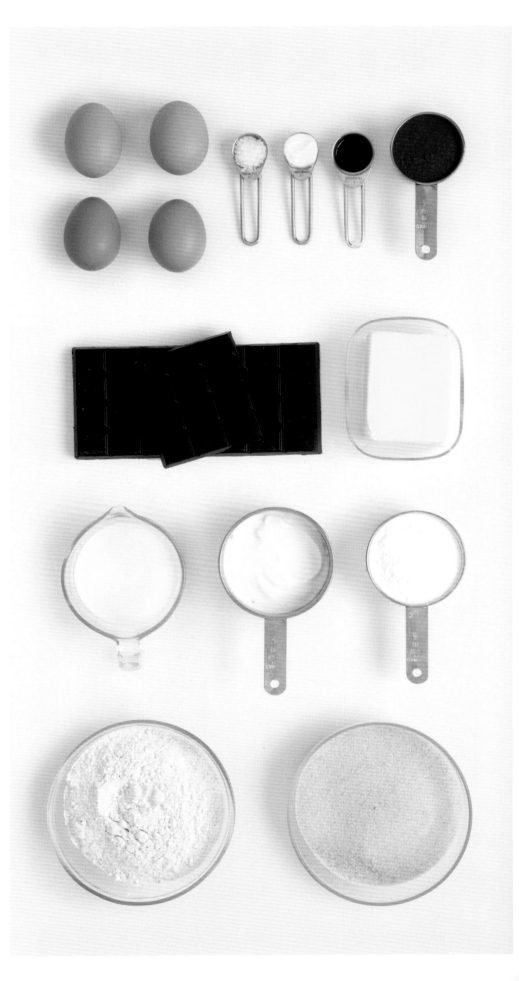

1

Rub a little of the butter around the insides of 2 shallow, round 8-inch (20-cm) cake pans, then line the bottoms with circles of parchment (baking) paper. Preheat the oven to 325°F/160°C/Gas Mark 3.

2

Break the chocolate into squares and put two-thirds (200 g) of it into a heatproof bowl. Put the bowl over a saucepan of barely simmering water, making sure that it does not touch the water, then let the chocolate melt for 5 minutes, stirring once or twice, until smooth throughout. Alternatively, microwave on high in 20-second bursts, stirring each time until smooth.

3

Put 1¾ sticks (200 g) of the butter into a large bowl, then add the superfine (caster) sugar, eggs, buttermilk or yogurt, vanilla, flour, and baking powder (and salt if using UK flour). Sift in the cocoa powder.

4

Using an electric mixer, beat everything together until smooth and creamy. Don't worry if you have any lumps of butter—they'll melt when the warm chocolate goes in.

5

Pour in the melted chocolate and beat again briefly until the batter is even and smooth.

6

Divide the batter equally between the prepared pans. Set aside the chocolate-coated bowl—you'll need it to make the frosting later.

7

Bake the cakes, both on the same shelf, for 35–40 minutes, or until risen in the middle, and a toothpick or skewer inserted into the middle of the cake comes out clean. Cool the cakes in their pans for 20 minutes, then turn them out onto a wire cooling rack to cool completely. The tops of the cakes are delicate, so take care as you do this.

8

While the cakes cool, make the frosting (icing). Put the rest of the chocolate and butter into the reserved bowl and melt together over a saucepan of simmering water, as in step 2.

FROSTING THE SIDES?
To frost the sides as well as the top of the cakes, you will need to increase the quantities for the frosting to: chocolate 5 oz (150 g), butter 3 tbsp (40 g), confectioners' sugar generous ½ cup (75 g), and cream scant 1 cup (225 g).

9

Take the bowl from the heat, sift in the confectioners' (icing) sugar, and add the cream. Stir to a smooth liquid mixture. It will thicken up to a spreading consistency as it cools. Do not chill it.

10

Use a spatula (palette knife) to spread half of the chocolate frosting over one of the sponge cakes.

11

Transfer to a serving plate. Top with the second cake, then spread the rest of the frosting over the top. Cut into slices to serve.

Strawberry Cream Cake

Preparation time: 20 minutes,
plus cooling
Cooking time: 25–30 minutes
Serves 10

This classic strawberry cream cake
has an almost all-in-one method,
and is quick to put together. Sponge
cakes are best enjoyed on the day
they are made, but a vanilla syrup
will help to keep them moist for
a day or two, stored in an airtight
container. For an (almost) classic
British Victoria sponge cake, see
page 399.

2 sticks (225 g) unsalted soft butter,
    plus extra for greasing
1 cup plus 2 tbsp (225 g) superfine
    (caster) sugar, plus an extra 3 tbsp
4 extra-large (UK large) eggs, at
    room temperature
2 tsp vanilla extract
¼ tsp fine salt
1¾ cups plus 1 tbsp (225 g)
    all-purpose (plain) flour
2 tsp baking powder
1 tbsp milk, if needed
10½ oz (300 g) strawberries (2 cups
    prepared)
1 cup (250 ml) whipping or heavy
    (double) cream
a little confectioners' (icing) sugar,
    to serve

1

Lightly butter two 8-inch (20-cm) shallow, round cake pans, then line the bottoms with circles of parchment (baking) paper. Preheat the oven to 350°F/180°F/Gas Mark 4.

2

Put the butter and 1 cup plus 2 tablespoons (225 g) sugar into a large bowl, then beat with an electric mixer until creamy and pale.

3

Add the eggs, 1 teaspoon vanilla, and the salt to the bowl. Mix the flour and baking powder together, then sift on top.

4

Mix again briefly until even and smooth. It's important not to overwork the batter, so stop as soon as everything is incorporated. If the batter seems stiff, add the milk and mix it in.

HOW FLOURS DIFFER
Depending on the kind of wheat used, the climate where you live, or even the brand you buy, flours can be drier or more damp, and this can affect your baking. This kind of cake batter should normally be soft enough to drop from the spoon, without being too stiff or too sloppy (although I've never found the latter to be a problem). Add the extra milk to your batter if you think it looks like it is on the thick side.

5

Use a spatula to scoop the batter evenly into the prepared pans, level the tops, then bake in the center of the oven for 25–30 minutes. If the cakes are cooking unevenly, they can be swapped around in the oven safely after 25 minutes or when evenly risen and firm. Open the door any earlier and the cakes may sink.

6

While you wait, make the vanilla syrup. Put 2 tablespoons sugar and 2 tablespoons water in a small saucepan and heat gently until the sugar dissolves. Take off the heat, then add ½ teaspoon vanilla extract and let cool.

7

When ready, the cakes will be evenly risen through to the middle, evenly golden, and slightly shrunken away from the sides of the pans. To be sure, insert a toothpick or skewer into the middle of one of the cakes. If it comes out clean or with a few damp crumbs, it's ready. If it comes out with any raw mixture, return to the oven for another 5 minutes.

8
Let the cakes cool in their pans for 15 minutes, then remove from the pans, peel away the lining paper and turn them onto a cooling rack, top side down and resting on the upturned parchment paper. This will stop the wires making marks in the tops of the cakes. Poke the upturned cakes all over with a skewer or cocktail stick, then spoon over the cooled syrup.

9
While you wait for the cakes to cool completely, coarsely chop half of the strawberries. Thinly slice the rest.

VICTORIA SPONGE
To make a classic British Victoria sponge cake (well, almost classic, because the true recipe has to adhere to some strict rules!), simply sandwich the sponge cakes with raspberry jam or preserves. You can add buttercream, if you like. Sprinkle the top of the cake with a little superfine sugar.

10
Pour the cream into a large bowl and add the rest of the vanilla, and the remaining 1 tablespoon sugar. Whip until thickened but not stiff.

11
Stir the chopped strawberries into the cream. Put one cake onto a serving plate, then spread with the strawberry cream.

12
Put the second cake on top, press it down a little, then top with the sliced strawberries. Dust with confectioners' (icing) sugar to serve.

Golden Citrus Drizzle Cake

Preparation time: 15 minutes
Baking time: 35 minutes
Makes 12 large squares,
or more fingers

In my experience, a citrus drizzle cake always disappears first from the table at a fête or bake sale, so I've re-created it as a square cake that's easy to make, slice, and transport. Corn flour (finely ground cornmeal) adds a golden glow to the inside, but if you prefer you can substitute the same amount of all-purpose (plain) flour.

For the cake

2 sticks (225 g) soft butter, plus
   extra for greasing
2 lemons
2 limes
1 tangerine, mandarin, or clemen-
   tine, with a vibrant orange skin
1 cup (200 g) superfine (caster)
   sugar
4 large (UK medium) eggs, room
   temperature
1 cup (125 g) all-purpose (plain) flour
1 cup (125 g) corn flour (finely
   ground cornmeal)
¼ tsp salt
2 tsp baking powder
½ cup (125 g) lemon-flavored or
   plain (natural) yogurt

For the topping

½ cup (100 g) superfine (caster)
   sugar, or granulated for extra
   crunch

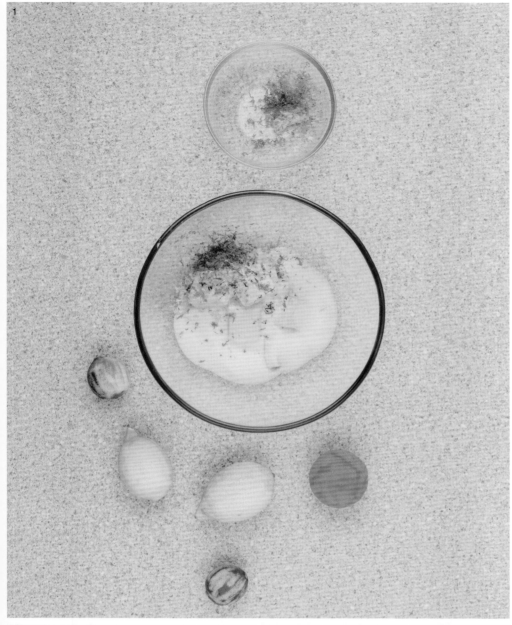

1

Preheat the oven to 350°F/180°F/ Gas Mark 4. Grease a 9-inch (23-cm) shallow square baking pan with butter, then line it with parchment (baking) paper. Finely grate the zest from all the fruit, taking care not to remove the bitter white pith just underneath the colorful outer layer. Put 2 teaspoons of the mixed zests into a large bowl with the butter and sugar, saving the rest for later.

LOVE LEMONS? LIME-AHOLIC?
For a straight-up lemon cake or lime cake, simply use the zest and juice from one kind of fruit (you'll need 4 teaspoons zest and ⅓ cup/80 ml juice). I find all orange a too sweet for a drizzle cake, so add a little lemon juice and zest for extra bite.

2

Using an electric mixer, beat the butter and sugar together until creamy and pale. Scrape the sides of the bowl down every now and again with a spatula, so that everything gets mixed.

3

Add one egg to the bowl, then beat it into the creamed mixture until completely combined, fluffy, and light. Add the rest of the eggs one by one, beating well each time. If the mixture starts to look at all slimy, add 1 tablespoon of the flour and it will become smooth again.

MAKE IT BIGGER
To make a sheet cake (traybake), grease and line a 9 x 13-inch (23 x 33-cm) traybake pan and double the quantities. Bake at 350°F/180°C/ Gas Mark 4 for 25 minutes, then at 325°F/160°C/Gas Mark 3 for 25 minutes, or until a toothpick or skewer comes out clean. Double the drizzle quantities, too.

4

Thoroughly mix together the flour, corn flour (cornmeal), salt, and baking powder, then sift half of it on top of the egg mixture. Using a spatula (palette knife) or a large metal spoon, fold it in until the batter is thick and fairly smooth.

5

Fold in the yogurt in the same way, then sift over and fold in the remaining dry ingredients. Scrape the batter into the prepared pan, level the top, then give it a sharp tap on the work surface to help remove any bubbles that can appear in this cake. Bake for 20 minutes, or until it is golden and has risen all over, then turn the oven down to 325°F/160°/Gas Mark 3. If it's browning too much on one side, quickly and carefully turn it around. Bake for another 15 minutes, or until firm to the touch and a toothpick or skewer inserted into the middle of the cake comes out clean, or with a few damp crumbs. Let cool in the pan on a wire rack for 30 minutes or until warm.

6

Meanwhile, squeeze the juice from 1 lemon, 1 lime, and half the tangerine, to make about ⅓ cup (80 ml). Poke 20 or so holes all over the cake using a fine skewer or a toothpick. Mix the sugar for the topping into the juice (do not let it dissolve), add any leftover zest, then spoon evenly over the surface of the still-warm cake.

7

Let cool completely. The sugar will become crisp and sparkly once the syrup soaks into the cake. Cut into squares to serve. If making the cake a day ahead, store it loosely covered or in a roomy container with a little air for breathing. This will keep the sugary crust crisp.

Peanut Butter Cookies

Preparation time: 15 minutes
Baking time: 10–12 minutes per batch
Makes 18

These have everything I look for in a peanut butter cookie: a slightly soft inside, a crisp outside, and a salty sweetness that means one is never enough. Like most homemade cookies, they are best eaten on the day of baking—no real hardship there! There's a make-ahead option if you prefer; see page 408.

1 cup (150 g) whole unsalted roasted peanuts, or see note
1½ cups (185 g) all-purpose (plain) flour
½ tsp baking powder
⅓ cup packed (65 g) light brown sugar
⅓ cup (65 g) superfine (caster) sugar
½ tsp salt
1 stick (110 g) butter, at room temperature
generous ⅓ cup (100 g) smooth peanut butter
1 large (UK medium) egg
3 tbsp honey

1

1
Preheat the oven to 350°F/180°C/
Gas Mark 4. Spread the nuts over
a baking sheet and cook for about
8 minutes, or until pale golden.
This step isn't essential if you're in
a hurry, but it adds an extra deep,
nutty flavor.

CAN'T FIND UNSALTED PEANUTS?
You could also use salted roasted
nuts (the snacking kind) for this
recipe. Skip straight to step 2
and add only a pinch of salt to
the dough instead of ½ teaspoon.

2

Chop the nuts with a knife, or use
a food processor until chunky.

3
Put the flour, baking powder, sugars,
and salt into a large bowl and mix
together. Cut the butter into cubes
and add it to the bowl with the
peanut butter.

3

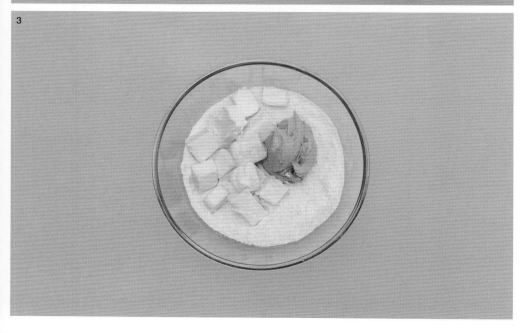

4

Rub the peanut butter and butter into the dry ingredients using your fingers and thumbs. To do this, use both hands to lift some of the butter, peanut butter and flour from the bowl. Gently pinch the butters and flour together as they pass through your fingers back into the bowl. Keep going, and eventually you will have a mixture that looks like fine crumbs. You can do this with a food processor, if you prefer. Beat the egg. Add two-thirds of the chopped toasted peanuts to the mixture, then the egg and honey.

5

Mix everything together with a blunt table knife or wooden spoon to make a rough, fairly sticky dough. Try not to overwork it, because this can make your cookies tough.

MAKE AHEAD
You can shape the dough into 2 logs about 3 inches (7.5 cm) across, roll each one in the nuts (chopped a little finer), then wrap tightly in plastic wrap (clingfilm) and chill or freeze. Slice and bake the cookies as you need them.

6

Line 2 flat baking sheets with parchment (baking) paper. Pinch off a walnut-sized ball of dough and roll it between your palms until smooth. Press the ball into the remaining chopped nuts, squishing it to a flatter disk. Place nut side up on the baking sheet, then repeat. Leave plenty of space between the cookies.

7

Bake for 10–12 minutes (13 minutes from frozen), or until evenly golden. Prepare the next batch of cookies while the first one bakes. Let cool on the baking sheets for a few minutes, then transfer to a rack to cool completely. Store in an airtight container and eat within 3 days.

Chocolate Chip Cookies

Preparation time: 20 minutes
Cooking time: 12 minutes per batch
Makes 18 cookies

If you like your cookies crisp, chewy, and full of chocolate pieces, then this recipe is for you. The basic cookie dough is a good all-round mix that you can adapt with lemon zest, raisins, chopped nuts, or whatever you like. For a sustaining chewy oat version, see the variation on page 412.

---

5 oz (150 g) chocolate (made up of milk, bittersweet/dark, or white, or a mixture of all three)

1 stick plus 2 tbsp (140 g) soft unsalted butter

1 cup (200 g) superfine (caster) sugar

1 large (UK medium) egg

1 tsp vanilla extract

2 cups (250 g) self-rising (raising) flour

¼ tsp salt, if needed (see page 12)

1
Coarsely chop the chocolate on a cutting (chopping) board.

2
Line 2 baking sheets with parchment (baking) paper and preheat the oven to 400°F/200°C/Gas Mark 6. Put the butter and sugar into a large bowl. Use an electric mixer to beat the butter and sugar together until pale and creamy. Separate the egg (see page 343), then add the yolk and the vanilla extract to the bowl. Lightly beat the white with a fork to break it up, then add 1 tablespoon to the bowl.

3
Beat the contents of the bowl together for a few seconds until creamy. Add the flour (and salt if using UK flour), then stir in with a spatula or wooden spoon. The mix will seem stiff, but that's fine.

4

Using a spatula, fold in the chopped chocolate. Be careful not to overwork the dough.

5

Roll the cookie dough into 18 or 20 rough walnut-sized balls and put them onto the prepared baking sheets. The mix spreads a lot as it cooks, so make sure the cookies will have enough room.

6

Bake the cookies one sheet at a time for 12 minutes, or until risen and golden at the edges with pale cracks. Remove from the oven, then give the baking sheet a sharp tap on the work surface. The cookies will deflate.

Let the cookies cool on their baking sheets until firm, then lift onto wire racks to cool completely, using a spatula (palette knife). Keep the cookies in an airtight container for up to 3 days.

GINGER OAT COOKIES
Add a total of 2 tablespoons egg white to the mixture after adding the yolk. Instead of the chocolate, stir in 2 teaspoons ground ginger, 2 finely chopped balls of preserved (stem) ginger from a jar, and a ½ cup (50 g) rolled (porridge) oats.

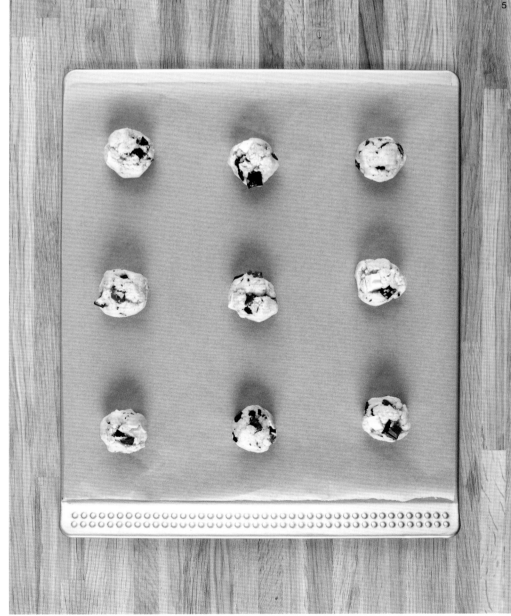

Iced Gingerbread Cookies

Preparation time: 20 minutes,
plus firming
Baking time: 9–11 minutes per batch
Makes about 14 gingerbread men,
or 24 smaller shapes

These fun little cookies are perfect for baking with children, because the dough can handle plenty of squishing and rolling without becoming tough. The level of spice should please adult tastebuds, too. For a darker color and bittersweet flavor, replace the golden syrup or corn syrup with molasses or black treacle.

For the cookies

1 stick (110 g) butter, plus extra for
   greasing
1 cup packed (200 g) dark brown
   sugar
⅓ cup (100 g) golden syrup, such
   as Lyle's—or use corn syrup
1 large (UK medium) egg
2¾ cups (350 g) all-purpose (plain)
   flour, plus extra for rolling
1 tsp baking (bicarbonate of) soda
1 tbsp ground ginger
2 tsp ground cinnamon
¼ tsp salt

To decorate

1 egg or 2–3 tbsp lemon juice
   (see note)
1⅔ cups (200 g) confectioners'
   (icing) sugar
dragees or sparkles (optional)

1
Put the butter, brown sugar, and syrup into a large saucepan, then gently heat until the butter has melted. Beat the egg.

2
Let cool for 5 minutes, then beat the egg into the pan. Mix the flour, baking (bicarbonate of) soda, spices, and salt, then sift into the pan. Stir together to make a shiny dough.

3
Turn out the dough onto the work surface, split it in half, then knead briefly to make 2 smooth balls. Squash into flat disks, wrap well in plastic wrap (clingfilm), then chill in the refrigerator until firm (this will take about 2 hours, or you can leave it overnight).

4
When ready to bake, grease 2 baking sheets with a little butter, then line with parchment (baking) paper. Preheat the oven to 350°F/180°F/Gas Mark 4. Lightly flour the work surface and use a rolling pin to roll the dough out so it's about ⅛ inch (3 mm) thick. Cut out shapes and carefully lift them onto the lined sheets, giving each one plenty of space. Squash together, reroll, and cut out the scraps (trimmings). You'll find the cookies come out of the cutter cleanly, if you dip the cutter in a little flour first.

5

For softer cookies, bake them for 9 minutes, or until golden all over (they will rise a little in the oven, then flatten out), or for cookies with snap, bake for 11 minutes or until a little darker. Let cool for 5 minutes on the baking sheet, then transfer to a wire rack to cool completely. Reuse the sheets for the rest of the dough.

TREE DECORATIONS

To make your cookies into Christmas tree decorations, punch a hole in the cooked dough (while still hot) using a small pastry (piping bag) tip (nozzle), or something like a pointy chopstick. Take care when handling the hot dough. Cool, then thread with ribbon to hang from the tree.

6

To make the icing, separate the egg (see page 343) and put the white in a clean bowl. Sift the confectioners' (icing) sugar on top, stir it in slowly at first to incorporate, then beat well until smooth. Either drizzle teaspoons of the icing over your cookies to decorate, or spoon into a disposable pastry bag or a food storage bag, snip off the end, and use it to pipe patterns. Decorate with dragees or sparkles, if you like.

ROYAL ICING

Icing made with egg white is known as royal icing. It is bright white and sets firmly. You can use store-bought pasteurized egg whites if you are concerned about using raw eggs, or replace the egg white with lemon juice instead. Start with 2 tbsp, then add more, if needed.

7

Let the icing set for about 1 hour, or until firm and dry, before eating, hanging on the tree, or packing into an airtight container.

Rocky Road

Preparation time: 10 minutes,
plus setting time
Makes 16 squares

OK, this isn't strictly speaking
baking, but I couldn't leave out
such an all-round people-pleaser
of a recipe. I use ginger cookies
(biscuits) in my rocky road, which
give it a spicy edge, but any crunchy
cookie will do, such as graham
crackers (digestives), or even Oreos
for a double chocolate hit.

---

4 tbsp (55 g) butter, plus extra for
    greasing
14 oz (400 g) bittersweet (dark)
    chocolate, around 60% cocoa
    solids
2 tbsp golden syrup, such as Lyle's,
    or use corn syrup
a pinch of salt
1 cup (125 g) mixed nuts
6 oz (175 g) crunchy cookies
    (biscuits) (about 1½ cups
    prepared)
1½ cups (100 g) marshmallows
generous ½ cup (85 g) plump
    raisins, or other dried fruit, such as
    chopped dried apricots
1 tbsp confectioners' (icing) sugar

1
Use a little butter to grease a
9-inch (23-cm) shallow square pan
or brownie pan, then line it with
parchment (baking) paper. To melt
the chocolate, first half-fill a medium
saucepan with water and bring it
to a simmer. Break the chocolate
into squares and cut the butter into
pieces, then put them into a large
heatproof bowl. Sit the bowl over
the pan of water, making sure that
the bowl doesn't touch the water.
(This is sometimes called a bain-
marie or double boiler.)

CHOOSING CHOCOLATE
If you can't find 60% cocoa content
chocolate, a mix of half 70% cocoa
and half 50% cocoa is fine.

2
With the pan over very low heat,
let the chocolate and butter melt
together, stirring now and again,
until smooth and silky. Now stir in
the syrup and salt and take the bowl
off the heat.

3
While you wait for the chocolate
to melt, coarsely chop any larger
nuts (such as brazils, if there are
some in your mix). Crush or break
the cookies into smaller chunks.
Snip the marshmallows in half.

4

Scoop about ½ cup (8 tablespoons) of the chocolate from the bowl and set aside. Toss all of the cookie chunks, nuts, marshmallows, and raisins, or whatever you are using, into the rest of the chocolate and stir well with a spatula (palette knife) until everything is well coated.

5

Spread the rocky road mixture into the pan, then spoon the reserved chocolate over the mixture to cover. It won't be perfectly smooth, but that's all part of the charm.

6

Let the rocky road chill in the refrigerator for about 3 hours, or longer if you like, until very firm. Remove from the pan, peel off the paper from the edges, cut into squares, and dust with the confectioners' (icing) sugar.

7

Store in the refrigerator or a cool place for up to 3 days.

TURKISH ROAD
Swap half the marshmallows for pieces of Turkish delight.

ROMAN ROAD
For an Italian panforte-inspired twist, replace half the raisins with finely chopped candied (crystallized) orange peel. Use amaretti cookies and add 1 teaspoon ground cinnamon and ½ teaspoon ground nutmeg, plus a pinch of ground cloves, if you like.

Fruit Scones

Preparation time: 15 minutes
Baking time: 12 minutes
Makes 10

A perfectly fluffy scone is a simple
pleasure: quick and thrifty to make,
but so delicious, especially when
served just warm with a thick cream
or butter and a good dollop of
jelly (jam) or lemon curd. The most
important thing to remember is
not to knead the dough, which will
quickly make your scones heavy.

3¼ cups (400 g) all-purpose (plain)
  flour, plus extra for dusting
2 tsp baking powder
¼ tsp baking (bicarbonate of) soda
¼ tsp salt
1 stick (110 g) cold butter
⅓ cup (60 g) superfine
  (caster) sugar
½ cup (85 g) golden raisins
  (sultanas) or your choice of
  dried fruit (optional)
scant 1 cup (225 ml) milk
2 tsp lemon juice
1 tsp vanilla extract
1 large (UK medium) egg

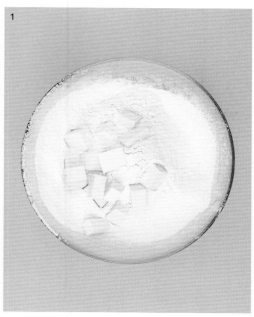

1
Preheat the oven to 450°F/220°C/
Gas Mark 7. Put a large baking
sheet in the oven to heat up. Mix
the flour, baking powder, baking
(bicarbonate of) soda, and salt, then
sift into a large bowl. Cut the butter
into cubes and add it to the bowl.

2
Rub the cold butter into the flour
until it looks like fine bread crumbs.
If you have a food processor, simply
process the butter into the dry
ingredients instead, then tip into
a large bowl.

COLD BUTTER
Fluffy, light scones need to be made
with really cold butter. If it's a hot
day and the butter begins to feel
greasy as you rub it in, put the bowl
into the refrigerator for 10 minutes
before continuing.

3
Stir in the sugar and the dried fruit,
if you're using it. I've made this a
separate step, because I've forgotten
to add the sugar so many times when
making scones, and I'm determined
that you won't do the same!

4
Heat the milk in a small saucepan
(or in the microwave) until warm, then
add the lemon juice and vanilla. Let
sit for a few minutes until it turns a
little lumpy. Beat the egg, then add
2 tablespoons of it to the lumpy milk
mixture. Set the rest of the egg aside.

MILK OR BUTTERMILK?
Souring the milk lightens the dough
by activating the baking soda and
boosting the rise. You can add ¾ cup
(185 g) buttermilk or yogurt instead,
and loosen with 4 tablespoons milk.
Omit the lemon juice, but still use
the egg.

5

Pour the sour milk evenly over the dry ingredients, working it into the flour with a spatula (palette knife). Keep mixing until all the liquid is incorporated and you have a soft, rough dough. Don't worry if you miss a few crumbs at the bottom of the bowl; it's best not to overmix it.

6

Flour your hands and the work surface thoroughly. Turn the dough out onto it and sprinkle a little flour on top. Fold the dough over itself a couple of times just to smooth it a little (it's essential not to overwork it), then pat it into a 1.5-inch (3-cm) thick round. Try to make sure the smoothest part of the dough ends up being the top.

7

Using a 2½-inch (6-cm) round cookie cutter, cut out 6 scones. Dip the cutter into some flour between each cut to stop it from sticking. Don't twist the cutter in the dough—the aim is to have a good, clean cut. Carefully press the remaining dough together and cut out the rest; remember not to overwork it.

8

Brush the tops of the scones with some of the remaining egg.

9

Remove the hot baking sheet from the oven and sprinkle it with flour. Carefully place the scones on it, spacing them out evenly. The heat will give the scones a head start.

10

Bake for 12 minutes, or until the scones are golden and well risen, and sound hollow when tapped on the bottom. You may need to turn the sheet after 8 minutes to be sure of an even color. Cool on a wire rack. For a softer crust, wrap in a clean, dry dish (tea) towel before cooling.

Malted Milk Chocolate Birthday Cake

Preparation time: 30 minutes
Baking time: 30 minutes
Makes 16 generous or
32 small pieces

There can be a lot of pressure to provide a homemade birthday cake that everyone will enjoy. This no-stress sheet cake (traybake) keeps well if you want to get ahead, and is deliciously chocolaty but not too rich. It's easily cut into squares once the candles have been blown out.

For the cake

1¼ sticks (140 g) soft butter

2¾ cups (350 g) all-purpose (plain) flour

¼ cup (25 g) unsweetened cocoa powder

2 tbsp malted milk powder, such as Horlicks

1 tsp baking (bicarbonate of) soda

2 tsp baking powder

¼ tsp salt

1½ cups packed (300 g) light brown sugar

1¼ cups (300 ml) milk

⅔ cup (150 ml) vegetable oil

1 tsp vanilla extract

For the frosting

7 oz (200 g) semisweet (dark) chocolate, about 50% cocoa solids

½ cup (120 ml) milk

¼ cup (25 g) unsweetened cocoa powder

2 tbsp malted milk powder

1¼ sticks (140 g) soft butter

2 cups (250 g) confectioners' (icing) sugar

a handful of chocolate candies

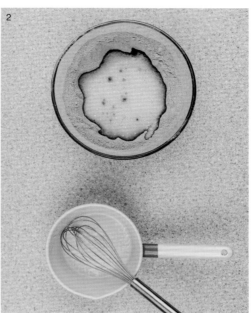

1

Preheat the oven to 350°F/180°C/Gas Mark 4. Make the cake batter first. Put the butter into a saucepan and melt it gently. Using a pastry brush, use a little of the butter to grease a 9 x 13-inch (23 x 33-cm) baking pan. Line the pan with parchment (baking) paper.

2

Put the flour, cocoa, malted milk powder, baking (bicarbonate of) soda, baking powder, and salt into a large bowl and use a whisk to mix and aerate. Add the sugar and break up any lumps with your fingers. Make a well in the center of the dry ingredients. Whisk the milk, oil, and vanilla into the melted butter and pour them into the well.

3

Use the whisk to draw the flour mixture into the liquid, slowly at first. Once mixed, beat until smooth and evenly blended. Pour into the prepared pan and level the top.

4

Bake for 30 minutes, until the cake has risen, is firm, and has slightly shrunken from the sides. A toothpick or skewer inserted into the center should come out clean. Let cool in the pan for 10 minutes, then turn out onto a cooling rack and cool completely.

5

For the frosting, break the chocolate into a heatproof bowl and place it over a saucepan of barely simmering water, making sure the bowl doesn't touch the water. Let the chocolate melt for about 5 minutes, stirring once or twice, until smooth. Alternatively, microwave in 20-second bursts, stirring each time. Let cool a little.

NO EGGS?
This cake is egg-free.

6

Heat the milk in a small saucepan or the microwave until steaming hot. Sift the cocoa and malted milk powder into a large bowl, then slowly stir in the hot milk to make a smooth paste. Let cool for a few minutes.

7

Now add the butter to the paste, sift in the confectioners' (icing) sugar, and beat together with an electric mixer until creamy. Follow with the melted, cooled chocolate to make a silky, soft frosting.

8

Transfer the cooled cake to a board or large, flat plate, then spread the frosting all over it. It will firm a little as it cools, so try to create your swoops and swirls fairly quickly.

9

Sprinkle the cake with the candies (sweets) and top with colored candles. Let the frosting set for a little while if you can, although it's delicious (if a little more messy) eaten immediately, too. The cake can be made up to 2 days in advance and kept in a cool place, well wrapped, or, if frosted, loosely covered on its board.

FLAG CAKE
For all the patriotic types out there, how about arranging the decorations in the colors of your national flag?

HALLOWEEN CAKE
Choose insect candies and other gruesome things to top the cake, or stand long, thin cookies up in the frosting to look like gravestones.

EASTER CAKE
Sprinkle the frosting with pastel-colored mini chocolate eggs.

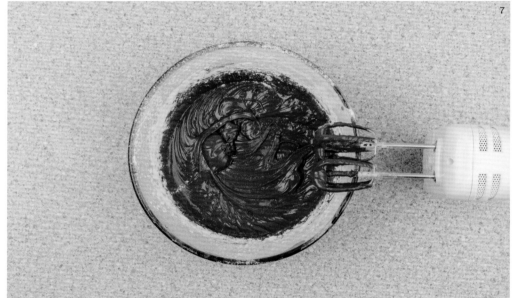

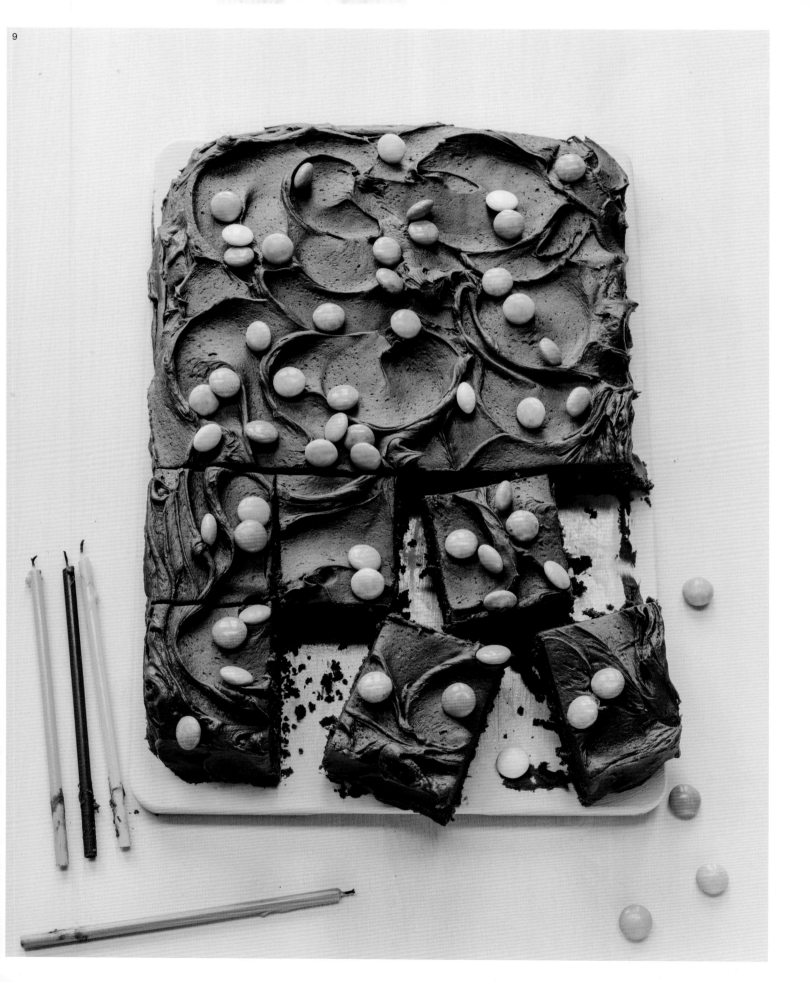

Cherry-Almond Streusel Slice

Preparation time: 20 minutes, or longer if you make your own dough
Baking time: 40–45 minutes
Cuts into 15 or 18 bars

Cherries and almonds are a classic pairing, but I've tried this with raspberries, sliced apple, and chunks of stone fruit (such as apricots or peach), too, each with great results. The contrast between the rich almond cake, pastry, and fruit is what makes this irresistible.

For the crust and streusel topping
1 quantity sweet shortcrust dough, made with all butter (see page 370 and note), or use 12 oz (350 g) store-bought dough
all-purpose (plain) flour, for rolling

For the cake layer
1½ cups (200 g) whole cherries, or 1 cup (150 g) pitted (stoned), fresh, canned, or defrosted
1¾ sticks (200 g) soft butter
1 cup (200 g) superfine (caster) sugar
4 large (UK medium) eggs
½–1 tsp almond extract (to taste)
1 cup (100 g) almond meal (ground almonds)
½ cup (65 g) all-purpose (plain) flour
½ tsp baking powder
¼ tsp salt
½ cup (150 g) cherry or raspberry jelly (jam)
a handful of slivered (flaked) almonds

For the icing (optional)
generous ½ cup (75 g) confectioners' (icing) sugar
2–3 tsp lemon juice

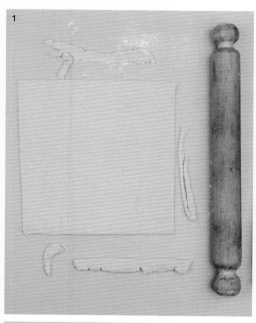

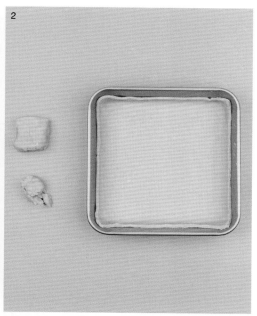

1

Preheat the oven to 350°F/180°C/ Gas Mark 4 and put a flat baking sheet in the oven to heat up. Cut one-sixth of the dough from the block and set it aside in the refrigerator—this will be used for the topping later. Roll out the rest on a lightly floured surface until it is just bigger than the bottom of a 9-inch (23-cm) shallow square pan, then trim it to neaten the edges. Keep any scraps (trimmings) to use later, and chill these, too.

ALL-BUTTER PASTRY
For a deliciously buttery crust you can use a total of 1 stick plus 1 tbsp (120 g) butter to make the dough on page 370, instead of the butter and vegetable shortening (fat).

2

Push the dough into the pan, letting it come a little way up the sides to make a rim of about ½ inch (1 cm). If the dough rips at all, just gently pinch it back together.

3

Remove the pits (stones) from the cherries, if using fresh, and cut them in half. To make the cake layer, put the butter and sugar into a large bowl and beat together until creamy and paler. Don't worry about incorporating too much air— a wooden spoon is fine. Add the eggs, almond extract (use the full 1 teaspoon if you like your cakes really almondy), and almond meal (ground almonds), then beat until everything is combined.

4

Mix the flour, baking powder, and salt in a bowl, then sift it onto the batter. Stir it in until smooth.

5

Spread the jelly (jam) over the dough, then spread the cake batter on top. It doesn't matter if some of it spills over the top of the dough and touches the side of the pan.

6

Sprinkle the prepared fruit over the cake batter, then tear the reserved pastry and scraps over it to make a streusel top. Sprinkle with the slivered (flaked) almonds. Carefully slide the pan onto the baking sheet in the oven. This will give a boost of heat to the bottom of the pan, helping the pastry crust to cook thoroughly.

7

Bake for 40–45 minutes, or until the cake has risen to the center, is firm, and a deep, glowing gold. Let cool in the pan. Once cooled, top with the icing. Sift the confectioners' (icing) sugar and slowly stir in enough lemon juice to make a smooth, flowing icing, then drizzle it liberally over the cake, letting it run off the spoon.

8

Let the icing set, then cut into 15 or 18 bars. Keep in an airtight container in a cool place for up to 3 days.

BAKEWELL TART
For bakers with a taste for British classics, line a 9-inch (23-cm) fluted tart pan with the dough, taking it right to the top of the pan (see page 362 for how to line a pan with pastry). Fill with the jelly, batter, and fruit, then sprinkle with the almonds. Bake as above, then drizzle with the icing and cut into wedges when cooled. Use halved candied (glacé) cherries instead of fresh fruit for the full effect.

Carrot Cake with Cream Cheese Frosting

Preparation time: 30 minutes
Baking time: 30–35 minutes
Makes 12 slices

Carrot cake is perfect as a first cake to make, because it's not only tasty, but also less likely to overcook and be dry, thanks to the water content in the carrots. If you'd like to make the cake in squares or cupcakes instead of layers, see the variations on page 436.

For the cake

1 cup (100 g) pecans

¾ cup plus 1½ tbsp (200 ml) vegetable oil, plus extra for greasing

2 cups (250 g) all-purpose (plain) flour

2 tsp baking powder

½ tsp baking (bicarbonate of) soda

2 tsp pumpkin pie spice (ground mixed spice); see note

½ tsp salt

1 cup packed (200 g) light brown sugar

1 orange

3 large (UK medium) eggs

5 (300 g) carrots (2¼ cups/250 g grated)

½ cup (85 g) raisins

For the frosting

1¾ sticks (200 g) soft butter

1¾ cups (400 g) regular (full-fat) cream (soft) cheese, cold

½ tsp vanilla extract

1 scant cup (100 g) confectioners' (icing) sugar

1
Preheat the oven to 350°F/180°C/ Gas Mark 4. Spread the nuts over a baking sheet and cook for 8–10 minutes, or until golden and toasty. Cool, then coarsely chop. Toasting nuts will add an extra depth of flavor, but if you're in a hurry, just chop the nuts and use them as they are.

2
While you wait, get everything else ready. Grease two 8-inch (20-cm) shallow, round pans with removable bottoms with a little oil, then line the bottoms with parchment (baking) paper. Mix the flour, baking powder, baking (bicarbonate of) soda, spices, and salt, then sift into a large bowl. Add the sugar and work it in with your fingers, breaking up any larger lumps, until evenly blended. Finely grate the zest of the orange into the bowl. Squeeze the juice.

HOW TO MIX YOUR SPICES
For a simple homemade pumpkin pie spice (ground mixed spice), combine 1 tablespoon ground cinnamon, 2 teaspoons ground ginger, ½ teaspoon each ground nutmeg and allspice, and ¼ teaspoon ground cloves if you have them. You'll have plenty left over.

3
Crack the eggs into a measuring cup (jug) with the oil, add 2 tablespoons orange juice, and beat together.

4
Trim, then coarsely grate the carrots. Pour the oil mixture into the dry ingredients and beat until smooth. Add most of the nuts, then the carrots and raisins, and stir until evenly blended. If the batter seems stiff, add another 1 tablespoon orange juice. Divide the batter between the prepared pans.

5

Bake for 30–35 minutes, or until the cakes are golden and have risen, and a toothpick or skewer inserted into the center comes out clean. Cool in the pans on a rack for 10 minutes, then turn out of the pans. Poke holes all over the cakes, and drizzle with a little orange juice. Cool completely.

6

To make the frosting, put the soft butter into a large bowl and beat well until creamy and totally smooth. Add the cream cheese and vanilla and beat until smooth and evenly blended. Now sift in the confectioners' (icing) sugar and work it in gently with a spatula.

FOR PERFECT FROSTING

The butter and cream cheese must be the correct temperatures, or the frosting can end up lumpy. If that happens, pass it through a sieve and no one will know. Do not overwork it once the sugar has been added, because this can loosen the texture.

7

On a serving plate, sandwich the cakes with a third of the frosting, spreading with a spatula (palette knife). Spread the remaining frosting over the top and the sides.

8

Sprinkle the reserved pecans over the top. The cake benefits from a little while in the refrigerator to settle. If it's a hot day, keep it there until you are ready to slice it.

CARROT SHEET CAKE (TRAYBAKE)

Use a 9 x 13-inch (23 x 33-cm) pan and bake for 40 minutes, or until a toothpick or skewer comes out clean. Frost, then cut into squares.

CARROT CUPCAKES

Also makes 18 cupcakes. Bake for 20–25 minutes, then cool and frost.

Fudgy Cheesecake Brownies

Preparation time: 20 minutes
Baking time: 30–35 minutes
Makes 16

A swirl of cheesecake topping gives these brownies a different look, and a delicious, creamy contrast to the dark fudginess beneath. Prefer a simple brownie? Just leave out the cheesecake topping and jump to step 8. And yes, the batter will give that shiny, papery crust we all love. Turn the page for more flavor options.

For the brownies

1¾ sticks (200 g) butter, plus extra for greasing

7 oz (200 g) bittersweet (dark) chocolate, about 60% cocoa solids (see note)

4 large (UK medium) eggs

1½ cups (300 g) superfine (caster) sugar

1 cup (125 g) all-purpose (plain) flour

½ cup (50 g) unsweetened cocoa powder

½ tsp salt

For the cheesecake topping

generous ¾ cup (200 g) regular (full-fat) cream (soft) cheese, room temperature

1 large (UK medium) egg

2 tbsp superfine (caster) sugar

1 tsp vanilla extract

1

Grease a 9-inch (23-cm) shallow square cake pan with a little butter, then line it with parchment (baking) paper. Preheat the oven to 350°F/180°C/Gas Mark 4. Make the brownie batter first. Melt the butter in a medium saucepan. While you wait, break the chocolate into pieces, then add them to the melted butter and take the pan off the heat.

CHOCOLATE IN COOKING
A good-quality 70% cocoa chocolate is often used for baking for its intense cocoa flavor. But it can sometimes seem a little sour and overwhelm a family-style treat, such as brownies. My preference is to use a bittersweet (dark) chocolate of around 60% cocoa, or a half-and-half mixture of 70% and 50%. This reduces the cost a little, too.

2

Let the chocolate melt until smooth, stirring now and again with a spatula.

3

Put the eggs and sugar into a large bowl. Using a whisk, beat together until frothy and a little thicker, just for 30 seconds or so.

4

Pour the melted butter and chocolate into the eggs and whisk to combine. Sift the flour, cocoa, and salt into the bowl.

5

Beat together using your (already chocolaty) whisk, until smooth and thick. Scoop about ⅓ cup (5 tablespoons) of the batter from the bowl and set aside, then scrape the rest into the prepared pan and smooth the top.

6

Now make the topping. Put the cream cheese into a large bowl, and add the egg, sugar, and vanilla. Whisk until smooth and creamy.

7

Spoon the cheese mixture over the brownie batter in the pan, then spread it into a thin layer using the back of a spoon or a spatula. Spoon the reserved brownie batter over the cheesecake topping. Drag a skewer, toothpick, or the tip of a knife through the cheesecake layer to create feathery swirls.

8

Bake for 30–35 minutes, or until the brownie has risen all over and jiggles just a little in the middle when you gently shake the pan. This is vital for a fudgy result. Let cool completely in the pan, then cut into squares. They'll keep in an airtight container for several days.

VARIATIONS
Add different flavors at step 5, and omit the cheesecake topping.

Classic Walnut Brownies: Fold 1 cup (100 g) chopped walnuts into the batter.

Sour Cherry & White Chocolate Brownies: Fold in ½ cup dried cherries and ⅓ cup (50 g) chopped white chocolate.

Peanut Butter Brownies: Warm 4 tablespoons peanut butter in a saucepan, then spoon it over the raw batter and swirl in with a knife.

Lemon-Glazed Ginger Cake

Preparation time: 20 minutes
Baking time: 50 minutes
Makes 12 slices

Everyone who tried this cake fell in love with it, including me! Making cakes this way with molasses or black treacle guarantees a deliciously dense and sticky cake, which keeps in an airtight container for at least a week. Don't worry if you don't have a bundt pan—see the instructions for making it in an ordinary 9 x 13-inch (23 x 33-cm) baking pan on page 444.

For the cake

¾ cup (180 ml) vegetable oil, plus extra for greasing

1¼ cups (100 g) crystallized ginger (or use candied/glacé ginger packed in syrup, drained)

1½ cups packed (300 g) dark brown sugar

½ cup (150 g) dark molasses (black treacle)

1 cup (250 ml) milk

3 large (UK medium) eggs

1 lemon ´

2⅓ cups (300 g) all-purpose (plain) flour

1½ tsp baking (bicarbonate of) soda

1 tbsp ground ginger

1 tsp ground allspice (or use cinnamon)

¼ tsp salt

For the glaze

scant 1 cup (100 g) confectioners' (icing) sugar

about 2 tbsp lemon juice

442

1

Preheat the oven to 350°F/180°C/
Gas Mark 4 and grease a 12-cup
or 10-inch (25-cm) diameter bundt
pan with a little oil, or use nonstick
cooking spray. Chop the crystallized
ginger into small pieces.

2

Put the dark brown sugar, molasses
(treacle), and milk in a saucepan and
let them melt gently together.

3

Take the pan off the heat, whisk in
the oil to cool the mixture, then add
the eggs and whisk until smooth.
Finely grate in the zest of the lemon.

4

Mix the flour, baking (bicarbonate
of) soda, spices, and salt, then sift
into a large bowl. Make a well in
the center by pushing the flour to
the sides of the bowl, then pour
in the wet ingredients. Add most
of the chopped ginger, saving some
for decoration later.

5

Using the whisk, mix the dry ingredients into the wet, going slowly at first. Once everything is mixed, give the batter a good beat until smooth and evenly blended. Pour into the prepared bundt pan.

6

Bake for 35 minutes, by which point the cake should have risen all over and be dark golden; but don't open the oven door yet or it will sink. Turn the oven down to 325°F/160°C/ Gas Mark 3 for a final 15 minutes of cooking. Test by inserting a toothpick or skewer into the deepest part of the cake; it should come out clean. Put the pan on a wire rack and let the cake cool completely.

7

To decorate the cake, sift the confectioners' (icing) sugar into a large bowl. Squeeze the lemon juice, then stir 4–5 teaspoons into the sugar until smooth. It needs to be thicker than you think, so see how it flows from the spoon before you add any more juice. Turn the cake out onto a serving plate, then drizzle with the icing.

8

Sprinkle the reserved chopped ginger over the cake, then let the icing set for at least 30 minutes.

NO BUNDT PAN?

No problem, simply make ginger-bread bars instead. Bake the cake in the same way, in a parchment-lined 9 x 13-inch (23 x 33-cm) baking pan, until a toothpick or skewer inserted into the center comes out clean. Drizzle with the glaze, or make double with 1¾ cups (200 g) confectioners' (icing) sugar and a little more lemon juice, then spread it thickly over the top of the cake. Let set, then cut into bars, wiping the knife clean before making each cut.

Skinny Blueberry Muffins

Preparation time: 15 minutes
Baking time: 25 minutes
Makes 12 muffins

Muffins are easy to grab and go, but I always want something with at least a nod to health in the morning. This butterless, fluffy muffin is good enough to rival the one from the coffee shop, without the guilt trip. The sweetness from the apple reduces the amount of sugar and fat needed, and there's added fiber from the fruit and flour, too.

For the muffins

1 lemon

1 cup (250 ml) milk

1 medium dessert apple

1⅔ cups (200 g) all-purpose (plain) flour

1 cup (120 g) whole-wheat (wholemeal) flour

1 tsp baking powder

1 tsp baking (bicarbonate of) soda

1 tsp pumpkin pie spice (ground mixed spice)

½ tsp salt

½ cup plus 2 tbsp packed (125 g) light brown sugar

⅓ cup (80 ml) vegetable oil

2 tsp vanilla extract

2 large (UK medium) eggs

1 cup (150 g) blueberries (fresh are best but frozen are fine)

For the glaze (optional)

generous ⅓ cup (50 g) confectioners' (icing) sugar

2–3 tsp milk

1

Preheat the oven to 400°F/200°C/Gas Mark 6 and line a 12-cup muffin pan with deep paper liners (cases). Grate the zest from the lemon (save it for later), then squeeze the juice from one half. Stir 1 tablespoon juice into the milk and let stand for a few minutes until it thickens and turns lumpy.

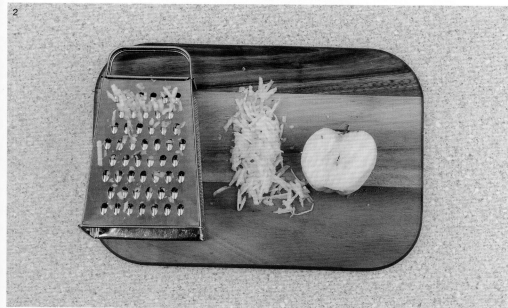

2

Meanwhile, grate the apple with a coarse grater, skin and all.

3

Mix the flours, baking powder, baking (bicarbonate of) soda, spice, and salt, then sift into a large bowl. This allows for the leavening (raising) agents to be thoroughly mixed with the flour. Return the bran from the whole-wheat (wholemeal) flour, which will collect in the sifter or sieve, to the bowl. Stir in the sugar, then make a well in the middle. Beat the oil, vanilla, and eggs into the now-lumpy milk.

4

Pour the liquid into the well. Add the apple and berries, too.

5

Stir the mixture together briefly to make a rough batter. Don't worry if there is still dry flour here and there.

6

Spoon generous heaping spoons of batter into the lined pan, or use an ice cream scoop, which helps do the job cleanly. They will seem full, but that's fine. Bake for about 25 minutes, or until they have risen well and are golden. Don't open the oven until every muffin has risen right to the center.

7

Make the glaze, if you like. Sift the confectioners' (icing) sugar into a bowl, then stir in the milk until smooth. Add the reserved lemon zest. Drizzle the glaze over the muffins.

8

Let cool, then eat the same day.

GET AHEAD
Muffins are always best baked fresh, so why not bag the wet ingredients, including the apple, and chill. Get the dry ingredients ready in a bowl. In the morning, combine the two mixtures and get the muffins in the oven in 2 minutes flat.

CHEESE & HAM CORNBREAD MUFFINS
For a savory option, switch the whole-wheat flour to corn flour (fine cornmeal). Use only 1 teaspoon sugar and omit the vanilla, spice, and fruit. Beat 2 teaspoons whole-grain mustard into the sour milk, egg, and use 4 tablespoons oil. Stir in ½ cup (50 g) grated mature Cheddar, ⅓ cup (50 g) chopped cooked ham and ⅔ cup (100 g) drained canned corn kernels (sweetcorn). Bake for 18 minutes.

Fruity Granola Bars

Preparation time: 20 minutes
Baking time: 35 minutes
Makes 12 bars

These satisfying bars are packed with good things to keep you going until lunchtime, and the butter and sugar have been kept to a minimum with no loss of texture or flavor. The recipe can be easily changed to include your favorite dried fruit, nuts, and seeds. Rolled (porridge) oats are the best choice for these bars because they stick together nicely.

2½ cups (250 g) rolled (porridge) oats (not the jumbo ones)
½ cup (50 g) unsweetened dried (desiccated) coconut flakes
½ cup (75 g) pumpkin or sunflower seeds
½ cup (50 g) slivered (flaked) almonds
4 tbsp (55 g) butter, plus extra for greasing
½ cup packed (100 g) light brown sugar
a pinch of salt
½ cup (160 g) honey
½ cup (85 g) soft dried apricots
2 tbsp fruit juice (apple works well), or use water
1 cup (140 g) dried berries and cherries (or use raisins or other dried fruit)

1

Preheat the oven to 325°F/160°C/ Gas Mark 3. Mix the oats, coconut, seeds, and nuts on a large baking sheet and bake for 15 minutes, stirring halfway through, until they smell toasty and are pale golden here and there. Meanwhile, grease a 9-inch (23-cm) shallow square baking pan, then line it with parchment (baking) paper. Put the butter, sugar, salt, and honey into a large saucepan and melt them gently together to make a syrup. Chop the dried apricots, or snip them with scissors.

2

Pour the toasted oats, seeds, and nuts into the saucepan, then add the fruit juice or water and the dried fruit. Stir well with a spatula until everything is evenly coated in the syrup. Press the granola into the baking pan and smooth it flat with the back of a spoon.

3

Bake for 35 minutes, or until golden all over, then let cool completely in the pan. Lift the baked slab of granola from the pan using the paper to help, then cut into bars using a large sharp knife. Rewrap in clean parchment paper and keep in the pan or an airtight container for up to 1 week.

Caramel & Walnut Coffee Cake

Preparation time: 25 minutes
Baking time: 20–25 minutes
Makes 12 slices

A stalwart of British tea shops and American coffee mornings, this cake deserves a place in cake lovers' hearts everywhere. I like to moisten the layers with strong coffee and finish with a crown of caramelized walnuts and frosting for a slightly flashier riff on the original.

For the cake

2 tbsp instant coffee granules, or ½ cup (120 ml) strong coffee

2¼ sticks (250 g) soft butter, plus extra for greasing

½ cup (50 g) walnut halves

1¼ cups (250 g) superfine (caster) sugar, plus 2 tbsp extra

5 large (UK medium) eggs, room temperature

2 tbsp milk

2⅓ cups (300 g) all-purpose (plain) flour

1 tbsp baking powder

¼ tsp salt

For the frosting and decoration

½ cup (100 g) superfine (caster) sugar (optional)

½ cup (50 g) walnut halves

1 tbsp instant coffee granules (or 1 tbsp strong coffee)

1 stick (110 g) soft butter

2 cups (250 g) confectioners' (icing) sugar

1 tbsp maple syrup (optional)

1
Preheat the oven to 350°F/180°C/Gas Mark 4. If using instant coffee, dissolve it in ½ cup (120 ml) just-boiled water and set aside to cool. Use a little butter to grease two 8-inch (20-cm) shallow, round cake pans, then line the bottoms with parchment (baking) paper. Finely chop the nuts.

2
Put the butter and sugar for the cake into a large bowl and beat with an electric mixer until creamy and pale. Crack in the eggs and add the milk. Mix the flour, baking powder, and salt together, sift them over the eggs, then beat together until creamy.

3
Using a spatula or large spoon, fold in the chopped walnuts and 5 tablespoons of the cooled coffee.

4
Spoon the batter into the prepared pans and level the tops. Bake for 20–25 minutes, or until risen, golden, spring back to the touch, and a toothpick or skewer inserted in the center comes out clean.

5
Let cool in the pans for 10 minutes, then turn out and cool upside down on a cooling rack. I like to peel the paper from underneath, put this on the cooling rack (cakey side down), then put the cakes on top of it. This prevents them from sticking to the rack. Stir the extra sugar into the remaining coffee, let it dissolve, then drizzle this all over the cakes. Let cool completely.

6

The frosting and topping can be simple, or less so, it's up to you. If you want the simple option, jump straight to step 8, use plain walnuts, and add 1 tablespoon maple syrup to the recipe instead of using the caramel. Or, if you're with me on the caramel, read on: Line a baking sheet with parchment paper. Put the sugar into a small saucepan or small deep skillet or frying pan, and heat gently. It will start to look patchy here and there. Don't be tempted to stir it at this point or it could seize, becoming hard and opaque.

7

Carefully swirl the melted patches of sugar over the dry parts, returning to the heat occasionally, to make an even-colored dark coppery caramel. If there is some sugar left, now you can give it a quick stir. Stir the walnuts into the caramel, then use a fork to transfer them one by one to the lined sheet to harden. When you've finished, add 1 tablespoon water to the pan and let it bubble to a runny, dark caramel.

8

If using instant coffee for the frosting, dissolve it in 1 tablespoon just-boiled water. Beat the butter until creamy, then gradually work in the confectioners' (icing) sugar. Once all the dry sugar has disappeared, beat it well until pale and fluffy. Add the coffee and 1 tablespoon of the caramel (or maple syrup), then beat again.

9

Sandwich the cakes with half of the frosting and top with the remainder. Top with the walnuts. The cake will keep well in an airtight container for 3 days. The layers can be frozen for up to 1 month, and the frosting and nuts can be made a few days in advance.

Blueberry-Cinnamon Crumb Cake

Preparation time: 30 minutes
Baking time: 35 minutes
Makes 16 squares

Great cakes for coffee time, these little fruity squares are also prime candidates for dessert, served just warm with a splash of cream. The batter, made with buttermilk, is tender and light and will accommodate just about any fruit you want to add; turn the page for some ideas.

For the cake

7 tbsp (100 g) soft butter, plus extra for greasing

¾ cup (150 g) superfine (caster) sugar

1⅔ cups (200 g) all-purpose (plain) flour

1 tsp baking powder

½ tsp baking (bicarbonate of) soda

¼ tsp salt

2 large (UK medium) eggs, room temperature

1 tsp vanilla extract

½ cup (125 g) buttermilk (or use low-fat plain/natural yogurt)

1 tbsp milk

For the fruit layers and crumb

1 tbsp plus 1 tsp ground cinnamon

4 tbsp turbinado (demerara) sugar

2 cups (300 g) blueberries, fresh or frozen, and defrosted

4 tbsp all-purpose (plain) flour

a pinch of salt

2 tbsp (30 g) butter, room temperature

1 tsp confectioners' (icing) sugar (optional)

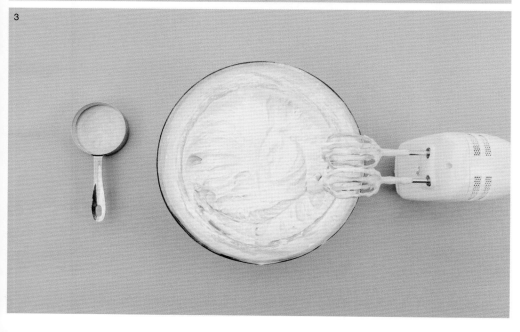

1

Preheat the oven to 350°F/180°C/ Gas Mark 4. Grease a 9-inch (23-cm) shallow square cake pan with butter, then line it with parchment (baking) paper. Put the butter and sugar into a large bowl and beat with an electric mixer until fluffy and light.

2

Mix the flour, baking powder, baking (bicarbonate of) soda, and salt, then sift them into the bowl. Add the eggs and vanilla.

3

Beat everything together until smooth, then beat in the buttermilk or yogurt and milk to make a smooth, creamy mixture.

4

Spoon half the batter into the prepared pan. Mix 1 tablespoon cinnamon and 2 tablespoons demerara sugar, then sprinkle half of this over the cake, followed by half the berries. Repeat the layers.

KEEP THEM SEPARATED
For defined layers, take care when spreading the second layer of cake batter over the blueberries, because they'll try to come along for the ride with the spatula. This will stop once you get going.

5

Make the crumb topping. Put the flour, salt, and remaining cinnamon, and demerara sugar in a bowl. Cut the butter into small pieces, add them to the flour, then rub together until the mixture looks like fine crumbs. When ready, squish some of the crumbs together to make big, cookie doughlike clumps.

6

Sprinkle the crumbs over the top of the cake, then bake for 35 minutes, or until it has risen all the way to the center, looks golden, and the crumb topping is crisp. Cool in the pan for 15 minutes, then lift out the cake using the lining paper and let cool on a rack.

7

Dust the cake with a little confectioners' (icing) sugar if you like, then cut it into squares to serve.

PEACH CRUMB CAKE
Replace the berries with 2 chopped ripe peaches.

APPLE & PECAN CRUMB CAKE
Thinly slice a tangy dessert apple, mix with ½ cup (50 g) chopped pecans, then layer as before. A few blobs of cream cheese would also make a tasty change.

Linzer Cookies

Preparation time: 15 minutes,
plus chilling
Baking time: 10 minutes per batch
Makes about 22

These lovely cookies are perfect
for giving at Christmas or Valentine's,
although the centers can be cut into
circles, stars, or whatever shape suits
the occasion. The buttery dough is
also a versatile go-to when you need
an elegant cookie to decorate (think
birthdays or baby showers), or as
a crisp bite to counter a creamy,
smooth dessert.

For the cookie dough

1 stick plus 4½ tbsp (175 g) soft
   butter, plus extra for greasing
⅔ cup (85 g) blanched hazelnuts
   (or use almond meal/ground
   almonds, see note)
½ cup (100 g) superfine
   (caster) sugar
1 large (UK medium) egg
1 tsp vanilla extract
1⅔ cups (200 g) all-purpose (plain)
   flour, plus extra for dusting
¼ tsp salt
½ tsp ground cinnamon
1 small orange, grated zest only
   (optional)

For decorating

1 tbsp confectioners' (icing) sugar
¾ cup (225 g) raspberry jelly (jam),
   or use Nutella or lemon curd

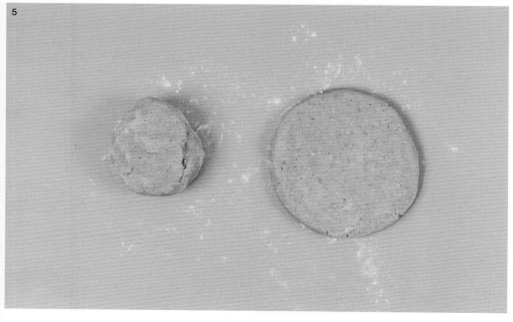

1
Preheat the oven to 350°F/180°C/
Gas Mark 4. Lightly grease 2 baking
sheets with butter, then line them
with parchment (baking) paper. Put
the nuts into a food processor with
1 tablespoon of the sugar, then
pulse until finely ground. Tip them
into a bowl.

DON'T OVERDO IT
Nuts can quickly turn from finely
ground to oily, clumpy, and unusable.
Pulsing the blades and using a little
sugar should avoid this.

2
Separate the egg (see page 343),
then put the yolk into the processor
bowl with the remaining sugar,
the vanilla, and butter.

3
Process the ingredients together
until creamy and evenly mixed.

4
Add the flour, salt, cinnamon,
and ground nuts to the processor
bowl. Finely grate in the orange
zest, if using, then pulse until the
ingredients form a soft dough ball.
You may need to scrape the sides
of the bowl down once or twice.

NO PROCESSOR?
Use ¾ cup plus 2 tablespoons (85 g)
almond meal (ground almonds)
instead. Beat the yolk, sugar, vanilla,
and butter in a large bowl, using an
electric mixer, until pale and creamy.
Work the remaining ingredients in
using a blunt table knife, then knead
briefly to a smooth dough.

5
Lightly dust the work surface with
flour, turn out the dough onto it,
then split it into 2 equal balls.
Flatten each ball into a saucer-sized
disk. Wrap in plastic wrap (clingfilm)
and chill for 20–30 minutes, or until
firm but not rock solid.

6

Sprinkle more flour on the work surface, then get ready to roll. Press ridges into one of the disks of dough with a rolling pin (this stretches it without overworking it, so keeping it tender). Turn the dough and repeat this ridging a few times, until it is about ¾-inch (2-cm) thick. If any cracks appear, pinch them together. Now roll the dough so it's about 3 mm (⅛ inch).

7

Using a 2½-inch (6-cm) fluted pastry cutter, stamp out 12 rounds. Next, using a small heart or star-shaped cutter (or the end of a wide icing tip/ nozzle to make a round hole), cut out shapes from the centers of half the cookies.

8

Carefully lift the whole round cookies onto one baking sheet, and the cookies with the holes onto the other. Squish the remains of the dough together (taking care not to knead it, or this can make the dough tough), reroll and stamp out more cookies until you have filled the baking sheets.

9

Bake the whole cookies for 10–11 minutes and the cutout cookies for 9 minutes, or until they are pale golden and smell nutty. Let stand for 2 minutes, then lift onto cooling racks and let cool completely. Repeat with the second batch of dough.

10

Use a fine-mesh sieve to dust the confectioners' (icing) sugar over the cutout cookies. Spoon about 1 teaspoon jelly (jam) over the whole cookies, then sandwich together with the cutouts. The basic cookies will keep in an airtight container for 3–5 days and are best sandwiched on the day you're going to eat them.

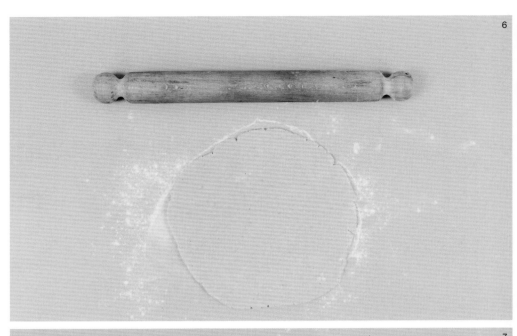
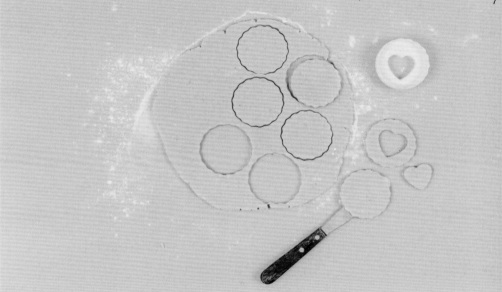
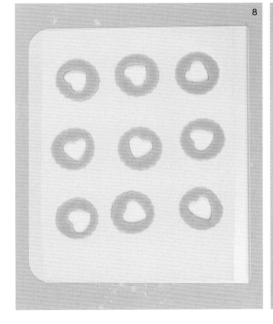

Coconut Layer Cake

Preparation time: 45 minutes
Baking time: 25 minutes
Cuts into 12 or 16 very tall pieces

Tall, frosted, and a little over the top, this cake is built from coconut sponge layers alternating with a silky-smooth coconut meringue buttercream and lemon curd layers. It's less sweet than a traditional American-style frosted coconut cake, but if you prefer it that way, see page 467 for an easy twist.

For the cake layers

½ cup (50 g) unsweetened dried (desiccated) coconut flakes

2 sticks (225 g) soft butter

1 cup plus 2 tbsp (225 g) superfine (caster) sugar

1 tsp vanilla extract

5 large (UK medium) eggs, room temperature

2⅓ cups (300 g) all-purpose (plain) flour

1 tbsp baking powder

½ tsp salt

½ cup (120 ml) regular coconut milk

To decorate

5 eggs (you only need the whites)

2½ cups (300 g) confectioners' (icing) sugar

a pinch of salt

1 tsp vanilla extract

2½ sticks (275 g) soft butter

½ cup (120 ml) regular coconut milk

1 cup (300 g) good-quality lemon curd

2½ cups (125 g) toasted coconut chips

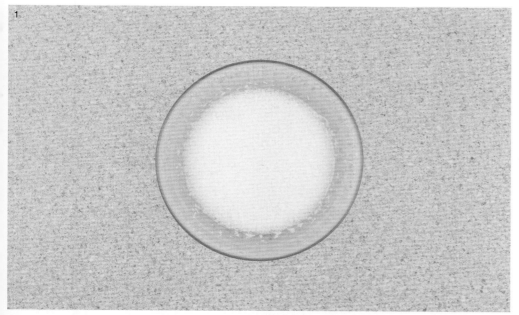

1
Soak the dried (desiccated) coconut in boiling water for 15 minutes (or longer if you can), then pour it into a sieve and press out the excess water. Use a little of the butter to grease two 8-inch (20-cm) shallow, round cake pans with removable bottoms, then line the bottoms with parchment (baking) paper. Preheat the oven to 350°F/180°C/Gas Mark 4.

2
Using an electric mixer, beat the butter, sugar, and vanilla together until creamy and pale, scraping down the sides of the bowl every now and again with a spatula. Beat in an egg until completely combined, fluffy, and light. Repeat with the other eggs, one by one. If it starts to look lumpy, add 1 tablespoon of the flour and it will become smooth again.

3
Thoroughly mix the flour, baking powder, and salt in a bowl. Sift half into the cake batter, then fold it in using a spatula or large metal spoon. Next, fold in the coconut milk, then fold in the rest of the flour mixture, then the drained coconut.

4

Using a spatula, divide the batter evenly between the pans and spread it flat.

TAKE A SHORTCUT
If you're in a rush, the cakes can be made using the all-in-one method. Add everything together, then add 1 extra teaspoon baking powder and beat.

5

Bake for 25 minutes, or until the cakes have risen, are firm, and slightly shrunken back from the sides of the pans. Let cool on a rack for 10 minutes, then remove from the pans and let cool completely.

6

For a four-layer cake, you'll need to cut each cake in half horizontally. Use a large serrated knife and first score a line first around the "waist" of the cake, cutting about 1 inch (2.5 cm) into it. Turn the cake with one hand and keep the knife in the other. Keep a steady hand and the start and finishing points should meet up. Cut the cake using gentle sweeps of the knife, keeping it parallel with the surface. Rotate the cake a few degrees after each cut. You will reach the middle and the top half will be freed. Repeat with the second cake.

NEED MORE PRACTICE?
If your cakes are uneven, don't worry, the frosting will cover it up. You could try inserting toothpick (cocktail stick) "markers" into the cake at equal intervals before you start cutting. These will help you cut evenly and rebuild the cake layers in their original positions later on.

7

Clean the mixer thoroughly. For the frosting, bring 2½ inches (5 cm) water to a simmer in a medium saucepan. Separate the eggs, then put the whites into a clean, large, heatproof bowl (one that will sit just on top of the pan), and sift in the sugar. Add the pinch of salt and beat together until smooth. Sit the bowl on the pan, then beat the whites for about 7 minutes or until thick and shiny. It's thick enough when you can stand a teaspoon upright in the bowl without it falling over. Beat in the vanilla.

SEVEN-MINUTE FROSTING
If you prefer to use classic 7-minute frosting as a thick and fluffy cake topping, then it's ready now. It's best spread immediately, then set for a while before cutting.

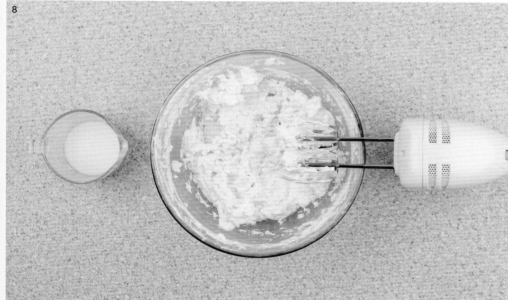

8

Scrape the meringue into another cold bowl, then beat for another few minutes until just about room temperature. Keep the pan of hot water—it may come in handy in a moment. Beat the soft butter into the meringue, 1 tablespoon at a time, waiting for each one to disappear completely before adding the next. You will find that the volume of the mixture falls at first, and may seem a little loose, but keep going.

9

The frosting will suddenly change from billowy to silky and thick as you add all the butter. When all the butter has been added, gradually beat in the coconut milk. If the mixture starts to feel lumpy, warm it gently over the hot water for a few seconds while beating, and it will loosen up again.

MERINGUE BUTTERCREAM
Although more time-consuming than ordinary buttercream, meringue buttercream is a great one to have up your sleeve for a really luxurious cake frosting. It's also delicious with cooled melted bittersweet (dark) chocolate whisked into it instead of the coconut. Meringue buttercream is good natured, and can be made a few days in advance, chilled, then rebeaten when ready to use. It pipes supersmoothly, too.

10
You're now ready to assemble the cake. Place one layer on a serving plate and spread with half the lemon curd. Top with the second layer of cake, then add about 1¼ cups (175 g) frosting and spread it evenly to the edges. Top the third layer with the remaining lemon curd.

11
Place the final cake layer on top, then spread the remaining frosting all over the cake and smooth it with a spatula (palette knife). Mound it on the top of the cake first, then spread it down and around the cake. Press the coconut chips up the side of the cake and sprinkle them over the top.

TOASTING YOUR OWN COCONUT
Spread the coconut chips over a large, lipped baking sheet. Bake at 350°F/180°C/Gas Mark 4 for 5 minutes, stirring halfway, until tinged with gold here and there.

12
Brush any excess chips from the serving plate. Keep the cake cool until serving. If making ahead, chill the cake, but let it come up to room temperature before eating it.

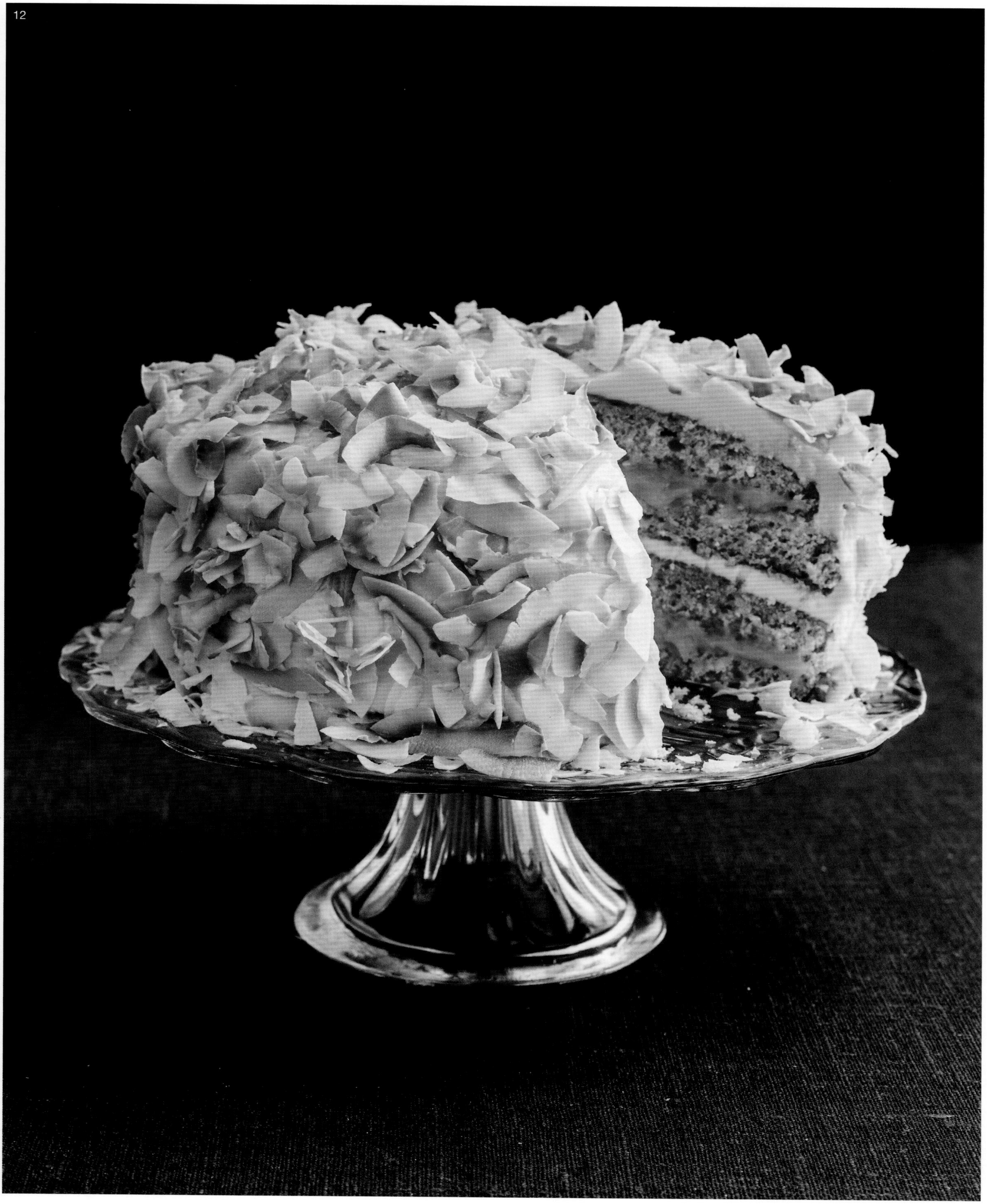

Sticky Pear & Pecan Toffee Cake

Preparation time: 20 minutes
Baking time: 50 minutes
Cuts into 12 slices

Many bakers have dreams of opening a little café with cakes on the counter and really good coffee. In mine, I'd be making this every day in fall (autumn), using plums, apples, or cranberries closer to the holidays.

For the cake
1 cup (150 g) soft pitted dates
2 sticks (225 g) soft butter, plus
    extra for greasing
1½ cups (150 g) pecans
2 medium, just-ripe pears
1 cup packed (200 g) light brown
    sugar
4 large (UK medium) eggs, room
    temperature
4 tbsp milk
2⅓ cups (300 g) all-purpose (plain)
    flour
1 tsp baking (bicarbonate of) soda
1 tsp baking powder
2 tsp ground cinnamon or pumpkin
    pie spice (ground mixed spice)
¼ tsp salt

For the toffee topping
½ cup packed (100 g) light brown
    sugar
2 tbsp butter
scant ½ cup (100 ml) heavy (double)
    cream
½ cup (50 g) pecans

1
First, soak the dates by covering them with boiling water. Let stand for 15 minutes, or longer if you like. Meanwhile, preheat the oven to 325°F/160°C/Gas Mark 3 and do the rest of the prep. Melt a little butter, then use a pastry brush to grease the inside of a 10-cup or 9-inch (23-cm) nonstick bundt pan.

NO BUNDT PAN?
Using a bundt pan gives this cake a wonderful texture and dramatic shape, but a greased and lined 9 x 13-inch (23 x 33-cm) baking pan does the job, too. Bake the cake at 325°F/160°C/Gas Mark 3 for 40 minutes or until it has risen in the middle, and a toothpick or skewer inserted into the center comes out clean.

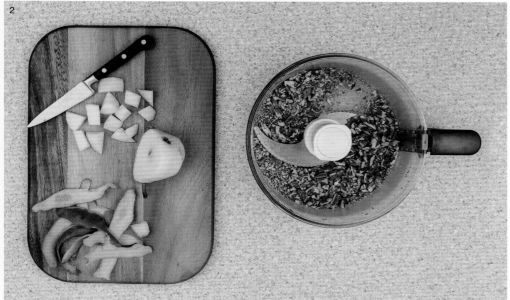

2
Finely chop the pecans in a food processor, then tip them out. Peel the pears, then cut them into fingertip-sized chunks, discarding the central core part.

3
Drain the dates through a sieve. Process the butter and sugar together until creamy and smooth, then process in the dates. Now add the eggs, milk, flour, baking (bicarbonate of) soda, baking powder, cinnamon, and salt and process to make a smooth cake batter.

MAKING IT BY HAND
This recipe is much easier with a food processor, but you can make it by hand, too. Finely chop the nuts, and chop the soaked dates as finely as you can, almost to a pulp. Mix the dates and other ingredients in a large bowl and beat until creamy and smooth. Fold in the nuts and pears and continue.

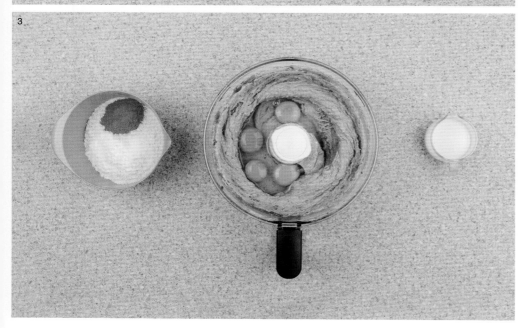

4

Unless you have a really big food processor, at this point you'll need to turn the batter into a bowl to fold in the pecans and pears. If you do have the room in the processor bowl, be sure to remove the blades before mixing. Spoon the batter into the prepared pan and smooth the top.

5

Bake for 50 minutes, or until the cake has risen all over and a toothpick or skewer inserted into the center comes out clean. Let the cake cool in the pan for at least 10 minutes. Give the pan a sharp tap on the work surface, then turn it out onto a cooling rack if serving cold, or a plate if serving warm.

6

For the toffee topping, put the sugar, butter, and cream into a medium saucepan. Heat it gently until the sugar has dissolved, then simmer briefly to make a silky smooth caramel sauce.

7

Stir the pecans into the sauce, then spoon it all over the cake. It will set firm and lose its shine if serving cold.

8

The cake will keep in an airtight container for up to 3 days, and will freeze well, without the topping.

TRY THIS
Make a double quantity of the toffee sauce, and serve the sauce and the cake warm, at the table, as a spectacular dessert. Great with cream or crème anglaise (custard) served alongside.

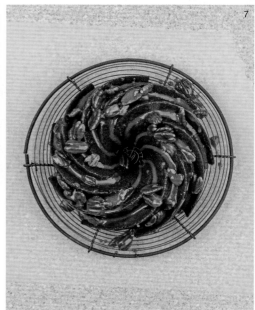

Frosted Cupcakes

Preparation time: 25 minutes
Baking time: 18–20 minutes
Makes 12 cupcakes

When I teach baking, the thing most students seem to want to master is a good piped cupcake. It does take practice, but you'll soon be swirling frosting like a pro. Here, the classic recipe gets an upgrade with a white chocolate frosting that is easy to flavor, color, and pipe. Too fancy? Use ordinary buttercream.

For the cupcakes
1½ sticks (175 g) butter
⅔ cup (150 g) buttermilk or low-fat natural (plain) yogurt
4 large (UK medium) eggs
1 tsp vanilla paste or extract
1 cup plus 3 tbsp (150 g) all-purpose (plain) flour
2 tsp baking powder
¼ tsp salt
¾ cup (175 g) superfine (caster) sugar
1 cup (100 g) almond meal (ground almonds)

For the white chocolate frosting
½ cup (120 ml) heavy (double) cream
3½ oz (100 g) white chocolate
1½ sticks (175 g) soft butter
½ tsp vanilla paste or extract
a pinch of salt
2 cups (250 g) confectioners' (icing) sugar
sprinkles, berries, or candies (sweets), to decorate (optional)

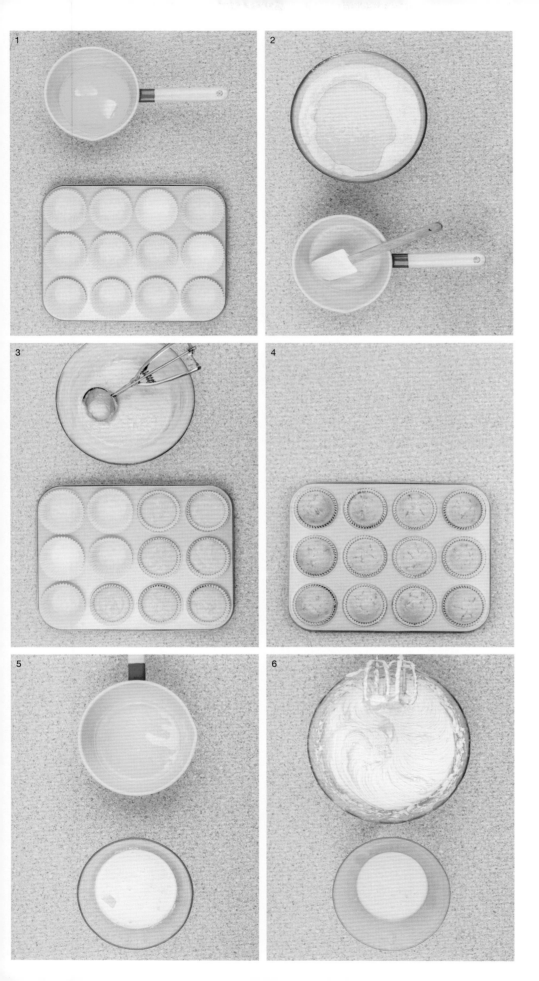

1

Line a 12-cup muffin pan with deep paper liners (cases). Preheat the oven to 375°F/190°C/Gas Mark 5. Melt the butter in a saucepan, remove from the heat, and let cool a little. Stir the buttermilk into the butter, then add the eggs and vanilla. Beat together with a fork until smooth.

2

Mix together the flour, baking powder, and salt, then sift into a large bowl. Stir in the sugar and almonds. Make a well in the center, then pour in the butter mixture.

3

Using a spatula or balloon whisk, quickly mix together until free of lumps, and runny. Fill the liners using an ice cream scoop, or hold the bowl over the pan while you spoon it in. The liners should be full.

4

Bake for 18–20 minutes, or until they have risen evenly, are golden brown, and smell sweet. Insert a toothpick or skewer into the middle of a cupcake; it should come out clean. Cool for 5 minutes, then transfer to a rack and cool completely.

5

To make the frosting, put the cream into a small saucepan and heat until the edges are just starting to bubble. Meanwhile, coarsely chop the chocolate and put into a small bowl. Pour the hot cream over the chocolate, then let it melt, stirring occasionally. Let cool.

6

Put the butter into a large bowl, beat well until creamy, add the vanilla and salt, then gradually beat in the confectioners' (icing) sugar until fluffy and pale. Gradually pour in the cooled chocolate, then beat to make a light, smooth frosting.

7

To frost with a spatula (palette knife), mound 2 tablespoons frosting onto the cake. For sloped sides, turn the cupcake clockwise in one hand and smooth counterclockwise with the other, holding the blade at a slight angle. Dip the knife into the frosting on top, turning it as before, to make an indent with a ridge. Clean the knife against the bowl's edge before each stage.

8

To pipe roses, cut the first 1-inch (2.5 cm) from a disposable pastry (piping) bag, insert a rose tip (nozzle), then spoon in the frosting until half full. Twist the bag at the top to create pressure at the tip. Start in the middle of the cake, then pipe outward in a spiral. Pipe evenly, keeping the bag upright. If you mess up, scrape the frosting back into the bag (avoiding crumbs) and try again. Twist the top of the bag to increase the pressure before piping each cake. Add decorative toppings, if you like.

CHOCOLATE OREO CUPCAKES
Use 1 cup (125 g) flour and 3 tablespoons cocoa powder in the batter. Make the frosting with dark chocolate instead of white, or crush Oreos into the white frosting. Top with half a cookie.

PEANUT BUTTER CUPCAKES
Replace 3 tablespoons butter with smooth peanut butter in the basic batter. For the frosting, replace the chocolate and cream with ¾ cup (175 g) smooth peanut butter. Top with Reese's Pieces.

PISTACHIO CUPCAKES
Grind 1½ cups (150 g) shelled pistachios in a processor and add 1 cup (100 g) to the batter instead of the almonds. Color the frosting green. Frost the cakes, and sprinkle with the rest of the pistachios.

Red Velvet Whoopie Pies

Preparation time: 20 minutes
Baking time: 10 minutes per batch
Makes 24 complete pies

If you feel like a change from cupcakes, whoopie pies are the answer. These attention-grabbing cakes are fun to make for Halloween or Valentine's. Unlike a classic whoopie, these are soft and delicate, like their namesake red velvet cake. Omit the food coloring if you prefer, for a pale, chocolaty look.

For the batter

1½ sticks (175 g) soft butter, plus extra for greasing
1 cup (200 g) superfine (caster) sugar
1 tsp vanilla bean paste or extract
2 cups (250 g) all-purpose (plain) flour
¼ cup (25 g) unsweetened cocoa powder
1½ tsp baking (bicarbonate of) soda
½ tsp baking powder
¼ tsp salt
3 large (UK medium) eggs
½ cup (125 g) buttermilk
1 tsp red food coloring paste

For the filling and decoration

1½ sticks (175 g) soft butter
14 oz (400 g) regular (full-fat) cream cheese, cold
1 tsp vanilla paste or extract
1¼ cups (150 g) confectioners' (icing) sugar
2 oz (50 g) white chocolate

1

Preheat the oven to 350°F/180°C/ Gas Mark 4. Lightly grease and line 2 baking sheets with parchment (baking) paper. Put the butter, sugar, and vanilla into a large bowl and beat with an electric mixer or a wooden spoon until creamy and light.

2

Mix together the flour, cocoa, baking (bicarbonate of) soda, baking powder, and salt, then sift them into a bowl. Put the eggs, buttermilk, and food coloring into the bowl with the butter and sugar.

3

Sift the flour mixture into the bowl, then beat to a smooth, bright-red batter. It will be thick and sticky.

4

Spoon the batter evenly onto the lined baking sheets, aiming for 48 balls, about 1 heaping teaspoon each. Leave room for the batter to spread as it cooks. I use a small cookie scoop to get a nicely uniform round shape, but you can push the batter off the end of a spoon with your finger, or pipe it instead. You'll need to bake them in several batches.

5

Bake the whoopies for 9–10 minutes, or until they have risen and are firm to the touch, but not crisp. Let cool for a few minutes on the sheets, then remove to a cooling rack and cool completely.

6

For the filling, put the butter into a large bowl and beat with an electric mixer until creamy and smooth. Add the cream cheese and vanilla and beat briefly until evenly blended. Sift in the confectioners' (icing) sugar and beat for another few seconds until smooth and creamy, or work it in gently with a spatula. If your kitchen is warm, chill the frosting while the whoopies cool.

7

Once cool, spread or pipe a generous amount of filling onto the flat sides of half the cakes, then top with the remaining halves and squeeze together gently so that the frosting shows at the sides.

8

Finely grate the white chocolate, then roll the edges of the whoopies in it to coat. It will stick to the filling.

9

Eat at room temperature the day they are made, or soon after. Keep filled whooopies in the refrigerator. If you are not filling them immediately, pack them, with parchment paper between the layers.

BANOFFEE WHOOPIE PIES
Beat 1 mashed ripe banana into the creamed butter and sugar. Use 2 eggs and 2¼ cups (280 g) flour and omit the cocoa. Sandwich with the filling plus 1 heaping teaspoon dulce de leche, then roll the edges in grated bittersweet (dark) chocolate.

PUMPKIN PIE WHOOPIE PIES
Use 1¼ cups packed (250 g) light brown sugar. Beat 1 cup canned (250 g) pumpkin puree into the creamed butter and sugar. Use 2 eggs, 2¼ cups (280 g) flour (omit the cocoa), and add 1 tablespoon pumpkin pie spice (ground mixed spice). Flavor the filling with the grated zest of 1 orange.

Vanilla Celebration Cake

Preparation time: about 1 hour
15 minutes
Baking time: 1 hour 30–40 minutes
Serves 20, or more

I'm often asked to make cakes for weddings, anniversaries, and birthdays, so I understand the pressure you might feel if you've been asked the same thing. You need a reliable recipe that keeps well, cuts cleanly, tastes good and looks fabulous. This recipe, with its luxurious white chocolate frosting, should do it.

For the cake

3 sticks (350 g) soft butter, plus extra for greasing
6 large (UK medium) eggs, room temperature
1¾ cups (350 g) superfine (caster) sugar
1 tsp vanilla paste
3 cups (385 g) all-purpose (plain) flour
1 tbsp plus 1 tsp baking powder
4 tbsp cornstarch (cornflour)
½ tsp salt
1¼ cups (300 g) buttermilk

For the syrup

¼ cup (50 g) sugar
½ tsp vanilla paste

For the frosting

1½ cups (350 ml) heavy (double) cream
6½ oz (175 g) white chocolate
3 sticks (350 g) soft butter
1 tsp vanilla paste
¼ tsp salt
5¼ cups (650 g) confectioners' (icing) sugar, or more if needed

1
Preheat the oven to 325°F/160°C/Gas Mark 3. Double-line the bottom and sides of a 9-inch (23-cm) springform or ordinary deep round cake pan. Separate 3 of the eggs and add the whites to 3 whole eggs. (You won't need the yolks.)

2
Using an electric mixer, beat the butter, sugar, and vanilla together until creamy and pale. Pour a little of the egg into the bowl, then beat in until fluffy and light. Repeat until all the egg has been used. If the batter starts to look a little lumpy at any point, beat in 1 tablespoon of the flour.

3
Mix the flour, baking powder, cornstarch (cornflour), and salt together in a bowl. Sift half of this into the cake batter, fold it in, then fold in the buttermilk. Follow with the rest of the flour mixture to make a smooth and fairly thick batter.

4
Spoon the batter into the pan and level the top. Make a slight dip in the center, which will encourage the cake to rise without a dome.

5
Bake for 1 hour 30–40 minutes, or until risen well, is golden, and a toothpick or skewer inserted into the center comes out clean. Check carefully: The cake may sink or seem heavy if underdone. Meanwhile, make the syrup: Gently heat the sugar in 3 tablespoons water until dissolved. Add the vanilla and set aside. Once out of the oven, let the cake cool in the pan until just warm, then poke 25 holes through it. Spoon the syrup over it, letting it soak in after each addition. Let cool completely in the pan. It can be wrapped and frozen for up to 1 month.

6

For the frosting, put the cream into a small saucepan and heat until the edges just start to bubble. Chop the chocolate into small pieces and put into a small heatproof bowl. Pour the hot cream over it, then let it melt, stirring now and again, until smooth and silky. Let cool completely.

7

Put the butter, vanilla, and salt in a large bowl, beat well until smooth and creamy, then slowly beat in the confectioners' (icing) sugar to make a fluffy buttercream. Gradually pour in the cooled white chocolate and beat to make a pale, silky-smooth frosting. If it seems too soft, add a little more sugar.

8

Split the cake horizontally into 3 even layers using a large serrated knife (see page 466). Stack it back together on a serving plate, spreading about 1 cup (200 g) frosting between each layer.

9

To cover the cake in a crumb coat for a perfect finish, mound 1¼ cups (250 g) of the frosting onto the cake, then spread it over the top and down the sides to the plate. Try not to lift the spatula (palette knife) off the cake, but move it in a fluid movement. Smooth, then chill for 10 minutes, or until firm.

10

Spread the remaining frosting over the cake as before, or leave the frosting ruffled and rustic. Store in a cool place (the refrigerator if it's hot) to let the frosting set. It can be wrapped and chilled for up to 2 days; bring to room temperature before eating. To top with flowers, tie together your favorite blooms, wrap the ends in plastic wrap (clingfilm), then sit them on top of, or to the side of, the finished cake.

Cranberry Stollen

Preparation time: 45 minutes,
plus rising and proving
Baking time: 30 minutes
Makes 2 family-size loaves

Several wintry trips to Germany have
given me a real fondness for stollen,
the richly fruited Christmas loaf with
the hidden treasure of marzipan
inside. The recipe makes two loaves;
one to eat straight after baking and
one to gift, or wrap well and stash
it in the freezer for up to 1 month.

For the bread

1 lemon

4 tbsp dark rum (or use orange juice)

1 tsp vanilla extract

1 cup (150 g) dried cranberries

1 cup (150 g) golden raisins
   (sultanas) or use chopped
   dried apricots

1¼ cups (300 ml) milk

1 tbsp (10.5 g) instant dry (fast-
   action) yeast

1 whole nutmeg, or use 1 tsp ground

4 cups (500 g) white bread (strong)
   flour, plus extra for dusting

1 tsp salt

generous ⅓ cup (85 g) sugar

1½ sticks (175 g) butter,
   room temperature

2 large (UK medium) eggs

9 oz (250 g) marzipan

To finish

4 tbsp (50 g) butter

4 tbsp (25 g) confectioners'
   (icing) sugar

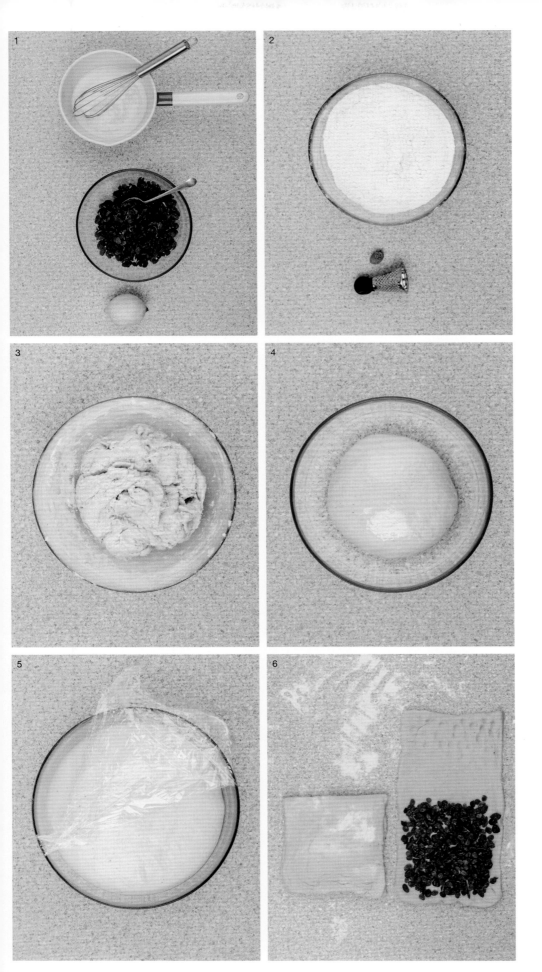

1

Finely grate the lemon zest and mix it with the rum or orange juice, vanilla, and dried fruit. Let macerate while you make the dough. Gently warm the milk in the microwave or in a saucepan, then whisk in the yeast. The milk must be only warm; if it's too hot, it will kill the yeast.

2

If using whole nutmeg, grate 2 teaspoons. Sift the flour into a large bowl with the salt, then add the nutmeg and sugar. Cut the butter into cubes, then rub it into the flour mixture using your fingertips, until it looks like bread crumbs.

3

Separate one egg (see page 343). Add the yolk and whole egg to the milk and yeast, and beat together. Using a wooden spoon, mix the liquid into the rubbed-in mixture to make a soft, sticky dough. Let stand for 10 minutes.

4

Dust the work surface with flour, then turn the dough out onto it. Flour the top of the dough and your hands, then begin to knead. Keep going for about 10 minutes, until the dough feels springy or elastic and silky smooth. Use more flour if you need to. Put the dough in an oiled bowl and cover with oiled plastic wrap (clingfilm).

5

Let rise in a warm place for 1½ hours, or until doubled in size.

6

Turn the dough out onto the floured work surface and cut it in half. Use your hands to press and pat each half into an 8 x 24-inch (20 x 40-cm) rectangle. Spread the soaked fruit over the bottom half of each one, then fold the top half over it.

7

Pat the dough out to about 6 x 10 inches (15 x 25 cm), then fold it in half again along the long edge; repeat this twice, or until the fruit is well distributed in the dough, but isn't escaping. You should end up with 2 rectangles about 6 x 10 inches (15 x 25 cm). If at any point the dough starts being too springy to handle, let it sit for a few minutes, then continue.

8

Roll the marzipan into 2 equal cylinders. Make a deep groove along the length of each piece of dough, then place the marzipan in it.

9

Roll one side of the dough over the marzipan. Press and pinch the edges together well to make a lip of dough, then shape the ends of the loaves into slight points.

10

Line a large baking sheet with parchment (baking) paper and lift the breads onto it. Leave room for rising. Cover with oiled plastic wrap (clingfilm) and let rise in a warm place for 1 hour, or until almost doubled in size. Preheat the oven to 375°F/180°C/Gas Mark 4.

11

Bake for 30 minutes, or until the breads have risen well and are dark golden brown. Melt the butter, then brush it all over the warm stollen and dredge with confectioners' (icing) sugar.

12

Let cool completely before wrapping and storing. Dust with confectioners' sugar again before bringing it to the table.

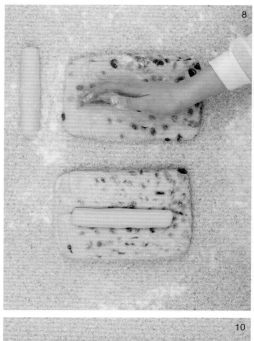

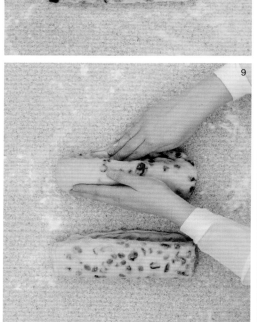

Whole Orange & Almond Cake

Preparation time: 10 minutes,
plus 2 hours for boiling the oranges
Baking time: 50 minutes
Serves 12

Whole oranges, skin and all, are cooked until completely tender, then blended with almonds, eggs, and a little olive oil in this Spanish-style, naturally gluten-free cake. Its texture is light but rich, with a marmalade-like quality.

---

2 medium oranges, about 6½ oz (185 g) each

2 tbsp extra virgin olive oil, plus extra for greasing

1¼ cups (250 g) superfine (caster) sugar

6 large (UK medium) eggs, room temperature

3 cups (300 g) almond meal (ground almonds)

1 tbsp baking powder (a gluten-free brand if needed)

¼ tsp salt

a handful of sliced almonds

thick Greek yogurt or crème fraîche, to serve (optional)

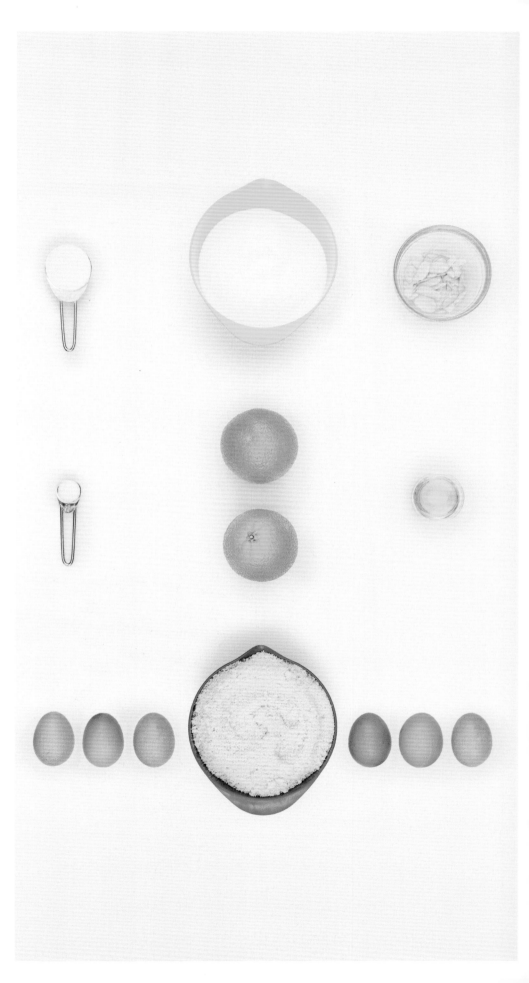

1
Put the oranges into a medium saucepan, then cover with water and a lid. Bring to a simmer, then cook for 2 hours, or until the oranges are soft when you poke them with a knife. The oranges will bob around a bit, so check them after 1 hour and turn them over to make sure they cook evenly. Add more water while you're there, if needed.

ORANGES IN THE MICROWAVE
If you have a microwave, cut the oranges in half (whole ones will explode), put into a microwave-proof bowl with a splash of water, and cover with plastic wrap (clingfilm). Pierce a few holes in the film. Cook on full power for 10 minutes, or until completely tender (it may take longer, depending on your microwave). Let cool for a few minutes before removing the wrap.

2
Grease a 9-inch (23-cm) round springform pan with a little oil, then line the bottom with parchment (baking) paper. Preheat the oven to 350°F/180°C/Gas Mark 4. Drain the oranges, and when cool enough to handle, cut into large pieces and remove any seeds (pips). Put them, skin and all, in a food processor. Add the sugar and pulse to a smooth puree.

3
Add the eggs to the processor, then process for about 1 minute until paler and thickened.

4

Tip in the almond meal (ground almonds), baking powder, salt, and oil and process for a few seconds to make a smooth, evenly blended batter. Using a spatula, scrape the batter into the prepared pan, smooth the top, then sprinkle with the sliced almonds.

5

Bake for 50 minutes, or until the cake is golden all over, has risen all the way to the center, and a toothpick or skewer inserted in the middle comes out clean. Remove and let cool in the pan for 10 minutes (the cake will sink back down to become flat), then run a spatula (palette knife) between the cake and the pan and unclip the sides. Let the cake cool on the pan bottom, on a cooling rack.

6

There's a trick to getting a cake with a loose topping onto a plate without any dramas. Put a flat plate upside down on top of the cake. Holding the plate and the pan securely, turn them both over. Remove the pan and parchment paper and replace with the serving plate. Holding both plates securely but without squashing the cake, turn it the right way up. Serve with thick Greek yogurt or crème fraîche.

Pistachio & Fig Biscotti

Preparation time: 20 minutes
Baking time: 1 hour
Makes about 36 biscotti

It's easy to make your own elegant biscotti, baked twice for just the right crunch, ready for dunking into coffee or sweet dessert wine after dinner, or crumbling over ice cream. I've chosen figs and pistachio for flavor and their graphic, colorful cross section, but any combination of dried fruit and nuts will work brilliantly.

---

2 tbsp olive oil, plus a little extra
  for greasing
½ cup (100 g) soft dried figs
  (or other dried fruit)
1 cup (200 g) superfine (caster)
  sugar
3 large (UK medium) eggs, room
  temperature
2⅓ cups (300 g) all-purpose (plain)
  flour, plus extra for dusting
1 tsp baking powder
½ tsp salt
1 orange
scant cup (100 g) shelled
  pistachios

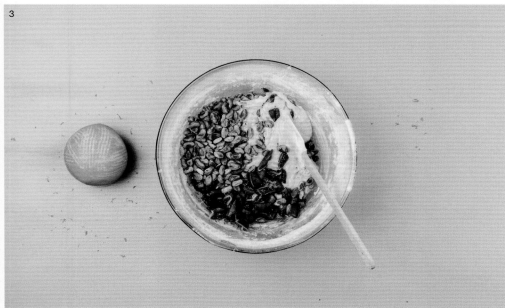

1

Grease and line a large baking sheet with parchment (baking) paper. Preheat the oven to 350°F/180°C/Gas Mark 4. Snip or cut the figs into small pieces.

2

Put the sugar and eggs into a large bowl, then whisk for a minute or so with a balloon whisk, just until the mixture feels frothy and a little more resistant as you beat. Whisk in the oil.

3

Mix the flour, baking powder, and salt, then sift them over the egg mixture. Fold together to make a dough. Finely grate the zest from the orange, then work it into the dough along with the nuts and figs, using a spatula (palette knife).

4

Sprinkle some flour on the work surface and turn the dough out onto it. Split the dough into 2 equal balls, dust each one (and your hands) with a little flour, then shape into a 8–10-inch (20–25-cm) log or sausage shape. The dough will be soft, so be gentle with it and pat it into shape rather than squeezing it too much. Lift it onto the prepared baking sheet.

5
Bake for 30 minutes, or until they have risen and turned pale golden. Let cool, and in the meantime turn the oven down to 325°F/160°C/ Gas Mark 3.

6
When the dough is firm and cool enough to handle, transfer it to a board and cut into ½-inch (1-cm) slices. Use a serrated knife and sawing action, because the dough is sturdy by this point. Spread the cookies over the baking sheet in a single layer. Use a second sheet if you want to bake all the biscotti at once.

GETTING AHEAD
The half-baked biscotti can be frozen at this point and baked from frozen when needed. Allow a few more minutes of baking time.

7
Return the biscotti to the oven and bake for another 30 minutes, turning them over halfway through, until dry, crisp and just golden. If you are baking 2 sheets at once, swap their shelf positions halfway through cooking, too.

8
Cool the biscotti on a rack, then pack in an airtight container until serving. They will last up to 2 weeks.

SPICED PECAN-CRANBERRY BISCOTTI
Sift 2 teaspoons pumpkin pie spice (ground mixed spice) into the flour. Replace the pistachios and figs with pecans and cranberries.

ANISE & ALMOND BISCOTTI
Work in whole blanched almonds instead of the pistachios, and add 1 teaspoon lightly crushed anise or fennel seeds.

Salted Caramel Shortbread

Preparation time: 45 minutes, plus setting
Baking time: 25–30 minutes
Makes 36 small cubes

If you're a fan of the salt and caramel combination but haven't tried it at home yet, this is a delicious way to experiment. The recipe is a twist on millionaire's shortbread, a classic childhood favorite of mine. It's now all grown up, and perfect as a bite after dinner.

For the crust

1 stick (110 g) soft butter, plus extra for greasing
¼ cup (50 g) superfine (caster) sugar
a pinch of salt
½ tsp vanilla extract
1 cup plus 2 tbsp (140 g) all-purpose (plain) flour

For the caramel

1 stick (110 g) butter
1 cup packed (200 g) dark brown sugar
4 tbsp golden syrup, such as Lyle's or corn syrup
½ tsp salt
1 (14-oz /400-g) can sweetened condensed milk

For the topping

7 oz (200 g) bittersweeet (dark) chocolate, 70% cocoa solids
1 tbsp vegetable or sunflower oil
½ tsp salt

1
Lightly grease a 9-inch (23-cm) shallow square baking pan, then line with parchment (baking) paper. Make the crust (base) first. Put the butter into a large bowl and beat well with a wooden spoon or an electric mixer until creamy and pale. Add the sugar, salt, and vanilla and beat again until even paler.

2
Sift the flour over the creamed butter and sugar. Using a spatula, gently work the flour into the mixture to make an even dough that starts to clump together.

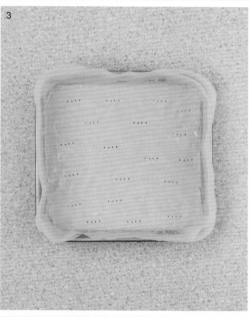

3
Press the dough into the prepared pan, then level and smooth it with the back of a spoon. Prick it all over with a fork, then chill for 10 minutes, or longer if you like, until firm. Meanwhile, preheat the oven to 325°F/160°C/Gas Mark 3.

4
Bake for 25–30 minutes, or until the shortbread is golden all over. Let cool completely.

QUICK SHORTCUT
If you prefer, buy 14 oz (400 g) all-butter shortbread cookies (biscuits). Crush them finely, then stir in 4 tablespoons (55 g) melted butter until evenly blended. Press into the pan, bake for 15 minutes, or until golden, then continue with the recipe.

5
Now for the caramel. Melt the butter, sugar, syrup, and salt together gently in a saucepan, then stir in the condensed milk.

6

Bring the caramel to a simmer, stirring constantly with a spatula, and let it bubble for 4 minutes, or until it thickens and smells like creamy toffee. It should be thick enough for the spatula to leave a trail in the caramel for a few seconds. Don't leave the pan or stop stirring during this step, because it can easily burn on the bottom.

7

Pour the caramel over the shortbread, then let cool completely.

8

Once the caramel has set and cooled, it's time to finish the layers. Melt the chocolate either over a saucepan of water or in the microwave (see page 309), stir in the oil, then pour this over the caramel. Sprinkle with the salt and let set at room temperature, or in the refrigerator if it's a hot day. The oil helps stop the chocolate setting too hard, which can make it difficult to cut.

9

When the chocolate is just set, mark it into squares (I use a ruler to get the lines perfectly straight), then chill until completely firm.

10

Cut into cubes to serve. For a really clean finish, wipe the blade of your knife with a slightly damp cloth between each slice. Store in an airtight container for up to 3 days.

MILLIONAIRE'S SHORTBREAD
To make classic millionaire's shortbread, simply reduce the salt to a pinch in the caramel, and omit it from the top, too. Use good-quality semisweet chocolate with cocoa solids of 30% (milk chocolate).

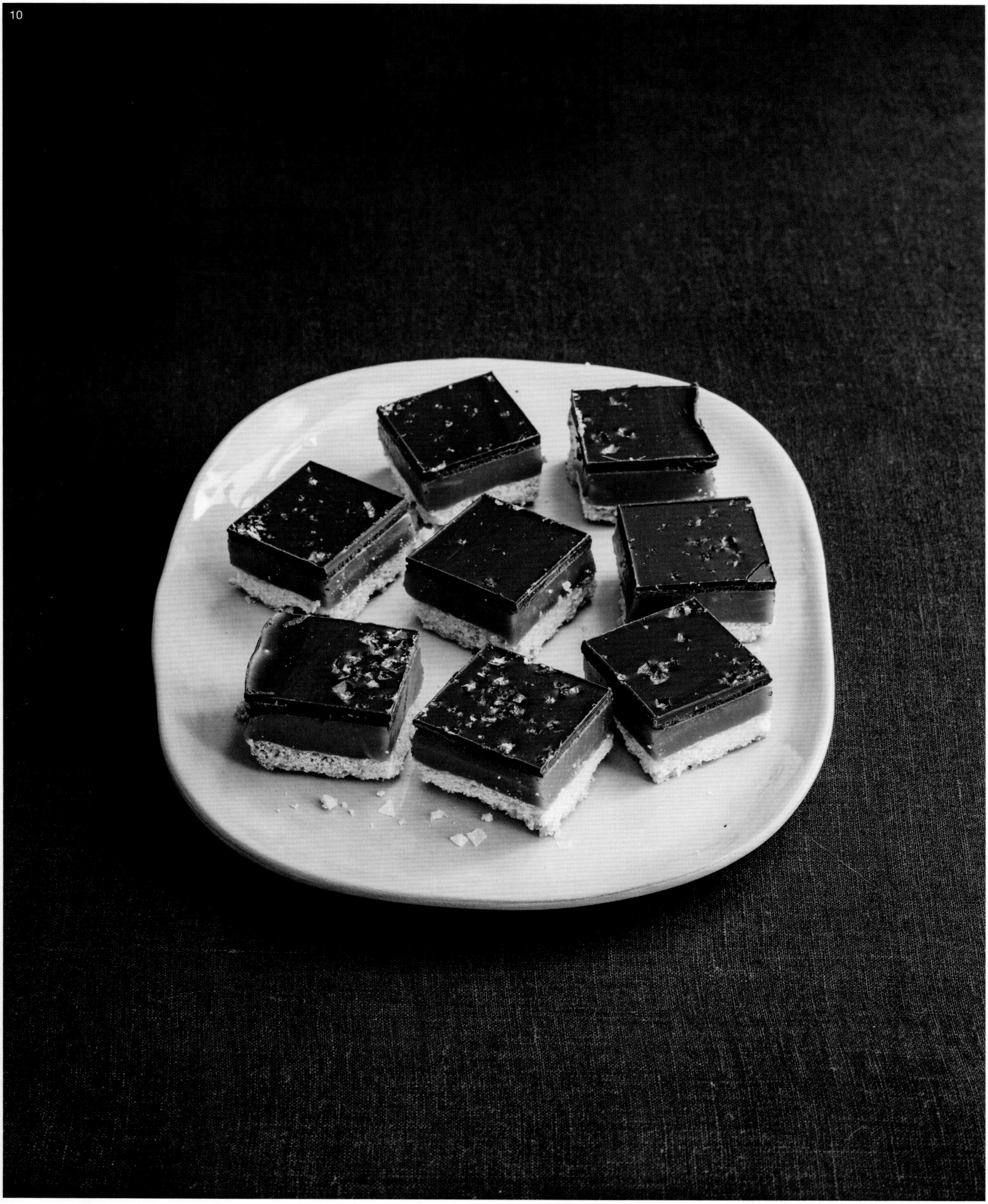

Favorite Jelly Roll

Preparation time: 15 minutes
Baking time: 10 minutes
Makes 10 slices

A jelly (Swiss) roll was one of the first things I ever baked with my mom, probably because it was so quick to make, and all the ingredients were in the cupboard. Although there are lots of steps, be assured that it's a simple cake, and one of the most popular among friends and family when I was creating the recipes for *What to Bake & How to Bake It.*

For the cake

½ stick (50 g) butter, plus extra for greasing

3 tbsp milk

4 large (UK medium) eggs, room temperature

¾ cup (150 g) superfine (caster) sugar

1 tbsp cornstarch (cornflour)

1 cup (125 g) all-purpose (plain) flour

¼ tsp salt

For rolling and filling

4 tbsp superfine (caster) sugar

¾ cup (250 g) raspberry jelly (jam)

1
Use plenty of butter to grease the base and sides of a 10 x 15-inch (25 x 37-cm) jelly roll (Swiss roll) pan or rimmed baking sheet, then line the bottom with parchment (baking) paper. Preheat the oven to 400°F/200°C/Gas Mark 6. Put the milk and butter into a small saucepan and heat gently until the butter melts. Set aside (it will need to be warm when you use it).

2
Put the eggs and the sugar into a large bowl and whisk with an electric mixer at medium speed until thick, moussey, and doubled in volume—about 5 minutes.

3
Stir the cornstarch (cornflour), flour, and salt together, then sift them on top of the eggs. Fold together well using a large metal spoon or spatula (palette knife), cutting and lifting the flour through the foam instead of stirring it. This will preserve the air bubbles and ensure a light and fluffy cake.

4
Pour the warm butter and milk around the edge of the batter bowl. Using the large spoon or spatula, fold until evenly combined. The liquid can pool at the bottom of the bowl, so be persistent, trying not to knock out too much air.

5
Carefully pour the batter into the prepared pan, then tilt it slowly from side to side, letting the batter run into the corners. If it still looks uneven, spread out the batter very gently with a spatula. Don't worry if you see a little dry flour or ribbons of butter—just work them in gently. The batter will completely fill the pan, but don't worry, it won't spill over as it bakes.

6

Bake for 10 minutes, or until the cake is golden, has risen, and the edges have shrunk away from the sides of the pan. Meanwhile, dust a larger sheet of parchment paper with 2 tablespoons sugar. Loosen the edges of the cake with a spatula (palette knife), then sprinkle the remaining sugar on top.

7

Swiftly flip the cake onto the sugared parchment paper. Carefully peel off the paper that lined the pan. Using a serrated knife, trim about ½ inch (1 cm) off from each edge. Score a line into the cake about 1 inch (2.5 cm) in from the short end nearest you. This will make it easier to roll.

8

While the cake is still hot, roll it up from the short end, rolling the sugared paper inside the cake. Don't rush things, and if a few cracks appear, don't worry.

9

Cover the cake in a clean dish (tea) towel and let cool until just warm.

10

Unwrap and unroll the cake, then spread it with the jelly (jam). Roll the cake up again, using one hand to guide it and the other to pull the sugared paper underneath it upwards. This will help keep the spiral fairly tight.

FILLING WITH CREAM?
To fill with whipped cream or buttercream, the cake must be cold. Whipped cream can go straight on top of the jelly. For buttercream, spread it out first, then cover it with jelly.

11

Place on a serving plate, seam side down. Best eaten on the day it is made.

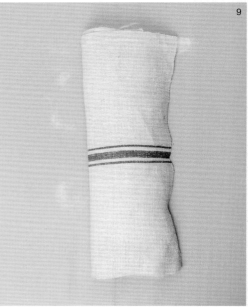

Planning a Menu

Whatever the occasion you're cooking for, a few quiet minutes planning the menu is always a good idea. I always do this—nothing tricky, just checking that what I have in mind will work together, fleshing out what will be cooked and when. Even if you are just doing a couple of plates for friends on a weeknight, it can help (especially with the shopping).

When it comes to what to serve with what, balance is the key word. Avoid repeating similar flavors, textures, and ingredients and remember we eat with our eyes, so color is important, too. Most of the dishes in this book were originally conceived as stand-alone favorites though many of them can sit together very well.

These are ideas more than instruction, and most savory recipes can be easily multiplied up or down to suit your needs. If you're feeding only a handful of people and want to make one of the larger desserts or baked items, then I'd recommend leaving the recipe quantities as they are.

For big get-togethers, a few well-prepared choices that can be served cold will keep serving simple and everyone happy, then you can concentrate on cooking something central to the meal. Why not cheat a little with a few bought items from the deli counter?

Finally, a note on style. For me, plating up for everyone in the kitchen is best saved for really formal entertaining (basically never in my house); on the whole I like to share from the table or a cleared-down work surface in the kitchen if space is tight, buffet-style. I carve and then bring the carved meat to the table, too. Then we all get to eat at the same time, and everyone can have have as much or as little of something as they want.

Bistro Supper
Coq au Vin (page 268)
Dauphinoise Potatoes (page 276)
Tarte au Citron (page 360)

Easier than Turkey Thanksgiving
Crab Cakes with Herb Vinaigrette (page 244)
Roast Chicken with Tarragon Sauce (page 204)—instead of asparagus, use long-stemmed broccoli
Maple-Roast Winter Vegetables (page 284)
Add some seasonal green vegetables, too
Pecan Cranberry Pie (page 388), Pumpkin Pie (page 352) or Sticky Pear & Pecan Toffee Cake (page 470)

Cozy Winter Gathering
Creamy Fish Pie (page 220)
Serve with simple wilted greens
Whole orange & Almond Cake (page 490)

Easy Veggie Fall Lunch
Goat Cheese & Polenta Stacks (page 256)
Vegetable Tagine with Chermoula & Couscous (page 252)
One-Crust Apple & Blackberry Pie (page 370)

Big Summer Lunch Party
Cheese and Onion Tart (page 128)
Potato, Bacon & Watercress Salad (page 290)
Roasted Vegetable & Feta Couscous (page 302)
Summer Pudding Trifle (page 324)
Muscat & Honey Poached Peaches (page 338)

Spring Lunch
Asparagus & Poached Egg with Balsamic Butter (page 178)
Roast Lamb & Rosemary Potatoes (page 232)
Serve with seasonal vegetables
Raspberry & Passion Fruit Mallow Meringue (page 342)

Halloween
Tomato and Thyme Soup (page 84) float halved mini mozzarellas in there as "eyeballs"
Spicy Pulled Pork (page 138)
Malted Milk Chocolate Birthday Cake (page 426) graveyard variation
Pumpkin Spice Whoopie Pies (page 478) variation recipe

Burger Night
Chimichurri-Style Burgers (page 264)
Slaw (page 124) from the Sticky BBQ Chicken recipe
Buy some good oven fries
Melba Sundaes (page 332)

Mother's Day
Breakfast Blinis with Smoked Salmon (page 46): make small pancakes as in appetizer info, below
Herb-Crusted Lamb with Pea Puree & Tomatoes (page 200)
Chocolate Profiteroles (page 366)

Independence Day
Sticky BBQ Chicken (page 124)
Hasselback Sweet Potatoes (page 292)
Green Salad with Seeds & Croutons (page 288)
Strawberry Meringue Cake (page 356) add some fresh blueberries for the red, white, and blue

Curry Night
Butternut Curry with Spinach & Cashews (page 160)
Lamb & Potato Curry with Fragrant Rice (page 224)
Mango & Black Currant Sorbet (page 334) you can omit the blackcurrant swirl

Watching the Game
Chicken Wings & Blue Cheese Dip (page 108)
Cheese Nachos with Guacamole (page 116)
Fudgy Cheesecake Brownies (page 438)

Special Dinner for Two
Spicy Shrimp, Fennel & Chile Linguine
(page 186)
Chocolate Mousse with Cherries
(page 378, recipe halved)

Lunch al Fresco for Two
Steak Tagliata & Artichoke (page 76)
Berry Ice Cream with a Crumble
Topping (page 328)

Family Barbecues
Sticky BBQ Chicken (page 124)
Roasted Vegetable & Feta Couscous
(page 302)
Potato, Bacon & Watercress Salad
(page 290)
Sticky Soy Ribs with Asian Slaw
(page 120)
Chimichurri-Style Burgers (page 264)
Hasselback Sweet Potatoes (page 292)
A fresh salad of your choice

Smart Barbecue
Spinach Ricotta Pockets with Roasted
Pepper Dip (page 100)
Lamb Kofte with Tzatziki (page 134)
Harissa Mackerel with Orange Salad
(page 174)
Grilled Halloumi with Pomegranate
Tabbouleh (page 62, recipe doubled)
Peach & Mozzarella Platter (page 66,
recipe doubled)
Goat Cheese & Polenta Stacks
(page 256)

Stylish Picnic
Spinach Ricotta Pockets with Roasted
Pepper Dip (page 100)
Cobb Salad with Honey Mustard
Dressing (page 68)
Cheese and Onion Tart (page 128)
Take along some smoked salmon,
pickles, good bread, cured meats from
the deli, etc.
Any sheet cake (tray bake)

Kid's Birthday Party
Easy Ciabatta Pizzas (page 112)
Malted Milk Chocolate Birthday Cake
(page 426)

Smart Spring Dinner
Lemon Basil Gnudi with Fava Beans
(page 208)
Herb-Crusted Lamb with Pea Puree &
Tomatoes (page 200)
Classic Baked Cheesecake (page 348)

Middle Eastern Feast
Store-bought mezze items, such as
hummus and olives
Fragrant Chicken with Quinoa Salad
(page 212)
Spiced Carrot & Herb Salad (page 294)
Fresh & Fluffy Flatbreads (page 298)
Whole Orange & Almond Cake
(page 490)

Flavors of Asia
Shrimp & Mushroom Laksa (page 86) -
serve small bowls as an appetizer
Sticky Soy Ribs with Asian Slaw
(page 120)
Vietnamese Herb & Noodle Salad with
Shrimp (page 72)
Finish with a fresh fruit salad

Cinco de Mayo
Spicy Pulled Pork (page 138)
Chimichurri-Style Burgers (page 264)
Mango & Black Currant Sorbet
(page 334) serve with a dash of tequila

Baking for the Holidays
Linzer Cookies (page 460)
Iced Gingerbread Cookies (page 414)
Cranberry Stollen (page 486)
Pumpkin Pie (page 352)

After Dinner/Host Gifts
Pistachio & Fig Biscotti (page 494)
Salted Caramel Shortbread (page 498)
Linzer Cookies (page 460)
Fudgy Cheesecake Brownies (page 438)

Baby Shower Treats
Frosted Cupcakes (page 474)
Fudgy Cheesecake Brownies
(page 438)
Linzer Cookies (page 460)
Blueberry-Cinnamon Crumb Cake
(page 456)

Index

Author's Acknowledgments

There aren't enough batches of brownies in the world to thank the folks listed here. Together we have made this book, and created the previous books that the recipes and images are taken from:

Everyone at Phaidon past and present. Ellie Smith, Emilia Terragni, Laura Gladwin, Beth Underdown, Michelle Lo, and Emma Robertson. Jennifer Wagner and Nico Schweizer for designing the original format, the design and production teams in-house, and Frédéric Tacer for the cover design of this book.

Angela Moore and assistants Pete, Julian, and Bruce; Steven Joyce and assistant Sandra Autukaite; and Liz and Max Haarala Hamilton, and assistant Ruth Carruthers for the photography. Particularly Liz and Max, for trekking to my home so, so many times. The photography for this book looks so simple, but was a devil to achieve.

My assistants for food styling and all that washing up. Marisa Viola, Katy Greenwood, Sophie Austen-Smith, Hannah Sherwood, and Lucy Campbell. And my wonderful mother, Linda, and Teresa Coen who both stepped in to save the day.

Recipe testing help, Katy Greenwood, Susan Spall, Michelle Bolton King, Cynthia Kruth, and all of our lovely friends who tested and tasted recipes for me and offered their take.

Finally, thank you to my family and friends, especially Ross, my parents, and parents-in-law, for your support, belief, and appetites. For Joseph.

Jane Hornby

The Publisher would like to thank Theresa Bebbington, Vanessa Bird, Jane Ellis, Julia Hasting, Sophie Hodgkin, Daniel Hurst, Lesley Malkin, João Mota, Tracey Smith, and Hans Stofregen for their contributions to the book.

NOTE ON THE RECIPES
Some recipes include raw or very lightly cooked eggs. These should be avoided by the elderly, infants, pregnant women, convalescents, and anyone with an impaired immune system.

OVEN TEMPERATURES

Celsius	Fahrenheit	Gas Mark
140°C	275°F	1
150°C	300°F	2
160°C	325°F	3
180°C	350°F	4
190°C	375°F	5
200°C	400°F	6
220°C	425°F	7
230°C	450°F	8

If you have a convection or fan-assisted oven, see page 9 for information about adapting your oven temperature.

Phaidon Press Limited
Regent's Wharf
All Saints Street
London N1 9PA

Phaidon Press Inc.
65 Bleecker Street
New York, NY 10012

phaidon.com

First published 2019
© 2019 Phaidon Press Limited
The recipes in *Simple & Classic* originate from the titles: *What to Cook & How to Cook It* © 2010; *Fresh & Easy* © 2012; and *What to Bake & How to Bake It* © 2014.

ISBN 978 0 7148 7811 9

A CIP catalogue record for this book is available from the British Library and the Library of Congress.

Commissioning Editor: Ellie Smith
Project Editor: Ellie Smith
Production Controller: Lisa Fiske
Photographs on pages: 308–311, 348–377, 402–409, and 414–505 by Liz and Max Haarala Hamilton
Photographs on pages: 39–57, 62–79, 100–103, 112–115, 120–127, 134–141, 148–151, 174–193, 200–215, 256–259, 264–267, 286–305, 324–347, 378–381, and 396–401
by Steven Joyce
Photographs on pages: 16–39, 60–61, 80–83, 96–99, 104–111, 116–119, 128–133, 144–147, 152–173, 194–197, 216–255, 260–263, 268–271, 274–285, 312–323, 384–395, and 410–413 by Angela Moore
Cover and chapter opener design
by Frédéric Tacer
Based on the original internal design for *What to Cook & How Cook It* by SML Office.

Printed in China